The Union
Reader

The Union Reader

Edited by

Richard B. Harwell

KONECKY&KONECKY

Konecky & Konecky
156 Fifth Ave.
New York, NY 10010

ISBN: 1-56852-153-7

Printed and bound in the U.S.A.

For
RUTH FOREMAN MOORE
and
LAUREN FOREMAN

Acknowledgment

To the Henry E. Huntington Library belongs, almost as completely as in Aesop's fable, the lion's share of the acknowledgments for this book. Not only is every item included in the volume present in the magnificent Civil War collections there, but the editor is indebted to the Huntington for making his search for appropriate selections thoroughly pleasant. His debt is to the whole library and the whole staff, but it is particularly great to Mr. John E. Pomfret, Director; Mr. Leslie Bliss, Librarian; Mr. Carey S. Bliss, Miss Mary Isabel Fry, Miss Gertrude Ruhnka, and Mr. Erwin F. Morkisch. For the graciousness which only a considerate publisher can display he is grateful to Mr. John L. B. Williams of New York. He is thankful for the generous help given by Floyd Cammack and Robert L. Talmadge. And for relief from the infinite troubles of typing and transcription he must thank Miss Elaine Mitchell.

RICHARD BARKSDALE HARWELL

October 8, 1958

Contents

Introduction   xvii

1861

Within Fort Sumter   3

    Within Fort Sumter; or, A View of Major Anderson's
Garrison Family for One Hundred and Ten Days. By
One of the Company [Miss A. Fletcher]. New York,
N. Tibbals & Company, 1861. 72 p.

Cheer, Boys, Cheer   24

    "Victory's Band" is in Beadle's Dime Union Song
Book, No. 2, comprising New and Popular Patriotic
Songs for the Times. New York and London, Beadle
and Company [1861]. 75 p.

Along the Border   27

    Address to the People of Maryland by the General As-
sembly, in Extra Session. Frederick, Beale H. Richardson, Printer, 1861. 4 p. and Reports Made by General
William S. Harney During His Command of the
United States Forces in Missouri . . . [Washington,
1861]. 32 p. (37th Congress. 1st Session. House. Executive Document, No. 19).

Rebels Ahead!   34

    The Hero of Medfield; Containing the Journals and
Letters of Allen Alonzo Kingsbury, of Medfield, Mem-

ber of Co. H, Chelsea Volunteers, Mass. 1st Reg.,
Who Was Killed by the Rebels Near Yorktown, April
26, 1862. . . . Boston, John M. Hewes, 1862. 144 p.

War in the West   40

History of the First Regiment of Iowa Volunteers. By
Henry O'Connor, a Private in Company "A." . . .
Muscatine, Printed at the Faust First Premium Print-
ing House, 1862. 24 p.

Fort Laramie   48

History of the First Regiment of Colorado Volunteers.
By Ovando J. Hollister. Denver, C.T., Thos. Gibson &
Co., Publishers, 1863. 178 p.

Battle of Port Royal   65

Abstract of the Cruise of U.S. Steam Frigate Wabash,
Bearing the Flag of Rear-Admiral S. F. Du Pont, 1861–
'62 & '63. New York, Printed by Edward O. Jenkins,
1863. 31 p.

1862

The Enemy Is Texas   75

Address of the Legislative Assembly of New Mexico.
. . . [Santa Fe, T.N.M., 1862]. *Broadside.* and His-
tory of the First Regiment of Colorado Volunteers. By
Ovando J. Hollister. Denver, C.T., Thos. Gibson &
Co., Publishers, 1863. 178 p.

Tardy George   96

Tardy George [by George Henry Boker]. New York,
Privately Printed, 1865. 4 p. and Soldiers of the Army
of the Potomac [address of Major General George B.
McClellan, March 14, 1862. Fairfax Court House,
Va., 1862]. [1] p.

One of the Strangest Naval Combats   101

The War in the United States, Report to the Swiss
Military Department; Preceded by a Discourse to the
Federal Military Society Assembled at Berne, Aug.
18, 1862, by Ferdinand LeComte, Lieutenant-Colonel,
Swiss Confederation . . . New York, D. Van Nos-
trand, 1863. 148 p.

Shiloh   111

The Battle Field of Shiloh. [n.p., 1862]. 6 p.

But You Must Act   122

The President to General McClellan. [Washington,
1862]. *Broadside.*

Unfit for Human Beings   125

One Year's Soldiering, Embracing the Battles of Fort
Donelson and Shiloh and the Capture of Two Hundred Officers and Men of the Fourteenth Iowa Infantry, and Their Confinement Six Months and a Half in
Rebel Prisons, [by] F. F. Kiner, Chaplain Fourteenth
Iowa Infantry. Lancaster, E. H. Thomas, Printer,
1863. 219 p.

The Capture and Occupation of New Orleans   137

General Orders from Headquaraters Department of
the Gulf, Issued by Major-General B. F. Butler, from
May 1st, 1862, to the Present Time. New-Orleans, E.
R. Wagener, Printer and Stationer, 1862. 35 p.

A Change in Virginia   144

Soldiers of the Army of the Potomac! [Address of
Major General George B. McClellan, June 2, 1862.
Camp Near New Bridge, Va., 1862] [1] p. Soldiers of
the Army of the Potomac! [address of Major General
George B. McClellan, July 4, 1862. Camp Near Harri-
son's Landing, Va., 1862]. [1] p. and To the Officers

and Soldiers of the Army of Virginia [address of
Major General John Pope, July 14, 1862. Washington,
1862]. [1] p.

We Must Learn Righteouness 149

Memorial of the Public Meeting of the Christian Men
of Chicago. . . . [Chicago, 1862]. 3 p.

Maryland Invaded 156

Report of Lewis H. Steiner, M.D., Inspector of the
Sanitary Commission, Containing a Diary Kept During the Rebel Occupation of Frederick, Md., and an
Account of the Operations of the U.S. Sanitary Commission During the Campaign in Maryland, September, 1862. . . . New York, Anson D. F. Randolph,
1862. 43 p.

I Think He Should Be Engaged 175

The Letters of Lincoln on National Policy . . . New
York, H. Lloyd & Co., 1863. 22 p. Officers and Soldiers
of the Army of the Potomac [address of Major General George B. McClellan, November 7, 1862. Camp
Near Rectortown, Va., 1862]. [1] p. and General Orders, No. 1 [of the Army of the Potomac by Major
General A. E. Burnside, November 9, 1862. Warrenton, Va., 1862]. [1] p.

Battle of Fredericksburg 180

Camp Fires of the Twenty-Third: Sketches of Camp
Life, Marches, and Battles of the Twenty-Third Regi-
ment, N.Y.V., During the Term of Two Years in the
Service of the United States . . . by Pound Sterling
[William P. Maxson]. New York, Davies & Kent,
Printers, 1863. 196 p.

A Day in a Hospital 185

Hospital Sketches, by L. M. Alcott. . . . Boston,
James Redpath, 1863. 102 p.

1863

The Grand Terpischorean Festival 203

Letters from the Forty-Fourth Regiment M.V.M.: a
Record of the Experience of a Nine Month's Regiment
in the Department of North Carolina in 1862–3, by
"Corporal" [Zenas T. Haines]. Boston, Printed at the
Herald Job Office, 1863. 121 p.

Chancellorsville 208

General Orders, No. 49 [of the Army of the Potomac,
May 6, 1863. Camp near Falmouth, Va., 1863]. [1] p.

The Second Louisiana 211

Washington and Jackson on Negro Soldiers. Gen.
Banks on the Bravery of Negro Troops. Poem—The
Second Louisiana, by George H. Boker. Philadelphia,
Printed for Gratuitous Distribution [1863]. 8 p.

Our Present Duty to Our Country 216

Our Stars . . . by E. Norman Gunnison, Second New
Hampshire Volunteers. Philadelphia, Ringwalt &
Brown, 1863. 120 p.

Gettysburg 223

General Orders, No. 67 [of the Army of the Potomac,
George G. Meade, Major General Commanding,
June 28, 1863. n.p., 1863]. [1] p. The Diary of a Lady
of Gettysburg, Pennsylvania, from June 15 to July 15,
1863 . . . [n.p., 1863]. 29 p. and General Orders, No.
68 [of the Army of the Potomac, July 4, 1863. n.p.,
1863]. [1] p.

The Fall of Vicksburg 238

Opening of the Mississippi; or, Two Years' Campaigning in the Southwest, a Record of the Campaigns,

Sieges, Actions and Marches in Which the 8th Wisconsin Volunteers Have Participated, Together with Correspondence, by a Non-Commissioned Officer [George W. Driggs]. Madison, Wis., Wm. J. Park & Co., 1864. 149, [1] p.

The Draft   244

"Grafted into the Army" is in The Bugle Call, Edited by George F. Root. Chicago, Root & Cady [1863]. and The Letters of President Lincoln on Questions of National Policy . . . New York, H. H. Lloyd & Co., 1863. 22 p.

The Gettysburg Address   248

Address of Hon. Edward Everett at the Consecration of the National Cemetery at Gettysburg, 19th November, 1863, with the Dedicatory Speech of President Lincoln and the Other Exercises of the Occasion . . . Boston, Little, Brown and Company, 1864. 87, [1] p.

The Battle of Chattanooga   250

The Three Days' Battle of Chattanooga, 23d, 24th, 25th November, 1864 [i.e. 1863]: Unofficial Dispatch from General Meigs, Quartermaster General of the United States, to the Hon. E. M. Stanton, Secretary of War. . . . Washington, D.C., McGill & Witherow, 1864. 8 p.

1864

Fresh from Abraham's Bosom   259

Old Abe's Jokes, Fresh from Abraham's Bosom, Containing All his Issues, Excepting the "Greenbacks," To Call in Some of Which, This Work Is Issued. New York, T. R. Dawley [c. 1864]. 135 p. and Lincolniana; or, The Humors of Uncle Abe; Second Joe Miller.

. . . by Andrew Adderup [pseud.], Springfield, Ill.
New York, J. E. Feeks [c. 1864]. 95 p.

Bushwhackers   263

Soldier's Letter [of the] Second Colorado Cavalry.
[Fort Riley, Kansas, 1864], Nos. 6, 8–10.

The *Alabama* and the *Kearsarge*   273

An Englishman's View of the Battle Between the *Alabama* and the *Kearsarge,* an Account of the Naval Engagement in the British Channel, on Sunday, June
19th, 1864, from Information Personally Obtained in
the Town of Cherbourg, as Well as from the Officers
and Crew of the United States' Sloop-of-War *Kearsarge,* and the Wounded and Prisoners of the Confederate Privateer. New York, Anson D. F. Randolph,
1864. 47, [1] p.

Andersonville   282

Narrative of the Privations and Sufferings of United
States Officers & Soldiers While Prisoners of War in
the Hands of Rebel Authorities, Being the Report of a
Commission of Inquiry, Appointed by the United
States Sanitary Commission; with an Appendix, con-
taining the Testimony . . . Boston, Published at the
Office of "Littell's Living Age" [1864]. 86 p.

Sherman   292

. . . Stirring Appeals from Honored Veterans; Democratic Statesmen and Generals to the Loyal Sons of
the Union: Views of Gens. Grant, Sherman, Dix, Wool,
Butler, Edward Everett, John A. Griswold, and Others.
Albany, Weed, Parsons and Company, Printers, 1864.
16 p. (Union Campaign Documents, No. 8.)

Sheridan at Winchester   300

"Sheridan's Battle of Winchester," in *Harper's New
Monthly Magazine,* XXX (1865), 195–200.

Victory for Christmas   321

The Army and Navy Gazette, Containing Official Reports of Battles: Also, Important Orders of the War
Department, Record of Courts-Martial, etc. . . . Washington City, Printed at the Office of F. & J. Rives,
1865. Vol. II (1864–65).

1865

Peace Conference   325

Peace: Message from the President of the United
States, Transmitting, in Compliance with the Resolu-
tion of February 8th, 1865, Information Relative to a
Conference Held at Hampton Roads with Messrs. A.
H. Stephens, R. M. T. Hunter, and J. A. Campbell.
. . . [Washington, 1865] 12 p. (38th Congress, 2d
Session. House. Executive Document, No. 59.)

The Second Inaugural   331

Inaugural Address, March 4, 1865. . . . [n.p., 1865]
3 p.

All Going Finely   335

The Army and Navy Gazette, Containing Official Reports of Battles: Also, Important Orders of the War
Department, Record of Courts-Martial, etc. . . . Washington City, Printed at the Office of F. & J. Rives,
1865. Vol. II (1864–65).

Raising the Flag at Sumter   342

General Orders, No. 50 [of the War Department,
March 27, 1865. Washington, 1865]. [1] p. and Rev.
Henry Ward Beecher's Fort Sumter Oration, April
14th, 1865. . . . [n.p., 1865] 24 p.

Index   355

Introduction

As the national memory of the American Civil War is dimmed with time the vision of the war is, more and more, portrayed in great bold strokes. We remember Sumter, Bull Run, and Gettysburg—that greatest of battles. We remember a farmhouse at Appomattox, tensed to silence and formality in marking the end of an era of noisy politics and noisier battle. We remember Lincoln and the giant shadow his figure has cast on American history. We remember Grant and Sherman, and Seward and Stanton. And John Wilkes Booth. We remember the Confederates: the nobility of Lee, the zeal of Jackson, the daring of Stuart.

But so much we forget.

The war was more than Lincoln and his generals and his Cabinet, more than battles and heroes. For more than four years war was our national life. War was the climactic event of a generation—of a century—of American life. It was, as its great leader said at the cemetery in Gettysburg, the test of the United States' national existence.

The story of the war has been told many times. Its vast literature still grows by, conservatively, a book a week. With the reports from the two contending sides in the same language and with the motivations of the two sections still influencing sectional thinking, this is a war which has a continuing interest and reality to Americans. Though historians' interpretations of the war have changed from generation to generation, shifting according to the emphasis of an outstanding historian or according to the fashionable thinking of a time, the facts of the war have not changed. Nearly a century after the fighting the closest we can come to those facts is still in the writings of the people of its own time. It is in their words that the war is fixed in print and on paper, for us as it was for them. Even if their facts may sometimes be wrong, even if their writings may often be crude or incomplete or prejudiced, who can gainsay what they wrote? What they described was the war as they saw it and lived it. This was the war they fought.

"The War of the Southern Rebellion," wrote J. B. Rogers, chaplain of the Nineteenth Wisconsin Volunteers in his *War Pictures* (Chicago, 1863), "is destined to create a literature of its own. Its history will be written by many hands, while its incidents and leading characteristics, above all the principles involved in it, will supply themes for discussion for a long time to come. The material for all reliable accounts of this great struggle must be furnished, in no small degree, by the testimony of eye-witnesses."

The Union Reader is a history by many hands. In nearly every case the writers were eyewitnesses, even participants in the events they described. In every case they were participants in the time, eyewitnesses to the most eventful days of American history. In their words lies the documentation of America at war—of Sumter, Bull Run, Port Royal, Shiloh, Seven Days, and on down the long list of battles. Equally the words of women working in the hospitals, of soldiers suffering the boredom of inactivity, of prisoners enduring far greater hardships are documentation of the times. As Chaplain Rogers wrote: "It is not altogether of battles that thoughtful people wish to read, even in the history of wars. Especially is this the case with those who read with some view to learn what war really is."

As were their opponents at the South, the Northerners of the sixties were tremendously conscious of their moment in history. There was, it would seem, a national urge to record the experiences of the war at every level of activity. These contemporary accounts as much as the work of later historians and the publication of the official records of the war make the American Civil War the best documented of all wars.

America in 1861 was still a new country. Just as the war was a test of democratic principle it was a test of democratic education. Never before had there been so literate an army. Such a soldiery was ready, and proud, to relate its experiences. Such a soldiery was capable of understanding printed orders and explanations. Nor, in the newness of universal education, was this country "with," as Henry Ward Beecher noted, "books and newspapers thick as leaves in our own forests, with institutions sprung from the people and peculiarly adapted to their genius" inured to the uses of propaganda. It was ripe for the printed word to be used in shaping the course of its history with especial freshness and effectiveness.

Unlike their Southern contemporaries, the Northerners were not impoverished for the materials of printing as the war progressed. Printing did not disappear in the South, but it survived against difficulties that seriously hampered its effectiveness. In the North supplies of paper, presses, and printers were readily available throughout the war. The publishing business was not nearly so concentrated in the big cities of the East as it would be later. The selections in *The Union Reader* include items from books printed in Muscatine, Iowa; Madison, Wisconsin; Denver; and occupied New Orleans; from governmental pamphlets issued at Santa Fe, and at Frederick, Maryland; and from ephemeral sheets produced from the Peninsula of Virginia to Fort Riley, Kansas. Presses were quickly adapted to camp use so that many units had their own regimental papers and every major command had its own field press. In his report to the Swiss Military Department Ferdinand LeComte, an observer with General McClellan's Army of the Potomac, noted: "There is not a village which has not its printing press and its journal. A head-quarters, as populous as many a village, might well pretend to the same privilege. I subjoin here, Mr. Counsellor, a specimen of the elegant pamphlets which our printers executed for us in the marshy woods of the environs of Yorktown. I should add that these pamphlets . . . simplify greatly the labor of the staff department."

Nor was the North impoverished of authors. Though little of literary note was published during the war, there was a wealth of talent among the practicing writers of the time. Some of this talent, such as Walt Whitman's, was redirected into active participation in the war effort. Other was used for purposes of literary propaganda. Even Bret Harte, in faraway California, wrote a special poem for *The Sanitary Commission Bulletin*. Edmund Clarence Stedman reported the war for the New York *World* and wrote topical poetry. Others who contributed to the anthologies of the day included Thomas Bailey Aldrich, Oliver Wendell Holmes, Charles G. Leland, James Russell Lowell, Fitz James O'Brien, and John Greenleaf Whittier. The novels were undistinguished, but there was a plenty of them. And the magazines—*Leslie's, Harper's*, the *Atlantic*—flourished. J. W. DeForest, later to achieve a distinguished reputation as a novelist, wrote reports from the armies for *Harper's*, and the *Atlantic* printed one of its most enduringly popular stories when it published Edward Everett Hale's *The Man without a Country*. Stephen Foster, Henry Clay Work, George F. Root, Patrick Gilmore, and a host of other professional song writers supplied the songs for the soldiers, but the amateurs helped too, particularly Julia Ward Howe with the great "Battle Hymn of the Republic." Of one collection of songs Hale wrote, in *James Russell Lowell and His Friends:* "Eager in everything in the way of public spirit, Professor [F. J.] Child made it his special duty to prepare a 'Song Book' for the soldiers who were going to the field. . . . He made everybody who could, write a war song, and he printed a little book of these songs, with the music, which he used to send to the front with every passing regiment." And, of course, the war was thoroughly documented in the publications of Congress, the personal and private reports of generals, and in the publication in the newspapers of every scrap of information their reporters with the armies could uncover.

General Sherman may or may not have said, "War is hell." It is certain that he wrote, in his letter of September 12, 1864, to the Mayor of Atlanta, "War is cruelty," and proceeded to prove it. War is cruelty, but it is also many more things. It is bravery and heroism, boredom and bombast, starvation and suffering. It is politics. It is tactics. It is fighting. But in the total General Sherman was right. War is cruelty. War is hell. If there is any lesson which should come out of the record of our own Civil War, it is summarized in that statement. And yet it is a lesson still to be learned.

The testimony of the participants in the days of '61 to '65 is vastly interesting. It is this testimony which makes up *The Union Reader*. It is not all here, far from it. Only bits and pieces can be encompassed in one volume. But these bits and pieces catch the spirit of the times from the fall of Fort Sumter to the reraising of the United States flag over its ruin. Each was written and published during the war itself, and many helped form the public opinion that, in turn, helped shape the further course of the war.

Few familiar pieces are included. Lincoln's *Gettysburg Address* and his *Second Inaugural* are known to every literate American. But almost none of the millions who have read Louisa May Alcott's *Little Women* know her charming *Hospital Sketches*, a chapter of which is reproduced here. Even fewer of those who know John Greenleaf Whittier's "Barbara Frietchie" have ever read the report of Dr. Lewis H. Steiner, inspector for the U.S. Sanitary Commission, which relates the incident in more prosaic form. Only the most fully initiated Civil War buff is likely to know that frank and truly remarkable regimental history from the Far West, Ovando Hollister's *History of the First Regiment of Colorado Volunteers*, or the broadside tirade against the Texans addressed to the citizens of New Mexico by their territorial governor in 1862. There is suffering in the prison narratives of F. F. Kiner and Prescott Tracy, heroism in the story of Fort Sumter, pure soldiering in the boyish account of the battlefield of Shiloh. The testimony of *The Union Reader* is, in fact, the essence of war itself.

"Blood ain't so cool as ink, John," wrote James Russell Lowell in 1862 in an admonition to Britain after the Trent Affair nearly precipitated war. But the words of those who participated in our Civil War run with blood as well as with ink. In these words, hot from the heart, that the Americans of another day wrote for each other their day remains alive. This, then, is their own story, the story of the war they fought. This is *The Union Reader*.

1861

Within Fort Sumter

ABRAHAM LINCOLN himself might well have written an
introduction for *The Union Reader*. He summarized
the background for war succinctly in an open letter
written June 12, 1863, to Erastus Corning and other
Democrats of Albany, New York, on the case of Clement
L. Vallandigham and arbitrary arrests. "Prior to my in-
stallation here," he stated, "it had been inculcated that
any State had a lawful right to secede from the national
Union, and that it would be expedient to exercise that
right whenever the devotees of the doctrine should fail
to elect a President to their own liking. I was elected
contrary to their liking; and, accordingly, so far as it was
legally possible, they had taken seven States out of the
Union, had seized many of the United States forts, and
had fired upon the United States flag, all before I was
inaugurated, and, of course, before I had done any official act whatever. The Rebellion thus begun soon ran
into the present Civil War; and, in certain respects, it
began on very unequal terms between the parties. The
insurgents had been preparing for it for more than thirty

3

years, while the Government had taken no steps to resist them."

This was the official point of view, and not without foundation. Southerners had certainly planned, propagandized, and prepared for secession. It is easy to overestimate, however, their preparations for war. The South wanted to "go in peace." Though some secessionists undoubtedly foresaw war and realized the desirability of preparing for it, to prepare for war would have canceled the propaganda of their position that secession was legal and that they could peaceably leave the Union. Had they made the war preparations implied by secession there might well have been no secession, no war.

It can be argued that the South lost its chance to achieve independence and establish the Confederate States when Fort Sumter was fired upon. If the South could not leave the Union in peace, she could not leave at all. For, once the war potential of the North could be mobilized, the South had little chance. Initial defeat or victory could hardly matter; in time the North could win by bringing to bear its might in arms and men, in matériel and technical achievement.

"The first gun that spat its iron insult at Fort Sumter," declared Oliver Wendell Holmes in a Fourth of July oration in Boston, 1863, "smote every loyal American full in the face. As when the foul witch used to torture her miniature charge, the person it represented suffered all that she inflicted on his waxen counterpart, so every buffet that fell on the smoking fortress was felt by the sovereign nation of which that was the representative.

Robbery could go no farther, for every loyal man was despoiled in that single act as much as if a footpad had laid hands upon him to take from him his father's staff and his mother's Bible. Insult could go no farther, for over those battered walls waved the precious symbol of all we most value in the past and most hope for in the future,—the banner under which we became a nation, and which, next to the cross of the Redeemer, is the dearest object of love and honor to all who toil or march or sail beneath its waving folds of glory."

Within Fort Sumter is a small book published in 1861 which purported to be "By One of the Company." Actually it was written by a Miss A. Fletcher, but her representation of life in the fort is sound and is corroborated by other accounts. Printed here is her story of the battle that began the war.

At two o'clock on Thursday, April 11th, a formal demand was sent by General Beauregard to Major Anderson for the evacuation of Fort Sumter. The Major's reply was as follows:

"SIR:—I have the honor to acknowledge the receipt of your communication, demanding the evacuation of this Fort, and to say in reply thereto that it is a demand with which I regret that my sense of honor and my obligations to my Government prevent my compliance.

"ROBERT ANDERSON."

The reception of this answer was immediately followed by a deputation from General Beauregard urging Major Anderson to evacuate, and proposing the most honorable terms, upon which he should be allowed to do so; but the Major, feeling his own strength, besides expecting the fleet from Washington, determined to hold out, and the deputation, after a long interview, in which they earnestly sought to persuade the Major to accept the offered terms, returned to Charleston to report their failure.

It was late on Thursday night when this interview closed; and at half past three o'clock, on Friday morning, the boat with its white flag, shrouded in darkness and mist, again drew up to the walls of Fort Sumter. It conveyed three of General Beauregard's Aid-de-camps, bearing the following notice:

"*Major Anderson:*

"By virtue of Brigadier General Beauregard's command, we have the honor to notify you that he will open the line of his batteries on Fort Sumter in one hour from this time."

Punctual to the minute, at half past four o'clock, the first gun was fired on Fort Sumter.

It was a dark, cloudy morning, not a star was visible, while a heavy mist covered earth and sea; but as through the sombre gloom came the brilliant flash of exploding shells from the batteries all around the bay, while the deep hoarse tones of talking cannon echoed over the waters, the scene was sublimely grand, and sensations wildly inspiriting swelled in every heart.

Major Anderson alone was calm, though the swollen veins of his temples, the dilating nostrils, the nervous lip, told that his great heart beat as ardently as any there.

He would allow of no hurry: he wished that his command

should husband their strength as it would all be needed. With this view he desired that they should breakfast before proceeding to action.

Their simple meal was soon prepared. For a week they had been on short rations of salt pork, biscuit and coffee, with a little rice. This rice, the last they had received, had reached them through a rough sea, and, the boat being leaky, had become saturated with salt water. It had then been spread out in an empty room of the barracks to dry, with the expectation of its being very acceptable when the biscuit should give out. That extremity was reached now. The last few biscuits were divided, and the cook was ordered to boil some rice; but, lo! the very first fire had shattered the windows of the room where the precious article was spread, and particles of glass were thickly strewn amongst the grain —the food was useless.

But they still had a little pork and plenty of coffee; and, thankful for this same, the brave fellows eat and drank, then filed in order to their places in the casements.

And all this time the enemy's shot rattled, thick and fast, around our stronghold, which did but little execution beyond affording the Major an opportunity of observing the efficiency of each battery employed against him, and of tracing the plan which he had to oppose.

At five o'clock day began to break; but the heavy masses of clouds which obscured the sky, the sullen swell of the dark waters, the grey mist which hung, like a sombre veil, over nature's face, only became more apparent as the gathering light increased.

Shortly after the huge clouds burst, and a deluge of rain rushed down upon the scene, as if commissioned to quench the matricidal fire leveled against Columbia's breast. But all in vain. The moaning wind—the splashing shower were scarcely heeded, or made but feeble sounds, while the hoarse bellowing of deep-mouthed cannon still rolled fiercely on. An hour, and the elements ceased to strive, the wailing storm was hushed, and a still but troubled sky looked down upon the scene.

Meanwhile the Fort Sumter garrison coolly prepared for action. Major Anderson divided his command into three reliefs of four hours each, for service at the guns; the first under charge of Captain Doubleday, assisted by Dr. Crawford and Lieutenant Snyder; the second under charge of Captain Seymour, assisted by Lieutenant Hall; and the third under charge of Lieutenant Davis and Lieutenant Meade. The laborers, over forty of whom were in the fort, were appointed to carry ammunition, help make cartridges and assist the gunners where their aid could be available.

All was now ready, every man was in his place, and still, before giving the word to fire, our kind commander walked around to administer his last charge.

"Be careful," he said, "of your lives; make no imprudent exposure of your persons to the enemy's fire; do your duty coolly, determinedly and *cautiously*. Indiscretion is not valor; reckless disregard of life is not bravery. Manifest your loyalty and zeal by preserving yourselves from injury for the continued service of our cause; *and show your love to me by guarding all your powers to aid me through this important duty.*"

This admonition, delivered in sentences, with anxious brow and broken voice, will long be remembered by those who heard it:—no doubt it was the fulcrum sustaining and steadying the power which cast such deadly force from Sumter's walls.

It was just within ten minutes of seven o'clock when the order was given to fire. The first shot was from a forty-two pounder directed against the battery at Cumming's Point. Three of our guns bore upon this point and seven on Fort Moultrie. The famous floating battery—which, by the way, did not float at all, but stuck fast on a point of Sullivan's Island—also received some attention, besides a new battery in the same neighborhood, which had only been unmasked the day previous.

Before our firing commenced—when the storm had cleared off sufficiently to enable us to see around us—we discovered a fleet, which we supposed to be our long-expected succor, outside the bar. The Major signaled them, but the shoals being heavy and the tide low, they could not possibly cross. Shortly after this a fragment of a shell struck and cut through one [of] the flag halliards; but the flag, instead of falling, rose on the wind, and, with a whirl, flung the remaining halliard round the topmast, by which it was held securely all day:— Long live our gallant ensign!

To return. Major Anderson having opened fire continued to pour it forth with good effect. Almost every ball went home. One of the Fort Moultrie guns was soon disabled; the roofs and sides of the building were penetrated by shot; the flag-staff was struck and the flag cut. The floating battery was struck seventeen times; its roof was penetrated, and several shots were sent square through it. The iron battery at Cumming's Point was struck several times, but not much impression was made. Two of its guns, however, were dismounted. The forty-two pound Paixhans of our lower tier worked well: not one of them opened her mouth without giving the enemy cause to shrink, while the ten-inch Columbiads of our second tier meant every word they said. The barbette guns were not manned. Early in the engagement three of them had been fired; but the number of shells descending upon the terreplain of the parapet, and the flanks and faces of the work being taken in reverse by the enemy's batteries rendered the danger of serving in the ramparts so imminent that Major Anderson quickly withdrew his men from them, and kept them in the casemates.

When the cartridges became scarce, the men not engaged at the guns were employed to make them; the sheets and bedding from the hospital being brought out and used for that purpose.

Noon came, yet Fort Sumter was not hurt: the proud stronghold had resisted every effort to do it serious injury. A new species of attack, however, was now resorted to. The solid pile which was impervious to cold ball might feel the influence of *hot shot,* especially as the barracks were constructed mainly of timber; and so a red, hissing shower rushed from Fort Moultrie on this treacherous errand.

The officers' quarters soon caught fire;—the roof of this elegant building, being taller than those adjoining, received the assault first, but the bursting of the cistern, on top, which occurred about the same time, prevented the conflagration from spreading. Still down came the fierce hot shot upon the doomed dwellings, and were it not for the leaking cisterns, each of which had been perforated by ball, the whole would have been quickly consumed.

The ball from the enemy's batteries continued to rattle against the fort, and the latter paid back the compliment with interest. A strong, determined will actuated our men, astonishing to find in so small a number, surrounded and hemmed in by an armament of thousands.

"Aye! there's a great crowd o' them against us!" exclaimed one, as he leaned for a minute behind the column of an embrasure, "but it's the Republic they 're fightin'—not us—and, in the name of the Republic, we 're able for them."

"To be sure we are!" was the hearty response, "seventy

true men to seventy thousand traitors, and the true side is the strongest!"

And at it they kept, loading and firing, firing and re-loading, without stopping for food or repose, except an occasional draught of coffee, to wash the powder from their throats, or a short rest for their weary shoulders against an arch or column.

Nor, all through the exciting day, did the officers ever flag in their duty. Cool, firm, and intrepid, with eyes like eagles, ears quick to hear, and limbs of agile motion, they saw every movement of the enemy, heard their leader's lightest command, and directed each action of their charge with a promptness and energy worthy the important occasion.

The day seemed short, too, full as it was with labor and excitement; and the hearts which beat with hope and enthusiasm heeded not the flight of time. They would fain fight on after day had closed; but the sun went down in lowering gloom, night gathered over us murky and chill, and Major Anderson ordered the firing to cease, and the men to eat some supper and to go to bed.

The only supper they had was a little pork and coffee; but this, with a good sleep, would afford them some refreshment, preparatory to the next day's toil; so they took it cheerfully and laid down.

Still the enemy's fire continued. Even when, at seven o'clock, a mighty storm arose, and rain descended with the force of a cataract, an occasional bomb from one of the batteries mingled with the fury of the elements, as if bidding defiance to nature as well as law.

The condition of the fort was now examined, and the injuries sustained were found to be as follows: The crest of the parapet had been broken in many places; the gorge had been struck by shell and shot, and some of these had pene-

trated the wall to the depth of twelve inches. Several of
the barbette guns had been injured; one had been struck by
a ball and cracked; one was dismounted and two had been
thrown over by a recoil. The lower casemates were uninjured, save one or two embrasures a little broken on the
edges.

But the internal structure had received the most damage
—the *wooden* building which had been treated to hot shot.
Nothing saved it from being consumed but the riddling of
the cisterns which sent the water flowing after the fire as
fast as the red balls kindled it; and now the copious rain
came down to quench every spark that might have remained
in wall or roof.

Yet the pretty edifice was in a sad condition: between fire
and water our pleasant quarters were spoiled.

And here we would say, in parenthesis, to military engineers: Never use timber to build the barracks of a fort, nor
raise the roof of your officers' quarters higher than the outer
wall, unless you calculate upon deserting your colors, turning traitor to your cause, and heading a host in attacking
that very fort. In such case you will find that having used that
material will serve your purpose—as did Beauregard.

That we should be again saluted with hot shot was pretty
certain, and, the cisterns empty and the rain storm over,
nothing could save the wood works from destruction. As
much of the officers' effects as could be removed, were, therefore, carried to the casemates—the privates, many of whom
were now sleeping soundly in their barracks, had not much
to lose.

The next morning rose fair and mild. The rain clouds had
discharged their burden, and now a clear, calm sky looked
down upon the scene. As day broke the firing from the enemy's batteries was resumed, and our garrison arose and

prepared to reply to them. The meagre breakfast of pork and coffee was again partaken, and at seven o'clock Fort Sumter opened fire, which was kept up vigorously during the remainder of the contest.

The first few shots directed at Fort Moultrie sent the chimneys off the officers' quarters, and considerably tore up the roof; nearly a dozen shots penetrated the floating battery below the water line, and several of the guns on Morris Island were disabled. The clear state of the atmosphere to-day enables us to see some of the effects of our fire upon the enemy—*all* the effects we do not expect ever to learn.

As anticipated, hot shot was fired again from Moultrie upon the doomed buildings inside Fort Sumter; and at a little after eight o'clock the officers' quarters were ablaze. All the men, not on duty at the guns, exerted themselves to extinguish the fire, but it spread rapidly, igniting here and there, as the red balls continued to drop, until every portion was in flames.

Attention was now directed to the magazines, which were situated at each of the southern corners of the fort, between the officers' quarters and the barracks. An intimacy with the internal arrangements of the fort had, doubtless, suggested to the gentleman in the opposite command the possibility of blowing up the garrison—hence the clever stratagem of firing the officers' quarters with hot shot; but against this danger Major Anderson provided by ordering all the powder to be taken from the upper magazines, and the lower magazines to be shut tight and thick mounds of earth to be heaped round the doors, through which no amount of heat could penetrate.

Afterwards, when the fire had spread through the barracks and reached the casemates, the Major ordered the powder, which had been removed thither from the magazines, to be thrown into the sea, and ninety barrels were thus disposed of.

As the fire increased the situation of the garrison was distressing beyond description. The water from the cisterns, followed by floods of rain, had saturated the riddled and broken buildings so that they burned with a hissing, smoldering flame, sending forth dense clouds of vapor and smoke, which soon filled the whole fort, rendering it difficult to breathe. The men were often obliged to lie down in the casemates, with wet cloths over their faces, to gain temporary relief.

Still the valiant fellows continued to serve their guns, and bomb after bomb, resounding from Sumter's walls, told that the spirit of American loyalty was not to be subdued, even by fire.

About half past twelve o'clock our flag-staff, which had been grazed several times, was shot through and the flag fell. Down, amid burning brands, surrounded by smoke and ruin, our war-worn ensign lay.

It was but a moment, and the next our young Lieutenant, Mr. Hall, rushed through the fire and, dashing all impediments out of his way, seized the prostrate colors. A buzz of admiration, mingled with words of fear for the officer's safety, and every man started forward, straining his eyes through the smoke until the object of quest emerged to view, begrimed with soot, choking and faint, his face and hair singed, his clothes scorched, and holding aloft, with almost spent strength, the rescued flag. A weak, but heartfelt cheer, from parched throats, greeted him as the precious burden was taken from his blistered hands, and he sunk down exhausted.

When the fire was all spent, the gay dwelling in ashes, and the noble fort was silent—standing, proud as ever, in stern, strong nakedness—Mr. Hall's epaulets were found on the spot from which he had raised the flag. In rushing through the fire they had become heated, and, oppressing his shoulders, he tore them off. They were now burnt—all but one little bunch of gold wire, which was embedded in ashes. That little relic is in the writer's possession; treasured as one of the precious trifles belonging to History's storehouse.

In fifteen minutes from the fall of the flag it was up again; a jury-mast was hastily raised, to which it was nailed, and it floated out as before. The honor of nailing it up belongs to Mr. Peter Hart, a New York gentleman, who had come to Fort Sumter some time before, to visit Major Anderson, with whom he had served in the Mexican war, and had remained at the fort as his guest. Though he took no part in the actual battle, yet he made himself useful to the garrison in many ways, of which this, recorded, is not the least.

And still the fire raged within and the cannon roared without. The flames increased in strength and volume, the air became heated all through the fort; but the more the little garrison suffered the harder they fought, and each ball that flew from their embrasures performed its errand well.

At about half past one P. M. a boat was seen approaching from Cumming's Point. Arrived at Fort Sumter a gentleman sprang from it, and, with a white handkerchief tied to the point of his sword to represent a flag of truce, he ran up to a port-hole, which he entered, saying to a soldier, whom he met,

"I wish to see the commandant—my name is Wigfall, and I come from General Beauregard."

The soldier went to inform Major Anderson, and Mr. Wigfall passed into the casemate where he met Captain Foster and Lieutenant Davis. To them he also introduced himself, stating that he came from General Beauregard. Then he added excitedly:

"Let us stop this firing. You are on fire, and your flag is down—let us quit!"

Mr. Davis replied,

"No, Sir, our flag is not down. Step out here and you will see it waving over the ramparts."

He ran out and looked up, but the smoke filled his eyes and he exclaimed, impatiently extending his sword:

"Here's a white flag,—will any body wave it out of the embrasure?"

Captain Foster said one of the men might do so, and Corporal Bingham, who was present, took it in his hand and jumped into the embrasure. And so the first white flag that waved from Fort Sumter was Senator Wigfall's handkerchief, tied to the point of that gentleman's sword!

But the firing still continued, when Mr. Wigfall said:

"If you will show a white flag from your ramparts, they will cease firing."

Captain Foster replied:

"If you request that a white flag shall appear there while you hold a conference with Major Anderson, and for that purpose alone, Major Anderson may permit it."

Major Anderson, at that moment came up, and the white flag was ordered to be raised.

"Major Anderson," said Mr. Wigfall, "you have defended your flag nobly, Sir. You have done all that is possible for man to do, and General Beauregard wishes to stop the fight. On what terms, Major Anderson, will you evacuate this fort?"

"Terms?" said Major Anderson, raising himself to his full height, and speaking with emphasis, *"I shall evacuate on the most honorable terms, or—die here!"*

Mr. Wigfall inclined his head;—respect for the glorious soul in that slight, frail form could not be withheld by even an enemy.

"Will you, Major Anderson," he then asked, "evacuate this fort upon the terms proposed to you the other day?"

"On the terms *last proposed* I will," was the reply.

"Then, Sir, I understand that the fort is to be ours?"

"On those conditions *only*, I repeat."

"Well, Sir, I will return to General Beauregard," said Mr. Wigfall, and, bowing low, he retired.

The white flag was then hauled down, and the American flag run up.

The Major now ordered that the firing should not be renewed, but that the men should take such refreshment as they had and rest a while. Poor fellows! they were nearly exhausted. Those who had not been engaged at the guns had been toiling to subdue the fire; and faint for lack of food, and suffocating with smoke, it was only their giant hearts sustained them through.

When the flames were at the highest the enemy blazed away the faster, in order to cut down the men who were working to extinguish the fire; but a Divine shield was over them, and *not one life of the gallant First was taken by traitor hands.*

Some "own correspondent" stated that the Major sent men outside the fort on a raft to procure water wherewith to quench the fire:—nonsense; there was plenty of water inside for the purpose, if there had only been hands enough to use it; but the guns must be kept manned, so only those who could be spared from that duty gave attention to the burning buildings.

Their exertions, however, were sufficient to prevent explosions and disaster to life. The fire was kept under, and prevented from communicating with the magazines, until every ounce of powder was removed out of our reach also, for, when hostilities ceased, we had but four barrels and three cartridges on hand.

But the fire had done its work, and was now gradually burning out. The barracks and officers' quarters were destroyed; and as the smoke thinned away, so that the eye could penetrate the scene, nothing but charred and smoldering ruins were visible.

About three o'clock P. M. a formal deputation came to Major Anderson from General Beauregard and Governor Pickens, proposing the same terms as had been previously offered, except that they were not willing the Major should salute his flag.

To this Major Anderson would not consent.

About six o'clock came another deputation, consisting of Colonel Pryor, Colonel Miles, Major Jones, and Captain Hartstene, and presented to Major Anderson General Beauregard's final terms. They were as follows. The garrison to march out with their side and other arms, with all the honors, in their own way and at their own time; to salute their flag and take it with them, and to take all their individual and company property; the enemy also agreeing to furnish transports, as Major Anderson might select, to any part of the country, either by land or water.

With all this Major Anderson was satisfied except the last clause. He would not consent to accept traveling accommodations from the enemy beyond the use of a steam-tug to convey him to the Government vessels outside the bar. . . .

And now all was arranged according to the Major's dictation, nothing remained but for the garrison to pack their effects and prepare to depart. This occupied great part of the night, and the next morning a Charleston steamer was in attendance to convey them to the fleet. The baggage was placed on board, then the men were drawn up under arms, on the parade, and a portion told off, as gunners, to salute their flag.

And now came the last solemn ceremony, to end even more solemnly than we expected. The guns began to fire. One after another their loud voices rolled out upon the Sabbath air until fifty were counted, and then—an explosion, a cry, a rush, and every gun was silent. A pile of cartridges, containing eighty pounds of powder, had been laid inside the bomb-proof, on the parapet, convenient to one of the guns. Among these cartridges a spark had fallen, and while the guns were firing, and the soldiers cheering, the powder exploded, tearing the strong sheets of iron, of which the bomb-proof was composed, into fragments, and scattering them abroad like feathers, at the same time sending a shock —a thrill of horror to every heart, for a group of men had been standing round, and Oh! where were they now?

A few moments and anxious faces were gathered to the scene of the disaster:—sad scene!—one of our brave fellows was dead—quite dead—rent almost in two; another was dying —fractured in every limb; another yet so mutilated that the Doctor only shook his head, and six others more or less injured.

The departure of the garrison was, of course, delayed by this accident—the dead and the wounded must be cared for; yet the process of evacuation must be concluded, and so, while with tender hands and moist eyes the soldiers removed their bleeding comrades, the flag, in vindicating whose honor this warm blood was spilt, drooped its proud pinions and slowly descended from the ramparts.

All that men in their circumstances could do was then done by the garrison for the dead and wounded: the former was prepared for decent burial, the latter tended with the kindest care.

The enemy, impatient to take possession of the fort, now arrived. Governor Pickens and General Beauregard with their aids landed and entered, but, seeing what had occurred, immediately tendered every assistance. A minister was accordingly sent for to Charleston, to perform the service for the dead, and physicians to take charge of those whom we should be obliged to leave behind living. Meanwhile a strong coffin was put together, a grave dug in the parade, and, shortly after the clergyman arrived, the funeral proceeded.

With military honors the scarcely cold remains were buried: the Major heading the procession with crape upon his sword. With the rites of the Church the coffin was lowered into the grave, and, awaiting the resurrection, when the justice of every cause shall be righteously proved, Daniel Howe was left sleeping in Fort Sumter.

The wounded men, all but two who were quite unfit to bear the voyage, were then removed to the steamer. These, under promise of the kindest treatment, were trusted to the hospitality of the South Carolinians; one of them, George Fielding was, therefore, conveyed to the Charleston Hospital, the other, Edward Galway, whose hours were numbered, was made as comfortable as possible in the fort.

These sad details arranged, Major Anderson issued his final orders for embarkation; and, carrying their flag and even its shattered mast, with band playing *Yankee Doodle,* the garrison marched out of the fort and went on board the steamer. As the Major emerged from the gate the music changed into *Hail to the Chief:*—simple tribute but no less heart-felt!

It was now late in the afternoon, and the garrison had eaten nothing since their scanty breakfast of pork and coffee;

it would, therefore, have been most desirable to have got out on board the transport without delay; but the state of the tide was such that the little steamer could not move, and all night she lay under the walls of Fort Sumter. Had they had only their own discomforts to think of, they would have felt more the inconveniences of that long delay without food or resting places; but thoughts of their dying comrade in the fort, whose groans almost reached their ears, filled their minds, even to the exclusion of self. Before they left, however, the sufferer was released. An officer came on board the steamer to inform Major Anderson of the death of Edward Galway, and to assure him that the deceased should be buried beside Howe, with the honors due to a brave soldier. . . .

Early on Monday morning, April 15th, with the rising of the tide, the Isabel, on board which our garrison lay, steamed out of the Charleston waters to where the United States vessels lay, waiting to receive the gallant freight. The little band were welcomed with cheers by the fleet, and the Baltic, on board which they were taken, felt honored by their presence. Every preparation had been made for their comfort, and nothing that could be done to atone for their past privation was neglected.

The Sumter flag, which had floated over the Isabel, was immediately hoisted on the Baltic, and a salute fired; and then Major Anderson was observed to bow his head and weep.

What, tears? Yes, Reader, tears! We don't conceal the fact. Great men can *feel*. It was told of Xerxes—why not tell it of our own loved hero? He looked up at his flag, tattered and begrimed, yet free as ever; he looked round at his comrades, wan and weary, but with hearts of stoutest metal, and emotion mastered him—he bowed his head and wept.

The Baltic was soon under weigh; and, after a pleasant run of three days reached Sandy Hook, where she was boarded by the Medical Staff from Staten Island, and quite a crowd of gentlemen who had come in boats, from New York, to meet her.

Here Major Anderson wrote the following dispatch to the War Department.

"STEAMSHIP BALTIC, off SANDY HOOK,
"Thursday, April 18, 1861.

"*Hon. S. Cameron, Secretary of War, Washington, D. C.:*
"SIR:—Having defended Fort Sumter for thirty-four hours, until the quarters were entirely burned, the main gates destroyed by fire, the gorge wall seriously injured, the magazine surrounded by flames, and its door closed from the effect of the heat, four barrels and three cartridges of powder only being available, and no provisions but pork remaining, I accepted terms of evacuation, offered by General Beauregard, being the same offered by him on the 11th instant, prior to the commencement of hostilities, and marched out of the fort, Sunday afternoon, the 14th instant, with colors flying and drums beating, bringing away company and private property, and saluting my flag with fifty guns.

"ROBERT ANDERSON,
"Major First Artillery."

It was a bright, sunny day as the Baltic steamed up New York Harbor, saluted by the firing of cannon from the forts, and by the ringing of bells and waving of flags from the city as she approached. The late garrison of Fort Sumter was drawn up on her quarter-deck, considerably restored in appearance by good food and rest; and the Major, surrounded by his officers, stood on the wheel-house, still looking pale and care-worn, his expressive features quivering with emotion as he acknowledged the salutations of the people.

All is now told—as far as a hasty sketch can tell it—of what transpired within Fort Sumter: of the energy, courage and determined will which sustained that little garrison to the last. And now you talk of promoting Major Anderson:—*promote Major Anderson!*—Could you promote the lion among beasts—the eagle among birds? could you exalt Sorata among mountains, or dignify the Amazon among streams? could you give distinction to the North Star, or brighten the sunbeam? as well might you attempt to elevate one who has arisen on the pinions of his own grand spirit to the hilltop of glory. No, fellow-countrymen, *you can not promote Major Anderson!* You can give no higher rank to the premier of his contemporaries—you can confer no prouder title on the HERO OF CHARLESTON HARBOR.

Cheer, Boys, Cheer

"WHAT A DEARTH we have in America," wrote George F. Noyes in 1863 in his *Bivouac and Battlefield,* "of good common songs! I have heard fire companies returning from a fire actually compelled to sandwich a good old hymn between two bacchanalian refrains, having quite exhausted their favorite melodies. 'We are bound for the land of Canaan' does not flow naturally from a great two-fisted, red-shirted fellow, nor could I ever enjoy hearing a crowd of roughs yelling out at the top of their lungs, 'I want to be an angel,' especially if they qualified each verse with an intermediate dash of oaths. In all seriousness, that man would be a public benefactor who would give our soldiers some simple patriotic songs, each with a good chorus, to lighten their weary marches and cheer their evening camp fires."

Many tried, but it was not until later in the war that Charles Carroll Sawyer, George F. Root, and Henry Clay Work really succeeded. In the meantime there was no dearth of songsters in which every conceivable tune was set with new words for the times. Here is Dan Emmett's

"Dixie" (in 1861 not yet completely a Southern song) with patriotic verses.

VICTORY'S BAND.
Air—*Dixie's Land.*

We're marching under the Flag of Union,
Keeping step in brave communion!
March away! march away! away! Victory's band
Right down upon the ranks of rebels,
Tramp them underfoot like pebbles,
March away! march away! away! Victory's band

CHORUS

Oh! we're marching on to Victory!
Hurrah! hurrah!
In Victory's band we'll sweep the land,
And fight or die for Victory!
Away! away!
We'll fight or die for Victory!

The rebels want a mongrel nation,
Union and Confederation!
March away! march away! away! Victory's band!
But we don't trust in things two-sided,
And go for Union undivided,
March away! march away! away! Victory's band!
Oh! we're marching, etc.

We're marching down on Dixie's regions,
With Freedom's flag and Freedom's legions.
March away! march away! away! Victory's band!
We're rolling down, a "Pending Crisis,"
With cannon-balls for Compromises,
March away! march away! away! Victory's band!
Oh! we're marching, etc.

Along the Border

THE NEW CONFEDERACY hoped to extend its domain over all the slaveholding states. To its first tier of states of the Deep South, Arkansas, Tennessee, North Carolina, and Virginia were added as the spring of 1861 progressed. There were vigorous secession elements in Maryland, Kentucky, and Missouri. Maryland was retained in the Union by forceful political action. Kentucky tried to remain neutral until it was too late for the Southern sympathizers to swing it to the Confederacy. Firm military action in Missouri soon put down the rebellious minority there.

These two pieces demonstrate the state of affairs on the border. First is the *Address to the People of Maryland by the General Assembly* of April 27, 1861. Next are two proclamations of General William S. Harney to the people of Missouri.

TO THE PEOPLE OF MARYLAND.

Resolved, by the Senate and House of Delegates,

That the "extraordinary state of affairs" in Maryland and the Republic, justifies and demands that we should adopt and publish the following Address to the People of Maryland:

Under the Proclamation of your Governor, we have assembled to act, according to our best judgments, for the true interest of Maryland.

That Proclamation has declared the present to be "an extraordinary state of affairs;" and all must admit the correctness of that assertion. We have been convened to do all that we have the constitutional authority and the mental ability of accomplishing, to provide for your safety and welfare during the pendency of the present unfortunate and terrible crisis. At the commencement of our labors, we feel it to be our duty to you and to your General Assembly to solicit your confidence in the fidelity with which our responsibilities will be discharged. We are Marylanders, as you are. We have families, as you have. Our interests are identified with yours. Our duty, our wishes and our hopes will be to legislate for the true interests of all the people of our State.

We cannot but know that a large proportion of the citizens of Maryland have been induced to believe that there is a probability that our deliberations may result in the passage of some measure committing this State to secession. It is, therefore, our duty to declare that all such fears are without just foundation. We know that we have no constitutional authority to take such action. You need not fear that there is a possibility that we will do so.

If believed by us to be desired by you, we may, by legislation to that effect, give you the opportunity of deciding for yourselves, your own future destiny. We may go thus far, but certainly will not go farther.

We know that the present crisis has materially deranged the usual current of business operations in every department. We shall devote ourselves to the duty of making this change as little inconvenient as possible to our constituents. We invite their scrutiny to our every action. If results do not realise our hopes and anticipations, we ask that you will, at least, extend to us the charity of believing that the failure has occurred from lack of ability, but not of will.

JNO. B. BROOKE,	JAMES F. DASHIELL,
THOMAS J. McKAIG,	J. J. HECKART,
COLEMAN YELLOTT,	S. J. BRADLEY,
H. H. GOLDSBOROUGH,	TILGHMAN NUTTLE,
D. C. BLACKISTONE,	F. WHITAKER,
C. F. GOLDSBOROUGH,	OSCAR MILES,
JNO. E. SMITH,	WASHINGTON DUVALL,
ANTHONY KIMMEL,	TEAGLE TOWNSEND,
J. S. WATKINS,	ANDREW A. LYNCH.

MILITARY DEPARTMENT OF THE WEST,
St. Louis, Missouri, May 12, 1861.
To the people of the State of Missouri and the city of
St. Louis:

I have just returned to this post, and have assumed the military command of this department. No one can more deeply regret the deplorable state of things existing here than myself. The past cannot be recalled. I can only deal with the present and the future. I most anxiously desire to discharge the delicate and onerous duties devolved upon me so as to preserve the public peace. I shall carefully abstain from the exercise of any unnecessary powers, and from all interference with the proper functions of the public offi-

cers of the State and city. I therefore call upon the public
authorities and the people to aid me in preserving the public
peace.

The military force stationed in this department by authority of the government, and now under my command, will
only be used in the last resort to preserve the peace.

I trust I may be spared the necessity of resorting to martial law, but the public peace *must be preserved,* and the
lives and property of the people protected.

Upon a careful review of my instructions, I find I have no
authority to change the location of the "Home Guards."

To avoid all cause of irritation and excitement, if called
upon to aid the local authorities in preserving the public
peace, I shall, in preference, make use of the regular army.

I ask the people to pursue their peaceful avocations, and
to observe the laws and orders of their local authorities, and
to abstain from the excitements of public meetings and
heated discussions. My appeal, I trust, may not be in vain,
and I pledge the faith of a soldier to the earnest discharge
of my duty.

WM. S. HARNEY,

Brigadier General U. S. A., Comd'g Department.
HEADQUARTERS DEPARTMENT OF THE WEST,

St. Louis, Missouri, May 13, 1861.

Official copy.

S. WILLIAMS,

Assistant Adjutant General.

MILITARY DEPARTMENT OF THE WEST,

St. Louis, Missouri, May 14, 1861.

To the people of the State of Missouri:

On my return to the duties of the command of this department, I find, greatly to my astonishment and mortification,

a most extraordinary state of things existing in this State, deeply affecting the stability of the government of the United States, as well as the government and other interests of Missouri itself.

As a citizen of Missouri, owing allegiance to the United States, and having interests in common with you, I feel it my duty, as well as privilege, to extend a warning voice to my fellow-citizens against the common dangers that threaten us, and to appeal to your patriotism and sense of justice to exert all your moral powers to avert them.

It is with regret that I feel it my duty to call your attention to the recent act of the general assembly of Missouri, known as the military bill, which is the result, no doubt, of the temporary excitement that now pervades the public mind.

This bill cannot be regarded in any other light than an indirect secession ordinance, ignoring even the forms resorted to by other States. Manifestly its most material provisions are in conflict with the Constitution and laws of the United States. To this extent it is a nullity, and cannot, and ought not, to be upheld or regarded by the good citizens of Missouri. There are obligations and duties resting upon the people of Missouri under the Constitution and laws of the United States which are paramount, and which, I trust, you will carefully consider and weigh well before you will allow yourselves to be carried out of the Union, under the form of yielding obedience to this military bill, which is clearly in violation of your duties as citizens of the United States.

It must be apparent to every one who has taken a proper and unbiased view of the subject, that whatever may be the termination of the unfortunate condition of things in respect to the so-called "Cotton States," Missouri must share the destiny of the *Union*. Her geographical position, her soil, productions, and, in short, all her material interests, point to this result. We cannot shut our eyes against this controlling fact. It is seen, and its force is felt throughout the nation.

So important is this regarded to the great interests of the country, that I venture to express the opinion that the whole power of the government of the United States, if necessary, will be exerted to maintain Missouri in her present position in the Union. I express to you, in all frankness and sincerity, my own deliberate convictions, without assuming to speak for the government of the United States, whose authority, here and elsewhere, I shall at all times, and under all cir-cumstances, endeavor faithfully to uphold.

I desire above all things most earnestly to invite my fel-low-citizens dispassionately to consider their true interests as well as their true relation to the government under which we live and to which we owe so much.

In this connexion, I desire to direct attention to one sub-ject which no doubt will be made the pretext for more or less popular excitement. I allude to the recent transactions at Camp Jackson, near St. Louis. It is not proper for me to com-ment upon the official conduct of my predecessor in com-mand of this department, but it is right and proper for the people of Missouri to know that the main avenue of Camp Jackson, recently under command of General Frost, had the name of *Davis,* and a principal street of the same camp that of Beauregard; and that a body of men had been received into that camp by its commander which had been notoriously organized in the interests of the secessionists, the men openly wearing the dress and badge distinguishing the army of the so-called Southern Confederacy. It is also a notorious fact that a quantity of arms had been received into the camp which were unlawfully taken from the United States arsenal at Baton Rouge, and surreptitiously passed up the river in boxes marked marble.

Upon facts like these, and having in view what occurred at Liberty, the people can draw their own inferences, and it cannot be difficult for any one to arrive at a correct conclusion as to the character and ultimate purpose of that encampment. No government in the world would be entitled to respect that would tolerate for a moment such openly treasonable preparations.

It is but simple justice, however, that I should state the fact that there were many good and loyal men in the camp who were in no manner responsible for its treasonable character.

Disclaiming, as I do, all desire or intention to interfere in any way with the prerogatives of the State of Missouri, or with the functions of its executive or other authorities, yet I regard it as my plain path of duty to express to the people in respectful, but at the same time decided language, that within the field and scope of my command and authority the *"supreme law"* of the land must and shall be maintained, and no subterfuges, whether in the forms of legislative acts or otherwise, can be permitted to harass or oppress the good and law-abiding people of Missouri. I shall exert my authority to protect their persons and property from violations of every kind, and I shall deem it my duty to suppress all unlawful combinations of men, whether formed under pretext of military organizations or otherwise.

WILLIAM S. HARNEY,
Brigadier General United States Army, Commanding.

Rebels Ahead!

THE SPRING OF 1861 was a time of preparation. There were no big battles. Men were being enlisted and trained for war. But they had little idea what was ahead of them.

Real war broke with sudden fury at Manassas in July, 1861. Confident Federal soldiers were turned back by the Confederates in a defeat humiliating for its unexpectedness.

The naïveté of the recruit, new to the army and new to battle, is apparent in this letter Allen A. Kingsbury of Medfield, Massachusetts, wrote his parents shortly after the battle. The wounded soldier did soon receive a leave but returned to the army in September and was killed in the Peninsular campaign the next April. His letters and his journal were printed in 1862 as *The Hero of Medfield.*

ARLINGTON HEIGHTS, JULY 25, 1861.

My Dear Parents:

Yesterday we moved from Camp Banks across the river to this place, which is just below Washington, and between Forts Corcoran and Albany. To-morrow our regiment will go to Fort Albany, which is about a mile from here. It is one of the outposts, and a very pleasant place; it commands the long bridge, the road from Fairfax to Washington, and the Potomac. It is in fact the post of *honor!*

I will now give you a description of our march to the field of battle, and of the battle itself. Tuesday, July 16, orders came to pack our knapsacks, and prepare to march. We rolled our rubber and flannel blankets up together and slung them across our shoulders in light marching order, filled our canteens with water and our haversacks with hard bread and salt pork for three days' rations. I put some coffee and sugar into my pocket for my own use, and it came very convenient, as we shall see. We left our knapsacks in the care of the sick and those who were not able to march. We started from camp about 4, P. M; went past the Michigan regiment's camp; they went with us. There were four regiments, the Mass. 1st, the Michigan 2d and 3d, and the N. Y. 12th. We were under command of Col. Richardson and Gen. Tyler. The first place of interest which we past was the chain bridge across the Potomac. It is quite long; on the hill above it are several cannon, in the centre of the bridge is a draw and a gate covered with wrought iron, with *port holes* through which to fire the cannon. The bridge is also fixed so that when a crowd of rebels get upon it, it can be pulled and precipitate them into the river, which is about thirty feet from the bridge, and is very rocky. As soon as we filed off the bridge our band struck up "Yankee Doodle." As we stepped upon the "sacred soil of Virginia" we marched at quick time, and there was some *cheering* I can tell you; but we little knew what we were to pass through. We marched on, however, over some of the worst roads I ever saw, worse, if possible, than the road to the top of Noon Hill. The roads are full of stones and gullies. Virginia is indeed a desolate country; most of the buildings are built of logs, the logs are hewed on the sides and placed above the other, and the cracks are filled in with mortar or mud; the chimnies are built on the outside, they are composed of large stones. Again I say it is a rough looking country; but I never saw black-berries so thick before. Would frequently "fall out of ranks," hop over the fence (Virginia fence) and pick our tin pots full in a very few moments, and then such large ones, it was perfect fun to pick them, and not at all unpleasant to eat them. We marched till 10, P. M., when we halted for the night. We camped on a low, marshy piece of ground in a place called Vienna, where the rebels fired upon the Ohio volunteers. We got to sleep about 11, P. M., we were so tired we did not eat any supper. We arose at sunrise next morning, prepared our breakfast of hard bread, salt pork, and cold water, but I had a cup of coffee, owing to the fore-sight of putting some in my pocket. We got under way as soon as possible. Saw the cars which contained the above soldiers when they were attacked by the rebels, the cars were riddled with bullet holes. The boys in my tent went out *"grubbing"* and brought in *peaches* and potatoes, so we had *peach sauce,* soft bread and new potatoes; quite a treat for us *half starved men!* We then proceeded on our march; were very much troubled for the want of water. I never suf-fered so much from thirst before. When we came to a brook or spring the soldiers would break their ranks and run for the water, but it was mostly so muddy and rily that it was hardly fit to drink, but yet it was *water!* Our regiment headed

the column. As we came upon the top of a hill it was a splendid sight to look as far as we could and see the road filled
with soldiers, horses and wagons. We went through places
where the rebels had had their camps and where they had
felled the trees across the road to prevent us from passing,
but they were soon cut away by our pioneers, who went
ahead armed with guns and axes. We stopped that afternoon at 3 o'clock, in a fine place where we staid all night;
there were 60,000 or 70,000 troops around us. We marched
about ten miles that day (Wednesday), and then I had to
go on *picket guard* all night; had about *one* hour's sleep;
very good after marching all day.

We were placed in a piece of wood with orders to fire
upon any one who should not halt and tell who he was. We
did not see any one, but could hear people walking about in
the woods. We got into camp about sunrise Thursday morning, found the boys all alive and stirring about getting breakfast and preparing to march. I made some nice coffee, which
went first rate. At 8, A. M., we started; as we went along
saw places where the rebels had had their camp; near noon
we came to places where their camp fires were burning. In
some places they had cooked dinner, but in their hurry to
leave they had thrown it away. In one place a wagon loaded
with flour was stuck fast in the mud; they had unloaded it,
stove in the heads of the barrels and left the flour in the
road. We were hurried forward as fast as we could go. Between 1 and 2, P. M., we stopped to reconnoitre and to send
scouts ahead. In about half an hour they returned and reported *rebels ahead!* We were up in a hurry, and two Co.'s
of infantry and one of cavalry were sent forward. When we
ascended a hill we could see men in a field about a mile distant—we could see the glittering of their bayonets. The General sent back for three pieces of artillery; when they were

ready we opened fire upon them; you ought to have seen
how they scattered and run into the woods. We fired some
three or four rounds among them, when very suddenly a
battery opened upon our left about a mile from us. We were
then ordered about, and taking a circle came out at the left
of our battery. We were then ordered into a field near some
woods. Two Co.'s, G. and H., with our pioneers who had
been ahead, commenced firing. Our Co. and Co. G. were
then ordered into the woods; we did not know what was
there, but we soon found out. We had got perhaps three
rods into the woods when a murderous fire was opened upon
us by the rebels from a masked battery; several of our men
were killed and wounded. Three of my comrades fell dead
at my side. Our Capt. then ordered us ahead, and on we
went. I saw a battery on a small hill. I saw an officer on the
embankment beside a cannon; I brought my rifle to my shoulder and fired at him. He threw up his arms and fell headlong
down the bank. A perfect volley of rifle shot then rained
around me; one bullet struck me on the breast, went through
my blanket and hit the eagle on my cross belt, and knocked
me down. Another ball cut off my cap box. Our Capt. then
ordered a retreat, and we started for the open ground. The
balls fell like hailstones around us, but I did not mind them;
was as cool as ice. When I had got out of the woods and was
walking along, a cannon ball struck the ground about a rod
behind me, and rebounding, hit me in the joint of the knee,
upon the under side, and knocked me down. I did not know
where I was for several minutes. When I got up I could
not stand. Two of the N. Y. 69th took me up and carried
me to the wagons. I did not think I was hurt much, but I
found I could not walk, so I was carried to the hospital at
Centreville, where I staid till Sunday, when I went out to
join my Co., but they would not let me, so I remained with

the wagons. At 5, P. M., an order came for the wagons to
retreat back towards Fairfax. I got on board one of the
wagons, rode all night, and next morning found myself in
Washington. I am quite lame now, so that I don't go round
much. I do not know what they will do with me. *I shall try
to get home* if I can. No more this time. *Don't worry about
me!* Love to all.

ALLEN.

War in the West

MEN from the great new states of the Northwest as eagerly volunteered as did the Yankees of New England. Their war was a different war, scattered over the plains west of the Mississippi, but no less war.

Henry O'Conner, in introducing his *History of the First Regiment of Iowa Volunteers,* addressed a letter to the Hon. S. J. Kirkwood, Governor of Iowa. In part, he wrote:

"The news of the fall of Fort Sumpter, on the twelfth of April 1861, although not wholly unexpected, aroused the people to a sense of the deep wrong and insult suffered by the nation and its flag. The proclamation of the President immediately following, called for seventy-five thousand volunteer troops, and apportioned to Iowa one regiment. The patriotism of the people, and the no less patriotic and prompt action of the State Government, furnished the regiment, clothed and ready for the field, at the designated point of rendezvous, (Keokuk,) within thirty days from the date of the President's proclamation; the chief embarrassment of the government and the principal disappointment of our citizens being in the fact that thousands who responded to the call and who have since proven their devotion to the cause of their country, could not then enter the service.

"The regiment, after its organization, spent five weeks in camp at Keokuk, preparing by company and battalion drill and the discipline of camp life, for the brief, severe, but glorious campaign which they afterwards went through in Missouri, with so much credit to themselves and honor to the State of Iowa.

"When General Lyon moved from St. Louis up the Missouri river to meet the rebel forces of Jackson and Price, then in position near Booneville, orders were sent to Iowa for what troops were ready, to proceed to Hannibal and thence across the country to the Missouri river at such point as he might be. Colonel Curtis, with his (the second) regiment, then at Keokuk, having received orders from the War Department for special service on the Hannibal and St. Joseph Railroad, moved on the twelfth of June at mid-night; and on the thirteenth, the day following, with four hours' notice, the First Regiment, under command of Colonel Bates, struck their tents at Camp Ellsworth, and embarked on two steamboats for Hannibal."

How life was in this Western campaign is related in O'Conner's letter of July 16.

CAMP SIGEL, GREEN COUNTY, MISSOURI,
Ten miles N. W. of Springfield, July 16, 1861.

FRIEND MAHIN: I am so much of a stranger to the *Journal* of late, that I scarcely know how to approach it. I am, as you see, very particular in dating my letter, not that there will be anything new to you in what I have to say, but that such of your readers as feel interested in the doings and misdoings of the First Iowa Regiment, may take map in hand and follow us through our long and somewhat tedious march; and perhaps some of them may wish to preserve it. I can vouch for its accuracy—elegance of style, of course, you cannot expect, when you consider that I am sitting *tailor fashion*, with the tail-board of a wagon across my knees for a writing desk, in a noisy camp of six thousand men, and over two thousand horses and mules—drums beating, fifes squealing, mules braying, horses neighing, men swearing, singing, and doing every thing but praying.

We are now encamped near the summit of the Ozark mountains, in a beautiful region, and what is still better, surrounded by a warm-hearted, Union-loving people, who are ready and willing to make any sacrifice for our beloved country. The soil is rich, but full of lime-stones, which show themselves on the surface of the ground about as thick as onions in Scott county, to the great annoyance of plowmen, and the especial annoyance of us poor devils who have to sleep on them every night. However, I must not get in advance of my story.

We left Keokuk, June thirteenth, thence to Hannibal by boat, next moving by rail to Macon City, thence to Renick by rail, thirty miles, where we remained one night, and commenced our march to Booneville. This is the point at which some unfriendly correspondent of the *Gate City* says we took to the woods and got cut off, a statement no less injudicious than erroneous, as I have no doubt it caused many a tear to be shed about our hearth-stones at home. We made the march to Booneville, fifty-eight miles, in two days and three hours, on three meals, and that it was a good one we need no better evidence than General Lyon's expression to Colonel Bates, that he knew of no better march even by regular soldiers. We staid in Camp Cameron, at Booneville, till the morning of the third of July, when, as a part of General Lyon's command, we started on our march for south-western Missouri, to any point where we could lay our hands on the traitor Jackson. We made what is usually denominated forced marches, twenty-four miles a day—except one day, when it poured down a drenching rain on us, we marched eighteen miles—the Iowa boys at the head of the column, with mud and water running off them in the shape of a mixture of rain and sweat—company A in the van singing national airs, under the leadership of that little nightingale from your office, Emerson O. Upham, who, by the way, has shown himself to be one of the toughest and best soldiers in the regiment. When we had marched eighteen miles and left the two Missouri regiments forty-five minutes behind, and their men dropping by the road-side by the score, the surgeon of Colonel Boernstein's regiment rode in a gallop to the head of the column, and told the General that unless he halted the column he would kill all the Missouri men. We halted right in the rain. The rain held up in an hour or two; we built a fire, dried our clothes on us, (the best way always to save taking cold,) got our supper of some healthy crackers and good coffee, ran round like antelopes, and in the evening, to the surprise of every one, and to the terror of the St. Louis boys, we had a skirmish drill. I believe it was at this point that General Lyon, who first called us Gipsies because of our ragged and dirty appearance, christened us the "Iowa Grey Hounds."

At Grand River, in Henry county, we came up with Colonel Sturgis' command, consisting of two volunteer regiments from Kansas, five hundred regulars, and four pieces of artillery, which, joined to our force of twenty-five hundred troops, put General Lyon at the head of a column of six thousand, with ten pieces of artillery. Crossing Grand river with such a force of men, wagons and horses, on a rickety old ferry boat, was, as you can perceive, a tedious process. It was prosecuted night and day, and the whole column taken over without a single accident to man or beast. We marched from there to the Osage river, at a point ten miles south-west of Osceola. Here, again, we had to go through the disagreeable process of crossing the troops on about the meanest thing in the shape of a ferry boat that I ever saw. But General Lyon was there, and the thing had to go ahead.

Just before starting over the river in the evening, some Union men came into camp and gave information to the General of about eight hundred secessionists being encamped at a point about twelve miles off. Colonel Bates was ordered to detail from his regiment a sufficient force to take them or break them up. Five companies—A, C, D, F and K— were accordingly detailed for that purpose, and got all ready to start, under command of Major Porter, silently, as soon as it was dark; when suddenly, and to the great disappointment of the boys, the order was countermanded. It appeared that a messenger had just arrived from Springfield with the intelligence that Colonel Sigel's command, of about fifteen hundred, were in Springfield surrounded by about eight thousand seccessionists, under the lead of Claib. Jackson nominally, but Ben. McCulloch really, for Jackson is not fit to lead a blind horse to water. He is a coward as well as a traitor. This news, of course, stirred up the old General, who seemed to feel sure of his game this time, having missed Jackson at Booneville.

We went on with the crossing, and got our regiment over by four o'clock in the morning; no sleep, with orders to march at five; made fires, hurried up our breakfast, swallowed it, and started at quarter past five. This was our great march, kept up through a hot sun until three o'clock. We camped, got supper, and at half-past five, when we were thinking of fixing our beds, the General's bugle sounded a forward march. Off we started, and after measuring off forty-five miles in twenty-two hours—recollect with the loss of two nights' sleep, and only three hours' rest—we fetched up in a corn-field, on the bank of a pretty stream; corn reeking with heavy dew, ground muddy from recent rains, men shivering, sleepy and hungry. We were ordered to get our breakfasts, what sleep we could, and be ready to march in two hours. Springfield, still thirty-five miles off, must be reached to-night. Of course, in this long march a great many fell back exhausted, but most of our regiment came up within an hour. Many dropped down in the wet and mud and went to sleep; some went to making a fire and stirring round to prevent chilling—myself among the latter. In a little over three hours we had got breakfast, sleep, rest, &c., &c., and were again on our weary, swinging march, but with many sore feet. We thought of nothing, however, but coming up with Jackson, when lo! after we had gone about five miles, the General received the news of Jackson's defeat by Sigel, and his subsequent hasty flight. Of course this rendered any more forced marching unnecessary; so after marching a few miles farther to a good creek, we encamped for the day, cooked, slept, washed ourselves, our shirts, &c. Next day,

Saturday, we marched to this place, where we have rested ever since.

We spend our time very pleasantly. The intervals between drill and parade are spent in looking up some delicacy in the way of bread, butter, chickens, &c. A good many wagons come into camp with those things, and those of the boys who have not gambled off their money have a little left.

I have given you a rough but faithful sketch of our soldiering for the last four or five weeks. How do you like it? It is better to read of, than to be a part of. Like others, perhaps, you will be astonished to hear that your correspondent stood the march all through without giving out or resorting to the wagons. Pretty fair for a soldier weighing only one hundred pounds. Our officers had not a much better time than the men. Captain Cummins is a perfect horse to march. It is rumored that he is going to Washington with a view of a commission in the regular army; or, failing in that, to get a company accepted, and then come home and raise it.

George Satterlee is acting Quartermaster, and on that account is very little with the company. He is unusually popular with the regiment, and his business knowledge and habits fit him admirably for the place.

Ben. Beach is, and always has been, a favorite with the company. Always at his place, wherever that is, impartial, modest and kind-hearted, he is seen and felt, but not often heard. He desires to raise a company and stay in the army, if he has a chance. I predict that he will make his mark as a soldier.

Colonel Bates has gained very much in favor with his men during this march. He evinced an anxiety for the comfort of his men which endeared him to them, and he assumes a respectful independence in the presence of his superiors which the citizen-soldier likes to see.

Lieutenant-Colonel Merritt and Major Porter have always been personally popular with the regiment. We have had none of those disgusting scenes of *whipping, bucking, gagging,* &c., in our regiment, but we have seen too much of it in the others while at Booneville and here, amongst regulars and volunteers—a great deal of it in the St. Louis regiment. In the First Kansas regiment, a young man named Cole was shot on dress parade, for killing a fellow-soldier. Four balls entered his body, and one his neck. He died instantly.

In a wayside grocery and gambling shop near the Osage river, two soldiers belonging to the regulars, were murdered. The grocery and house were burned by order of the General, and the grocery keeper, who proved to be the murderer of at least one of the men, was taken, tried before the General, convicted, sentenced to be hanged, and is now under guard awaiting execution as soon as the General shall order. He deserves his fate richly. He is an old offender. These are incidents of news.

I had almost forgotten to say a word about General Lyon. A man rather below the middle stature, with no surplus flesh, red hair and whiskers, fast ripening to grey, small blue eyes—vigor, energy, fearlessness, and a dogged determination to accomplished his purpose at all hazards, are the prominent traits of his character. Finish the picture yourself—I must close to get this to Springfield.

We expect to be home about the twentieth or twenty-fifth of August, and will be glad to see the people, whether they will to see us or not.   **H.**

Fort Laramie

ONE OF THE MOST INTRIGUING of all personal narratives of the Civil War is Ovando J. Hollister's *History of the First Regiment of Colorado Volunteers*. Not only is it one of the rarest of Civil War books, it is also one of the freshest and frankest accounts of army life.

Born in Massachusetts in 1835, Hollister nevertheless qualifies as a "first citizen" of three Western states. He farmed on the Kansas frontier in the 1850's, succumbed to the gold fever and moved to Colorado, where he was living in 1861. After the war he removed to Utah, where he died in Salt Lake City in 1892, an honored citizen of the Mormon capital.

The *History of the First Regiment* is wonderful reading, a fine combination of frontier and army narratives. Hollister himself described it in the book's introductory paragraphs: "I propose to write a History of the First Regiment of Colorado Volunteers; its organization and discipline at Camp Weld; campaign in New Mexico, with notices of the most striking features of that Territory, and the conditions and strength of the Regiment at present [1863].

"I make no pretensions to literary merit or taste. The work was originally written for my own amusement, with no thought of publication. The fact that the members of the Regiment wanted it, and were willing to pay for it, induced me to have it published. It is common, in such cases, to beg indulgence for the constant use of the personal pronoun, but as I am a broken down soldier, consequently as low as I can get on the social ladder, I submit my work to the gentle public to judge of as they please. . . . As a record of our marches and fights, should we unfortunately never have any more, it will, I trust, be of some value. It will at least be a tie to bind us together in the days that are to come."

These portions of the book's first three chapters tell the early history of the regiment.

In the latter part of July, 1861, three men were sitting at dinner, round a rough table in a rougher country—the mining district of South Clear Creek. To those familiar with the style of living in the mountain placers, it will perhaps be unnecessary to say that their meal was neither extra in quality nor profuse in quantity. Judging from the appearance of the country and people, mining at that time was not exceedingly inviting or profitable. If they could make grub out of their claims they were satisfied; flattering themselves with the various wild things they *would* do when they struck the pay-streak. Through a strong hope in the future and a stronger faith in luck, the industrious and sanguine persevered in their hard, thankless task, while the bummer and loafer avoided all labor that was not necessitated by the state of their larder. That of our friends was nearly empty, and as this spasmodic gold-digging was intensely disagreeable, they were discussing their bread and beef and the chances of "raising the wind" in some easier way, at the same time.

Casting their eyes about for a new lode, the state of the country, plunged in a gigantic civil war, attracted their attention, and the idea of taking advantage of the patriotic uprising of the nation's heart and of the hard times in the mines, to raise a company of volunteers for the war, thus securing commissions for themselves, struck them as being a lode, which, once open, might be worked with ease and profit. Accordingly, Sam. H. Cook, who was perhaps the most self-reliant and decisive of the three friends, instantly struck off a few advertisements for Volunteers to form a mounted company, proceed to the States and enter the service under Jim Lane, with whom Cook had been somewhat associated in the Kansas war of '56. These bills, which promised service to the admirers of Lane, under the very eyes of their loved chief—an immediate return to America—a sentiment sufficiently powerful of itself to enlist a company—and which chose the mounted arm of the service as the field of the projected company's future action, were posted in conspicuous places through the mines, and owing to the skill with which they were drawn, eighty or more men had engaged in the enterprise by the middle of August.

Cook was to be Captain—the others Lieutenants. One named Nelson, having been in the service before, consequently somewhat posted on military affairs, was to be First —the other, named Wilson, ambitious and energetic, yet lacking the self-reliance with which Cook was so bountifully provided, was to be Second. With this programme they were well pleased, as it was calculated to advance their personal interests.

Soon, advertisements under the auspices of one W. F. Marshall, appeared in the Denver papers, inviting proposals for the transportation of the company to Leavenworth. The expenses of the trip across the plains were to be defrayed by a contribution of five dollars from each enlisted man.

About the 20th of August they all repaired to Denver, expecting to start for the States as soon as the requisite transportation could be procured. But Gov. Gilpin, unwilling to have these men leave the Territory, where he was then recruiting a Regiment of Volunteers, tried to induce them to remain and form one company of the First Colorados. Having pledged his honor that they should be well mounted, armed and equipped, and have active service "till they couldn't rest," they concluded to stay.

They were furnished quarters on Ferry Street, West Denver, and immediately proceeded to elect officers—commissioned and non-commissioned. It seems the W. F. Marshall mentioned above was an old acquaintance of Cook's, and had held a commission as Second Lieutenant in the Kansas Militia, under Lane. For this reason, and his services in enlisting men, he was the Captain's choice for Second Lieutenant, if not for First; but the Company disliking his haughty style and reserved manner, would not have him First nor even Second, until Wilson, at Marshall's earnest entreaty waived his claims and withdrew his name from the canvass.

Wilson became Orderly Sergeant, the hardest and most thankless position in the business. The other non-coms. were indicated by those who had secured the most important positions, rather than elected by the men.

As the Ferry Street quarters became too small for the increasing number of the company they were moved down to the old Buffalo House, where they remained two or three months. A corral just below and across the road contained the company horses, and was used as a guard house. There was no trouble in getting out at the back side, however, and prisoners confined in the corral enjoyed the freedom of the town.

A guard was stationed before the doors of the Captain's and Orderly's rooms, to prevent privates from passing in. Here the non-coms. chiefly congregated, while the privates occupied the upper story. Judging from their appearance, they were well possessed of the idea of their own importance. The finest clothes in market were none too good, and these, with the skill of the barber and tailor, made a very tangible contrast between these fifteen day soldiers, and recruits who were constantly coming in. Collisions between them and the town secesh occurred occasionally, but they never resulted in anything serious. The men were obliged to remain in quarters, a pass being necessary even to go up town.

A picket guard was stationed every night on various routes leading into Denver, to prevent surprise from domestic traitors or Texans, who were supposed to be coming in force. Then again cartridges would be issued and orders published for all to sleep on their arms, ready for action at a moment's notice. The idea of there being any necessity for these precautions was jeered at by us, but the cry of "wolf, wolf," was persisted in, till many no doubt trembled for safety.

Finally the wolf came. The company was put in fighting trim instanter. Time passed, and men breathed hard and quick. Perhaps they thought of home, and the loving ones there awaiting them. Orderlies galloped through the streets as if the fate of empires hung on their movements. Small bodies of troops hurried to their assigned positions, and suspense had become painful, when some enterprising scout came in with the news that the fancied host of Texans was a drove of stock, "Oh! what a fall was there," etc.

At that time the other companies of the Regiment, excepting A and B, were in embryo, and straining every nerve to entice recruits. A sketch of their organization would not perhaps come amiss.

Soon after the war broke out it became patent to every one that some force would be necessary to preserve Colorado to the Union. Gold was first discovered by Georgians, and the Southern element had always been well represented in our society. In view of this fact, and with the idea of strengthening the forts in the lower portion of the Territory, Gov. Gilpin during the summer recruited two companies of volunteers.

After the battle of Bull Run the disaffected in Denver boldly avowed their principles, raised a Secesh flag, which, however, did not fly long, secretly bought up arms, and in various ways commenced marshaling their forces to seize our infant Territory. But the Governor and other public men were alive to the emergency. They knew it would not do to stand idly by while the active, turbulent factionists were preparing to make their deadly spring, *a la* C. F. Jackson, in Missouri. The capture of Forts Bliss and Fillmore, in Arizona, by "Baylor's Babes," and their reported march on Santa Fe, decided the Governor, and in the last days of August J. P. Slough, Captain of Co. A, was appointed Colonel; S. F. Tappan, Captain of Co. B, Lieut. Colonel; J. M. Chivington was commissioned Major . . .

Recruiting offices were opened in Denver, at Gregory, Idaho, and beyond the Range; and in two months the required complement of men was obtained. A site was selected for barracks on the Platte, two miles from the centre of Denver City, and called Camp Weld, in honor of the then Secretary of the Territory. At a cost of $40,000 comfortable and sufficient barracks were constructed, and as fast as the companies were filled they went into quarters there. Notices like the following were occasionally seen in the daily papers.

"Yesterday Capt. S. F. Tappan, with Co. B, numbering 101 men, arrived from the mountains and went into quarters at Camp Weld. The men look hale and hearty, and are in excellent spirits." . . .

By means of drafts on the U. S. Treasury, the Governor defrayed the expense of raising clothing and sustaining his Volunteers, though this irregular proceeding afterwards environed him with trouble and finally cost him his office. Government was slow to endorse his action, and it is said never would have done so but for the meritorious service of the Regiment in Mexico. This idea was prevalent among the men for six months, and caused much lawlessness and insubordination that might otherwise have been avoided.

The men having enlisted with the idea of going to the States and taking an active part in the war, were dissatisfied with the inactivity of Camp Weld, and the idea of something in Gilpin's proceedings which would prevent their entering the service under their present organization, rendered them reckless. They have been publicly accused as "chicken thieves, jayhawkers, turbulent and seditious, a disgrace to themselves and the country." Grant it true. Suppose they plead guilty. Was there not much in the attendant circumstances to palliate their little irregularities? The fact that man's inactivity is the Devil's opportunity, and the prevalent though erroneous idea that they would never be recognized or paid, gave some excuse for the slight peccadilloes of the Volunteers at Camp Weld. Believing that every candid man will view it as I do, I leave the subject with the assertion that notwithstanding all that has been said, east, west, north or south, about their jayhawking proclivities, there is not a manlier, better disposed thousand men in the United States service than the First Colorados.

All the arms in the country were purchased, not so much for the use of the volunteers as to prevent traitors from getting them. Owing to our judicious state of preparation, Colorado escaped the civil convulsions that have desolated portions of our once happy country.

For the better equipment of his Regiment, the Governor had already sent to divert southward a train of arms proceeding from Camp Floyd to the States. This train was known to be in the vicinity, and fears were entertained for its safety. An escort, numbering sixteen, under command of Lieut. Nelson, was sent out to protect it on the way in. They started September 6th, full of the idea of their good fortune in being mounted and on their first service, and of escaping from the restraint imposed in quarters, which, though novel, was disagreeable. They proceeded with light hearts as far as Crow Creek, where they met the train and turned back with it. But danger seeming to thicken, at least to the apprehension of the authorities, another detail of twenty men, under Lieut. Marshall, was sent out on the same errand, on the 10th inst. We furnished ourselves with rations for six days, and a pair of blankets apiece, which we packed on two ponies.

At our first camp, on St. Vrain's Creek, a dispute occurred in the party as to whether bacon, used to oil firearms, would or would not make them rust. Little Hawley had ten dollars that said bacon grease was the best that could be used. Jude, on the other side, would bet ten dollars, but he had not got it with him. He put up five—the balance to be staked at the time of trial. As soon as the money was up, the crowd adjourned to an adjoining grocery, procured two buckets of milk and a gallon of whisky, and bound the bet by drinking the stakes. The betters joined us, and as neither ever mentioned it again, the merits of the case are still in the dark.

Next morning an express passed us. He said a few words to Marshall, probably of an alarming nature, for we left our pack animals on Little Thompson and hurried on. About dark we came in sight of Box Elder, when the orders "Form Fours"—"Trot"—"Gallop"—"CHARGE!" followed in quick succession, and Nelson, alarmed at so unusual an approach, ordered his men under arms, and prepared to give us a warm reception, should we prove enemies. On nearing the sentinels, our column was halted with some difficulty, and after recognition we quietly proceeded into camp.

On the ensuing day we came back to Cache-a-la-Poudre, where a messenger met us, with dispatches from the Governor. They contained orders for Lieut. Marshall to proceed, with his detail, on the Horse Creek route, towards Fort Laramie. It was thought a train of arms had left that place for Denver, on the strength of Gilpin's representations.

As we had only provided for a six days' trip, it seemed hard to start on a six weeks' one; but our newly fledged zeal was mounting as eagles' wings, and made small account of obstacles.

After bidding Nelson's party good bye (fresh friendships are always tender) we pressed a wagon and harness, hitched up our horses and started down the river. We had a good supply of flour, fifteen pounds of bacon and three of coffee. Our culinary department contained two frying-pans—minus handles—two small tin coffee-boilers and a few tin cups. Flour was mixed in the mouth of the sack and baked before the blaze. Thus furnished, we struck across the desert, two hundred miles in extent, between the mouth of Cache-a-la-Poudre and Laramie. Not a man in the party had ever been in the country before, though two citizens of Denver accompanied us as guides.

Our first day's travel was down the Cache-a-la-Poudre.
Though late in the haying season, but little grass had been
cut. It was a good indication of the quality of the soil. Ten
miles below Laporte there is some good bottom, especially
on the north side; but sandy, barren streaks, destitute of
vegetation, are common in the best of it. These are from two
to ten rods wide—the edges as well defined as if a mowing
machine had cut out the barren strips. I thought that was
the case till we passed over some. On the stream, as a whole,
there is much good land—more that is worthless. The small
breadth in crops is heavily burdened. But few people live
here though every claim is occupied by a cabin. We camped
near the mouth of the creek.

Next morning we struck across six or eight miles, to Crow
Creek. There was but one water hole in the lower part of its
course, and we were lucky enough to find it, and a small
quantity of bacon and coffee hanging in a tree. We traveled
up this creek two or three days. The lower part was dry,
with occasional patches of low, scraggy-topped cottonwoods,
among which great inky ravens were always wheeling and
screaming. The upper, was running full of muddy water—the
effect of a heavy storm in that vicinity. Antelope abound in
this region. There was not an hour in the day when they
might not be seen "on a thousand hills."

One day the writer was sent out to get one. He rode along
for a time without success. Having got some distance ahead,
he came to a flock of several hundred, scattered over a large
bottom. Antelope, when scared, first huddle together before
they "skedaddle." Knowing this, our hunter approached as
near as possible under cover, then dashing boldly on them,
his horse at his best speed, his eye on the sight and finger
on trigger, visions of roast venison dancing through his brain,
he had just selected his mark when his horse suddenly

stopped. He went *on* at about the same gait till his momentum became exhausted and he stopped. His gun went a piece farther, discharged itself and it stopped. By the time he had gathered himself, gun and horse together again, the antelope were viewing his outfit over their left shoulders, from a high hill about three miles off. A dog-hole was the innocent cause of this ludicrous finale of his hunt. Owing to the state of our commissary we were anxious to kill some game, but our efforts were uniformly unsuccessful. . . .

Fort Laramie, like all Government posts in the Western Desert, is built with little regard to system or defensive purposes. It consists of the usual accommodations for officers and men, quartermaster and commissary buildings, hospital, sutler's store and stables. It is handsomely situated on the north bank of Laramie Creek, a mile above its junction with the Platte. Beyond, a high ridge, upon the crest of which the gray rocks crop out, supporting here and there a stunted growth of pine, extends nearly to the junction, hiding the Platte from view. On the south the sand-hills approach within rifle-shot, and altogether the situation appears cramped and encroached upon by the desert. There is but little arable land in the vicinity, and that is of a light sandy texture. Nothing but necessity can make the desolate place endurable to white men. Two companies of the Second Dragoons and one of Infantry, form the garrison at present.

When we arrived on the ground the soldiers gathered round, anxious to hear from the world. They, too, had been alarmed by rumors of Texan invasion, and were half minded to take us for enemies. Subsequent usage proved that we were viewed as intruders at least. There were unoccupied quarters in the Post, and plenty of supplies; yet we could get no quarters, no clothing, and only wormy, condemned bacon and hardbread for rations. The soldiers swore that Col. Alexander, commanding the Post, was an old "Secesh," and I guess they were right. He hated us not only as interlopers, in which light Volunteers are detested by all Regulars, rank and file, but as opposed to him politically—enemies on principle—and he treated us accordingly.

We pitched camp on the north side of the Platte, as near the Post as possible. The sand-burs were thick and the feed poor, but it was the best we could do. A fine grove of cottonwoods enhanced the beauty of the place. Sober Autumn, with his nipping frosts and withered leaves dancing down to their burial, while the wild wind moans their requiem through the bare branches, was rapidly advancing—but summer resigned her sceptre with reluctance. A shade was still indispensable to comfort. The river channel averages a hundred yards in width, muddy and shallow, with numerous bars in sight at low water. Fording is hard on account of loose cobbles at the bottom.

They had no transportation at Laramie, and we had to send to Denver for it. As we were to remain here till it returned, we set about enjoying ourselves as well as we could. Sometimes we went over to the Post to see them mount guard, but the cavalry drill was the most interesting. The horses were large and spirited, and in splendid condition. Prancing and curveting from excess of life, when they charged in platoons down banks and over ditches where it seemed they could hardly pass safely in a walk, it required nerve and practice to keep the saddle. Nor did these daring horsemen, who covered themselves with glory on many bloody fields in Mexico, always come off scatheless—two or three men being seriously injured and their horses stove up while we were there. In this school of the trooper we first saw the opening bud that promised danger and excitement enough by the

time it should ripen into the hard and glorious fruit of victory. In camp, a slack-rope was stretched for gymnasts; a
broken iron axle answered for dumb-bells; and foot-racing,
jumping, wrestling, boxing, tumbling, and fishing with a
seine borrowed from the Post, filled the time.

One incident that occurred here will perhaps pay for telling. Lieut. Marshall had bought a lot of tobacco, and the
Sergeant issued it to the men as they needed it, keeping an
account with each. One of the boys, named Frank, draws a
plug or two, and has it charged to another, called Jem. Jem
is a Sucker. How he came to wander so far from the paternal
acres has never ceased to be a wonder. He is not a fool—far
from it—only troubled with a mild type of simplicity. Guile,
or the idea of guile, has never entered his brain. Nothing
can prevent a crowd from having their fun with such a character. Jem soon learned that he was charged with sundry
plugs of tobacco on the Sergeant's books, and as he made no
use of the weed he naturally became wrathy. Hints were
dropped by one and another to bait him until he demanded
a public investigation of the affair. This was what the boys
wanted, and a court-martial was promptly organized for the
trial of suspected persons. Jem's suspicions had been adroitly
directed to Frank as the guilty party, and Frank was accordingly brought before the court. The oath administered to
the witnesses being to the effect that "they wouldn't tell the
truth nor nothing like the truth so help them grog," there
was no difficulty in proving Frank's innocence, and that of
others who were suspected. During the progress of the case,
which was conducted with due solemnity, Jem sat among
the crowd as sober as if he thought himself on trial for his
life. It was finally proved to the satisfaction of the court, that
Jem himself had drawn the tobacco; and when the President
so decided, and fined him four dollars and costs, he looked as

blank as if struck by lightning. The boys told him it was too bad—outrageous—but Frank was mad, and going to maul him for falsely accusing him, unless he paid the fine in "rot" immediately. As the pleasantest alternative thus offered, Jem forked over the four dollars, and a party started to the Post for whiskey. They returned in due time, with two quarts —three parts of it inside of them, however. Jem drank a small swallow, to see how his money tasted. He got excited. "It was his first spree." "D—n the expense." "Who wouldn't get drunk a thousand miles from home, and 'rot' only two dollars a quart?" "He must learn to play cards." "He would be a man or a long-tailed rat.". . .

That evening we had a new sport. The cook threw a burning brand at some one who was molesting him. Its streaming passage through the air suggested the idea. Forthwith, fires appeared in different quarters of the grove, and soon the air was full of brands. It was a picture in miniature, of Farragut below New Orleans. One by one the boys joined in the sport till the whole camp was engaged. Jem was there. He engineered both sides. Was the North in the ascendant? There was Jem pawing fire and bellowing like a Stentor, "Charge! Chester, Charge!" "Down with the rebels." "Give 'em hell." "We'll whip 'em, by G—d we'll whip 'em." Was the South uppermost? Jem had flown, and his lank figure, split to the armpits, stood out boldly from the midst of the blaze, where, with hat and shirt off, arms blackened to the shoulders, the sweat pouring down his smoky face in streams, he scattered fire like Vulcan forging thunderbolts; and ever as the fight lulled were heard his lusty cheerings, "We'll whip 'em—the d—d abolitionists—we'll give 'em Bull Runs till they can't rest." Jem was a tiger that night. The battle ceased towards morning. The South got cleaned out. One by one their men came over to the North, until their chief was left alone. He fought to the last, but was finally disarmed and taken prisoner.

Soon after this occurrence Marshall and Pott contrived a plan for their sport if not for ours. It was evening, and a young moon was beginning to cast shadows. We were ordered to "Fall in," and Marshall drilled us in various motions of the arms and legs, while Pott stretched a rope between two trees close by. Soon Marshall brought us into line near the rope and ordering the "charge," stood by to see the fun. Away went the men at their best speed till their shins struck the rope, when they rolled over and over in the sand-burs. Then we agreed that each should sing, speak, or tell a story. Some, took their turns agreeably. Contumacious subjects were forced to the bar and "compelled to give in evidence." Several popular songs were "did," but—

> "Cot tam dat shnaik vot pites mine Shon,
> He 'sh all over plack, mit fite shpots on;
> He laish in ter grass, and he fistle mit him tail.
> Cot tam dat Cot tam shnaik to Hail,"

carried away the palm. The tune was like a Virginia fence, jagged on both sides. It was rich. But Jude, the laughing, boisterous, buck-eye butcher had gone to bed. His turn came at last. He said he was sick. It was no go—out of bed and away went Jude, with a dozen after him. They lassoed him, after a long race, and brought him on the stage. He was dressed—in a shirt. He began, "Blaze with your serried columns, I will not bow the knee." Poor fellow! he is dead now; died as he lived—laughing. We laughed at first. His theme, his attitudes and gestures—extra-theatrical—were so incongruous with his costume. But as he warmed with his subject, he thundered the old Chief's defiance with such truth that we forgot he was acting, and almost expected him to leap among us with a tomahawk, and seal his words with deeds. Had his skin been a shade or so darker the illusion would have been perfect. We were satisfied and the curtain fell.

There was a large encampment of Ogalallah Sioux on Laramie Creek, three or four miles above the Post, that we often visited. They were assembled in Council, preparatory to taking the war-path against the Pawnees. Their temple of ceremonies was a large booth, constructed by planting parallel rows of long slender withes in the ground about ten feet apart. The tops were then bent in and fastened together, and this frame-work filled in with small brush, basket fashion, was closed up at one end, the entrance festooned with pine boughs and wild flowers and it was ready for use. First comes the inevitable smoke. Seated in a circle round the council fire, the pipe, an iron tomahawk with hollow head and perforated handle, is filled and lighted. Each in succession takes three whiffs, invariably pouring the smoke through the nostril, till it is burned out. Then comes the dance in which all participate. Forming in a circle, facing inward, hands joined, when the music strikes up they slowly move round, chanting Ha! ha! ha! Ha! ha! ha! through all the variations of the scale, though with a certain uniformity that claims a distant relation to tune. Time is kept by beating tin-pans and gourds. As their wild, untutored music rises and falls on the breeze, weird shadows from the dark forests of the east float before you. Readily assimilating, they assume a terrible shape, and midnight massacre alights in the circle and seems at home. You turn with disgust from the tawny brutes and wonder if they *are* the descendants of King Philip and Tecumseh.

Now comes a scene told of in books, but seldom witnessed. Some young braves are to be initiated. With sharp knives, they open great gashes in their breasts and shoulders. Two men seize the subject, pierce the quivering flesh between the cuts, with oak splints a half-inch in thickness. A pony is hitched to these and the intervening flesh torn out. Others are suspended in the air by the splints. Scourges are applied till the back and thighs are completely lacerated. During these operations not a muscle betrays their torture. More impassable than the chiefs and warriors who look on, they inflict these cruelties on themselves to prove their fortitude and courage. They are now admitted to the council and war-path as braves.

Such scenes were of daily occurrence while the encampment lasted. Whatever of savage grandeur in the Indian character they conjured from the records of history or romance, was speedily dissipated on entering a lodge. The squaws, miserable and emaciated, were baking human excrement on shingles for food, while the bucks were usually engaged lousing themselves. The squalid misery of these wasted creatures is past belief, and must be seen to be appreciated. Utter and speedy extinction is their only cure. Association with our race injures rather than benefits them. It has already done its work. Their ruin is accomplished.

Battle of Port Royal

IN THE EAST there was continued skirmishing along the battle line in northern Virginia, but no big battle followed that at Bull Run in the remainder of 1861. It was a time of stalemate, of regrouping, of enemies feeling out the positions and the strength of one another.

But Union troops gained an important victory farther south. On November 7, 1861, the Union fleet, under the command of Admiral S. F. DuPont and operating with the army, captured Port Royal, South Carolina, and gained its first foothold on the rebel shore.

The firsthand account of that operation reprinted here is from a small pamphlet published in 1863, *Abstract of the Cruise of the U.S. Steam Frigate Wabash . . . 1861–'62 & '63*, apparently written by a veteran of the crew. Its author is unknown, the pamphlet being signed "Marlinspike."

[October] 29*th*. General Sherman and staff came on board, and were saluted with 13 guns. Got under way, as also the whole fleet, in order of sailing, *Wabash* leading. The fleet consisted of 23 naval vessels, and about 50 transports with troops.

NOVEMBER, 1861

4th. After experiencing a very heavy gale, in which the transports *Governor* and *Peerless* went down, *Union* and *Osceola* ashore, and the crews captured by the rebels, we arrived off Port Royal, most of fleet at anchor, and the rest heaving in sight. The light draft gunboats stood in over the bar to reconnoitre; first shot from enemy's batteries.

5th. Got under way and stood in over the bar, anchoring inside, being greeted with cheer upon cheer from the transports while crossing.

6th. At anchor, preparing for action, sending down topgallant masts, snaking down stays, reefing preventer slings to the yards, and getting everything in readiness, with as much coolness, as if we were going into port to pay off; pay off we certainly meant to, but in a sort of coin that was rather too hot for the recipients to hold, and too heavy to retain. During the preparations several small rebel gunboats were crossing and recrossing the channel apparently landing troops.

BATTLE OF PORT ROYAL

Nov. 7th. At 8.08 A. M., "all hands up anchor." At 8.18 anchor catted and ship under way; 8.50 stopped the engine, the starboard spring being foul of the propeller; 9 propeller clear of hawser. Beat to quarters to engage the enemy, the forts on Hilton Head and Bay Point, and the enemy's steamers lying near the latter; 9.17 all ready for action; stood for the enemy, starboard guns trained well forward on Bay Point; fort called "Fort Beauregard;" 9.27 enemy opened fire

from Hilton Head; fort called "Fort Walker;" shot fell short;
immediately enemy opened from Bay Point; fire answered at
once from our forward pivot gun; shot good; our port broadside was also at once brought to bear upon Hilton Head fort,
and a heavy gun masked about 500 yards below the fort.
At 9.45 *Bienville* ranged alongside on starboard bow; 9.53
ceased firing from the *Wabash* until the ship turned to present the starboard battery at Hilton Head; 10.03 reopened
fire with forward pivot gun; made signal for close action
with fort on Hilton Head; kept up terrific and well-directed
fire from starboard battery; received a shot which cut in
two the starboard lower studdingsail boom, and carried
away jewsharp of sheet anchor; 10.15 a shot carried away
the paunch batten of mainmast; 10.30 none of our guns bearing, we ceased firing. Between 10.15 and 10.30 an 80-pound
rifled shot passed through our mainmast, near the centre,
about 25 feet from the deck; two other shots successively
cut away both mainstays about 25 feet from collars, and a
fourth shot cut away the end of the spanker boom at taffrail;
10.35 resumed firing from our port battery; 10.37 ceased firing except from pivot guns. Ship turned; 10.40 trained starboard battery to play upon Bay Point; our shot fell short;
10.50 ceased firing, ship turned round; 11.15 ship's head
S. S. E.; 11.18 fired the forward pivot gun on the starboard
side at Hilton Head—shot too high. Ship now ran in within
600 yards of Hilton Head; 11.26 opened with all starboard
battery and both pivots; trained, knocked down enemy's
flagstaff. The firing from our guns admirably accurate; 11.40
ceased firing, except from pivot guns; guns no longer bearing
upon the fort; ship turned round; 11.50 reopened fire from
our port battery and pivots. Our jib halliards cut twice, main-
topgallant stay cut away; 11.52 received a heavy shot in
starboard main chains, which carried away the lower dead-

eye and laniard of the maintopmast backstay, topsail halliards, and smashed in the hammock rail. Starboard battery
manned to play upon Bay Point; 11.54 received a heavy shot
through the starboard head-rail, and stranded the port fore
swifter; 11.55 our starboard mizen horse-block shot away,
and upper part of starboard after port badly chipped; also
cut off inside of sheave hole of starboard arm of spare main-
topsail yard; shot came from Hilton Head; 11.56 port battery
manned to bear upon Hilton Head; 11.58 ceased firing from
gun deck; 12 a 42-pound shot from Bay Point, struck the
deck port side at No. 16 gun, knocked a hole in the deck,
wounded four men, carried away forward truck of the gun
and broke into the hammock netting; also Thomas Jackson,
(cox.) captain of the gun, had his leg shot away at the thigh;
was removed to cock-pit, and died within an hour; the others
were injured by splinters; the shot went no farther than the
hammock netting, and was kept by the ex.-officer as a souve-
nir; 12.05 received a spent shot from "Fort Walker" at cop-
per line under port counter; 12.10 ceased firing, ship turning
round; gave biscuit and grog to the crew at their guns. 1.15
reported by signal from gunboat *Ottawa* that "Fort Walker"
was abandoned. 2 P. M. starboard battery manned, ran within
500 yards of the fort, and fired both pivot guns into it; fire
unanswered; ceased firing; 2.12 commander John Rodgers,
(aid to flag-officer,) left the ship in one of our boats, with
flag of truce to visit the fort; 2.15 reported from mast-head
that about 1000 men were in full retreat for the woods; 2.20
the American flag flying upon the enemy's ramparts; 2.45
anchored near and abreast of "Fort Walker," and proceeded
to land our marines, Lieut. Barnes taking a company of 50
small-arm men in the tug *Mercury*, to land at the fort. "Fort
Walker" was taken possession of by Commander C. R. P.
Rodgers of the *Wabash*, and at 5.45 formally turned over to

the command of Brigadier-General Wright and his brigade; at 4 P. M. secured the guns and went to supper. 800 shell and shot were fired from this ship alone.

As we approached the forts the enemy's flotilla was in line of defence on our starboard bow, near Bay Point. At 9.40 the enemy's largest gunboat stood across the head of the bay, evidently to annoy this ship; the forward pivot gun was vigilantly handled to answer from either bow. At 9.45, as the enemy crossed our bow, he discharged a shell which struck very near our port bow. We immediately answered from our pivot gun.

The enemy's gunboats then ran out of range, where they remained until near the close of the engagement, when they disappeared up the river. At 10 P. M., Lieutenant Barnes and his command returned to the ship. The enemy had retreated in utter rout and confusion, without attempting to carry away either public or private property. The ground was covered with the arms of the soldiers, and the officers retired in too much haste to take their swords; even the dinners of both officers and men were left on the fire cooking, and ready to be partaken of by the victors. The scene of the battle must have been grand and terrific to those who had the opportunity of witnessing it from the decks of the transports. The battle was spoken of by men, who had been under fire more than once during their life-time, as terrible, and described the *Wabash* a destroying angel as she hugged the shore, men stationed in the chains, calling the soundings with cool indifference, slowing the engine, as to only give her steerage way, signalizing to the vessels their various evolutions, at the same time raining shells with the precision and calmness of target practice. It can be truly said, that when in close action the men were only getting warm, thinking about going in with a will; what the effect would have been had it lasted an hour longer it is difficult to say, as nearly all the spectators acknowledged they could compare it to nothing but "hell upon earth." The conflict at an end, the usual duties of the ship were resumed as if no such occurrence had happened, as plenty of men can testify in stronger terms than can be written. The weather during the day was

LIST OF VESSELS IN THE ACTION.

Wabash,	44	guns.
Susquehanna,	18	"
Mohican,	7	"
Seminole,	6	"
Pawnee,	11	"
Unadilla,	6	"
Ottawa,	5	"
Pembina,	4	"
Isaac Smith, guns thrown overboard in gale.		
Vandalia, towed by I. Smith,	22	"
Bienville,	11	"
Seneca,	4	"
Curlew,	6	"
Penguin,	7	"
Augusta,	10	"
Mercury,	2	"
R. B. Forbes,	1	"
Pocahontas,	6	"

REBEL SIDE.

Fort Beauregard,	20	guns.
Outwork,	5	"
Fort Walker,	23	"
Outwork,	1	"

and 5 steamers, from 2 to 3 guns each.

pleasant, light winds from the north-east, and smooth sea. The loss in the whole fleet was eight killed, six wounded seriously, and seventeen slightly.

10th. Sent mail and despatches on board United States steamer *Bienville* for New York. After divine service all hands mustered on quarter-deck, and an order from Flag Officer DuPont, thanking the officers and men for their gallantry and skill during the bombardment of the 7th, was read.

19th. H. B. M. frigate *Immortalité* came in and anchored; saluted the flag with twenty-one guns and Flag Officer with thirteen, which was duly returned.

On the Sunday following the battle a number of our men went on shore to have a look at the damage that was done by our guns; they found the fort, as a matter of course, in possession of the soldiers, but were greatly surprised to find they were not allowed to go inside without a pass from the commanding officer. Such rules and regulations may be all very well, but it certainly seemed rather hard for those very men who had fought for the place, and were the means of placing the army in the position they then held, to be refused from visiting it. However, be it as it may, some of our shellbacks murmured at it, and one, who was getting rather frosty through servitude and years, determined to see the General himself;—the name of General does not abash Jack in the least; a General to him is no more than any one else, but the case is different when Commodore or Captain is mentioned, he is then all attention and respect, and they are the only titles that he supposes himself bound to take any cognizance of—so our old Barnacle-Back started for the quarters of the General, and bolted right in, demanding to see him. It happened that he alighted in the midst of the General's staff, and himself among them. One of the officers desired to know what he wished? "What do I wish, is it? Well, I wish for a second pass to go into the fort; I did not know before that a man had to have two passes to go to one place." "How, two passes," asked one; "have you had one before?" "No," returned Jack, "I sent one on shore Thursday, in the shape of a nine-inch shell, and I thought it sufficient." Jack got his pass, and visited the fort.

1862

The Enemy Is Texas

IN THE SPARSELY SETTLED Territory of New Mexico the traditional enemies had been, first, the Indians and, second, the Texans. War gave the Texans an opportunity to exercise their ambitions for expansion and, early in 1862, they invaded New Mexico in the name of the Confederate government.

Facundo Pino, President of the Council of the Territory, and J. M. Gallegos, Speaker of the House, issued on January 29 an impassioned plea for resistance. "Now is the day to feel the tinglings of the ancient, and unconquerable Castilian blood, that our ancestors brought to this land. The fire-sparks are deathless in every drop. —Now is the day for the flame, that shall conquer and consume."

The complete text of Pino and Gallegos' "Address of the Legislative Assembly of New Mexico" is printed here. Following it is another section from Hollister's *History of the First Regiment of Colorado Volunteers.*

The New Mexicans unaided were no match for the Texans. Aid was sent from the North. Hollister's narrative for March, 1862, tells of the Coloradans' march to help in New Mexico and the Battle of Glorietta Pass which ended Confederate hopes of conquest to their west. In the battle the Confederates held the field, but the destruction of their train effectually ended their New Mexican campaign.

Interesting and entertaining as it is, Hollister's account must be taken with at least a small grain of salt. Each side exaggerated the importance and the violence of the battle, and each side claimed overwhelming victory. In an undated letter of many years later Hollister wrote book collector John Page Nicholson: "I do not know where a copy of the pamphlet can be found, & saving that it might be of use to you, I sincerely hope there is not one in existence. I was so exceedingly crude, & it is so ditto, that I never think of it without mortification. Some of the incidents are colored, somewhat, to make a story, such as . . . the raiding of Mexican towns, stealing blankets, chickens, &c. In fact there is nothing in the whole book that I can now tolerate, & I wonder that I could have put my name, fool that I was at the time, to such stuff."

ADDRESS OF THE LEGISLATIVE ASSEMBLY OF NEW MEXICO.

MANIFESTO OF

The Council and House of Representatives to the Inhabitants of the Territory of New Mexico.

FELLOW CITIZENS:

Being at the close of the present session of your Legislative Assembly, and knowing from this Capital, the danger that threatens you, we have thought it well, to address you this

MANIFESTO

That a savage tribe of Indians should be your enemies, and plunder and murder, is not a thing new or unexpected. Such has been *their* habits, since our brave ancestors first possessed the Valley of the Rio Grande. But we have now another enemy less excusable than the barbarians, because he has grown in the midst of civilization, and enlightenment.

Without any fault or even offense of yours, your honor and property, your families and children are now in peril, by an enemy you have not injured, and whose invasion of the peace, security, and integrity of your soil and homes, you have not provoked.

This enemy is Texas and the Texans. With their hostile armed regiments, rebels to the Government of the United States, to whose protection and flag, our good faith, our duties, our confidence, interests and hopes turn and belong, they have come upon us, in violation of every principle of right, of justice and friendship. They threaten you with ruin and vengeance.— They strive to cover the iniquity of their marauding inroad, under the pretence, that they are under the authority of a new arrangement they call a Confederacy, but in truth is a rebel organization. But this pretence cannot deceive. They come to subsist upon the substance of our property and industry. They are without money or credit.

They come to destroy the Government under which we have lived, prospered, and been happy, and whose protection and care we need. They come to turn from their places, those in offices and authority among you, and to erect by military despotism alone, a power to oppress, to harrass and crush you. You are free and unmolested in your religion, and they who are in violation of every thing held sacred by our religion pretend to come to protect our religion already protected.

They pretend to relieve you from the expenses of Government, when they have no Government, that can bring into our Territory one dollar of money or credit.

To even eat for a day, they must take and plunder your cattle, your sheep, your wheat, corn and beans. They must plunder from our people, all their living. Could they succeed in their infamous and iniquitous attempts, they have no way of subsisting, but upon the substance of our people. A lawless body of men, banded together, hoping to kill or conquer us, would then be established among us, and our shame, injuries and sufferings, we will not attempt to describe.

May a just and avenging God, not withdraw his arm from us, and leave our people to the insults, wrongs, dishonors, cruelties and oppression, that these Texan invaders will inflict, the moment they shall have the power! We must not forget they are our ancient enemies. Twenty years ago they came with intents like they now come. Then they were overcome, and the integrity of our soil vindicated. In 1849, they strove to set up their power over our people, and sent their agents among our people, to carry out their schemes, but our people stood firm, and the General Government silenced Texan pretension.

Taking advantage of the troubles in the United States, they have now come hoping to succeed. Their long smothered vengeance against our Territory and people, they now seek to gratify.

We are a free people, and our fathers ever abhorred negro slaves and slavery.— Our enemies found their rebellion upon pretences touching the negro, negro slaves and slavery. They have set up their rebel organization upon those elements, and boast in the face of a Christian world, of their skill and wisdom in building upon such foundations.

We have condemned, and put slavery from among our laws. It is not congenial with our history, our feelings or interests. The marauders come to destroy our enactments, and force upon us by the cannon and rifle, slave institutions, against our will, protests and tastes.

We have no interests to promote, by being drawn within the destinies of the rebels and rebellion. All in that direction is danger and ruin. Listen not to their agents or emissaries, whether sent for mischief, or shall be found as traitors, living among us. In the midst of our wrongs and dangers, neutrality is without excuse. He that is not for us, is for the rebels and rebellion, and his sympathies favor the invaders.— The Texans may circulate their seditious papers and proclamations, by traitors to us among our people. Be not deceived by these pretensions. Put far from you, the language and sentiments of treason.— Touch not the poison. A serpent's fang is in it. Expose your loyalty to no suspicions. Look to the Government for reward for your services. Forfeit no claim by giving any favor to the enemy. Trust the justice and generosity of the Government. We are well assured, that we will be relieved from the assessment, placed upon us. The matter is brought to the attention of Congress. We have no doubt of liberality being extended to us. Could our enemies gain advantages and *even* battles, they could not long profit by their success. But success cannot crown so iniquitous, so unholy a cause. Success is impossible where there is not the treachery, the cowardice, weakness or folly, that condemned to undying infamy, the conduct, the affairs and surrender of Fort Fillmore. The time has fully come to wipe out that shame.— The army feels it, the people and the whole government feel it. The means of your complete success, in driving the enemy from our limits, are in our hands, large columns of well armed, well disciplined, and well prepared United States American troops, are ready for the fight. These are commanded by officers, who should know the whole art of war. It is their education and profession. We would recoil from even the approach of the thought, that they have not the spirit, courage, conduct, skill and judgement, that must lead the elements under their command, to victory and glory. May they and their troops, win fame that shall dazzle with its brightness, and honor that shall endure as the mountains. With our native soldiery, and volunteers, our pride, our solicitude and sympathies, are too deep for expression. Side by side as they are, with the veteran regular soldier, they live at a time and are actors in the scenes when they may win wreaths of glory and renown, for themselves, their children, and their children's children's generations.— We know they have spirit and courage.— Let us trust to their love of country, justice and honor.

In one sense, the period and event upon us, is fortunate. The enemy is accustomed to sneer at our valor, and depreciate our force and capacity. Never did time, present to outraged men, a fairer field in which to save a country, punish an enemy, and make a name, that invaders shall ever dread, than now surrounds us. Now is the day to feel the tinglings of the ancient, and unconquerable Castillian blood, that our ancestors brought to this land. The fire-sparks are deathless in every drop.— Now is the day for the flame, that shall conquer and consume. The remains of our intrepid and glorious ancestors, slept in no grave, that did not entomb a hero. Their pride and honor could endure no invader. To violate truth, and to commit cowardice, their high souls scorned and abhorred.— Now is the day to show ourselves worthy of our ancestors. Now is the day in which we can make a bright name, that shall shine throughout the union and through time. Let not the veteran Regular surpass you in daring. Emulate the boldest daring he has the spirit to attempt. Let him who commands know no fear like defeat, no dishonor like flying from the face of the invader. Drive off the audacious invader, and then the Indian marauders can be exterminated. If the invader gets a foothold further within the country, there are many modes of depriving him of any profit by his advance, more than the plunder he will gather. This people will never consent to his rule, his military, his slave despotism. The brave and just from neighboring sections will come to our aid. Already reinforcements of Regiments are organized to march to our assistance. They are coming with strong arms and hearts, and will join us in driving off all enemies. The Texans will be driven from our soil. Let no one despair. Our troops are ready and eager to win their laurels and security.

Let every Mexican in the Territory rally to the brave in the field; your fathers, sons and brothers. Let no discouragement or alarm disturb you. Your deliverance from enemies is at hand. Be true, be faithful, and be courageous; then your native land will be full of songs, in honor of your glorious deeds, and New Mexico blaze with fame, and her sons and daughters glow with pride when wheresoever they may travel hereafter through the Union or other lands, they shall find how great the benefit and distinction will be, in being known as the sons and daughters of New Mexico.

FACUNDO PINO,
PRESIDENT OF THE COUNCIL.

J. M. GALLEGOS,
SPEAKER OF THE HOUSE
[T.]N. M. Jan. 29, 1862

We left camp about 8 o'clock, the infantry detachment immediately in advance. The cavalry numbered 210, and marched in the order of their rank, our company being second in the column. Our whole force numbered nearly 400, commanded by Major Chivington. As we advanced leisurely, scouts kept coming in, confirming the intelligence received last night. We thought likely we would meet a force of Texans during the day, but it is doubtful if many realized the issues involved in the meeting. If we had we would have stolen a longer and tenderer look at some of our comrades, whose countenances were soon to be robed in *death*.

We passed Pigeon's Ranche, gained the summit of the divide, and were proceeding down the road, when our picket came charging back with the Lieutenant in command of their artillery a prisoner, crying, "We've got them corralled this time." "Give them h—l, boys." "Hurrah for the Pike's Peakers." Instantly the ranks closed up, the cavalry took open order by fours, and we rushed forward on the double-quick. Knapsacks, canteens, overcoats and clothing of all kinds were flung along the road as the boys stripped

for the encounter. How our hearts beat! That tremendous
event, the burden of history and song, a *battle*, burst on our
hitherto peaceful lives like an avalanche on a Swiss village.
Were we worthy of the name we bore? A few minutes would
tell. On turning a short bend we entered the canon proper
and came full on two howitzers, less than two hundred yards
off. These were attended by a company of mounted men,
displaying a saucy little red flag emblazoned with the emblem of which Texas has small reason to be proud. San Ja-
cinto expresses all the glory of that arrogant, impotent State,
while language is inadequate to describe the narrowness and
insolence of her public policy or the moral and intellectual
degradation of her outcast society. On seeing these "lions in
the path," the infantry divided, a wing flew into either hill,
and the fight commenced. Capt. Howland's company parted
either way and filed to the rear in confusion, leaving us in
front. A couple of shells whizzed over our heads and we in-
stinctively crowded to the left to get out of range. All was
confusion. The regular officers in command of the cavalry
plunged wildly here and there, and seemed to have no control
of themselves or of their men. Every one was talking—no one
talking to any purpose. Major Chivington was placing the
infantry in position, and Cook's cavalry awaited orders, while
the shells went tearing and screaming over them. The Texans soon found their position in the road untenable and retired rapidly with their little red clout a mile or so down the
canon, where their infantry was concealed in the rocks on
either side, and posted their howitzers to command the road.
We followed cautiously until within an eighth of a mile of
the battery, which seemed throughout to be more occupied
in keeping out of our way than in trying to do us injury. Here
we halted behind a projecting point while the infantry were
collected from the hills, and together with the mounted men,

except Cook's company, deployed right and left to outflank the enemy's new position. Major Chivington, with a pistol in each hand and one or two under his arms, chawed his lips with only less energy than he gave his orders. He seemed burdened with a new responsibility, the extent of which he had never before realized, and to have no thought of danger. Of commanding presence, dressed in full regimentals, he was a conspicuous mark for the Texan sharp shooters. One of their officers taken prisoner averred that he emptied his revolvers three times at the Major and then made his company fire a volley at him. As if possessed of a charmed life, he galloped unhurt through the storm of bullets, and the Texans, discouraged, turned their attention to something else.

At this time, so far as I could judge, the battle was progressing finely. Our flankers were rapidly approaching them, and it was arranged that simultaneously with their attack on the wings, we should charge the centre. True, their battery commanded the road, but we had seen that move before with more celerity than grace, and as the event proved, we had only to go down after it to drive it from the field. The ground was unfavorable for the action of cavalry; the road was rough, narrow and crooked; a deep trench, worn by the water and which the road crossed occasionally, running alongside, rendered it impossible to approach a battery but by column in the fair face of it; our horses were weak and thin, and there was every chance to conceal a heavy support. But obstacles only stimulate the daring and determined. The enemy had a strong natural position, and to dislodge them it was necessary to walk into their affections without ceremony. About four hundred yards below us, the canon bent abruptly to the left, then directly resumed its old course, leaving a high, steep, rocky bluff, like the bastion of a fort, square in our front. On this point the enemy had posted a

full company, and at its base, on a smaller mound, their battery was stationed and had now worked diligently for an
hour. Below this we could not see, but personal observation
of the closest kind soon convinced us that the bluffs and
road were alive with Texans, for some distance. As soon as
the order to charge left the Major's mouth we were on the
wing, fearful lest our company should win no share of the
laurels that were to crown the day. As we approached the
point mentioned above, the old United States musket cartridges, containing an ounce ball and three buck-shot, began
to *zip* by our heads so sharply that many, unused to this
kind of business, took them for shells, and strained their
eyes to see where the spiteful bull-dogs were. There were
none to be seen. Divining our intentions, they had turned
tail again and vamosed. Instead, however, we met a redou-
bled shower of lead, rained on us from the rocks above. Capt.
Cook was among the first hit. An ounce ball and three buck-
shot struck him in the thigh, but did not unseat him. Forty
rods further down, his horse stumbled and fell on him badly
spraining his ankle, and he got another shot in the foot. As
the battle swept down the canon like a hurricane, he limped
one side and escaped further injury. We still had a leader as
cool and fearless as Cook—Lieut. Nelson. Slightly halting at
the bend in the road where the fire from small arms was
indeed terrific, and discharging a few shots from our revolvers at the rocks above, we dashed around the point, broke
through their centre, trampled down their reserve, and
passed away beyond the fight in pursuit of the coveted artillery. But it was too fleet-footed for us, and we returned in
time to help Lieut. Marshall, with the two rear sections,
clean out the reserve. They had been stationed in the road,
and though somewhat confused and scattered by our sudden
advent among them, made for cover and stood like a tiger

at bay. By this time, the infantry, under Capts. Downing, Wynkoop and Anthony, came down on them like a parcel of wild Indians, cheering at the top of their lungs, regardless of the shower of bullets raining among them. It was a fine evening, and the boys felt like fun; they were full of *vim* as they could hold. The Texans, terrified at the impetuosity of the attack, broke and fled in every direction.

Personal incidents make quite an episode in this hand to hand encounter. Boone and Dixon took fifteen fellows from a house which they could have held against fifty. As they were being disarmed, somebody cried out "Shoot the s——s of b——s." "No, I'm d——d if you do. I'm d——d if you do. You didn't take 'em. I took these prisoners myself, prisoners of wah. Fall in thar, prisoners. Forward, double quick," and away went Boone to the rear with them.

Lowe's horse fell with and partly on him, badly wrenching his knee, in the ditch just around the corner where the fire was hottest. Hastily disengaging himself from his horse, he jumped over a bank to gain some shelter. He was confronted by a stalwart Texan captain, who, with a cocked pistol bearing on him, "guessed Lowe was his prisoner." Lowe sprang on him like a cat, and after a violent struggle disarmed and marched him to the rear.

Logan, already wounded in the face, observing a fellow behind a rock, leveled on him, when he called out that he was wounded and wished to surrender. Logan dropped his aim and advanced to disarm him, when he coolly drew up his pistol and fired. The ball, which was meant for a centre shot passed through Logan's arm. "O, you son of a b——h," exclaimed Logan, "I'll kill you now. G——d d——n you." And suiting the action to the word, put a bullet through his head. He lived long enough to tell his brother that his death-shot had been given after he was wounded and a prisoner. Logan

being in the hospital at Pigeon's, which the Texans occupied
after the second fight, heard them talking about it, swearing
they would hang the perpetrator of the atrocity if they could
lay hands on him. Whereupon he informed them he was the
man that did it, and gave his reasons. His story, backed by
his wounds, proved entirely satisfactory, and he and the
Texans were on the best of terms until they were separated.

Dan. Rice, who claims no kin to the great showman,
opened a show of his own on the occasion of a certain bone-
heap yclept "Rice's Battery," depositing him on the road
where the leaden hail fell thickest and there leaving him to
his fate. What he did, or rather did not, I cannot tell, but
those who saw it say there was humor in it of the broadest
kind.

Many of the boys were unhorsed in the charge, and some
of the horses escaped entirely, which should be credited no
doubt to profit.

We were obliged to make prisoners of some forty or fifty
—all there were in the road; for when they found us in their
midst, as if descended from the clouds, they forgot that one
of them was equal to five of us, and insisted on surrendering.

In half an hour after the charge the enemy had disappeared and the firing ceased. It was too dark to follow them.

Slowly and sadly we gathered our dead and wounded and
returned to Pigeon's Ranche, as there was no water in the
canon where we were.

A reinforcement of five hundred men, with the howitzer
battery, Capt. Claflin, arrived just as we did, and the woods
rang for half an hour with their cheering.

No cheers came from me. I was sick at the wounds of
Dutro, and spent the night watching his life ebb away.

Thus ended our first battle. We had driven them from
their position under every disadvantage; killed and disabled

fifty at least, and captured one fourth of their entire number. If we had had two hours more daylight our victory would have been still more decisive. Darkness favored their escape.

The action, though small, was conducted with great spirit and judgment. Officers and men came to the scratch with enthusiasm. The impression made on the enemy paved the way for success in subsequent encounters. They cared little for death—we cared less. By their own admission they never expected to whip us till the last man had bit the dust.

The feelings of men in battle is a subject of interest to people generally. I am persuaded there are but few brave men by nature. Battle brings all speculation to a point. Life and death stare each other in the face. Life, however miserable, against death that ends all. Until actually engaged, the most of men suffer excessively from suspense. In the midst of a fight they partake more or less of the demoniac spirit surrounding them. The "thunder of the captains and the shouting" has an awful inspiration of its own. Man glories in his mad power and fear is forgotten. But the men who go into battle with pleasure, depend upon it, are mighty scattering. Many, whose patriotism is unaffected and pure, would flinch at the last moment but for self-respect. That I believe is the only boon *more* precious than life.

Our loss was 5 killed, 13 wounded and 3 missing. How we escaped so cheaply God only knows, for we rode five hundred yards through a perfect hailstorm of bullets. Many were the men lying behind rocks, almost near enough to knock us off our horses, taking dead rests and firing as we passed. Among the conflicting emotions of that evening, not the weakest was one of disappointment in the character of the foe we had met. "Why, they ought to have killed the last one of us," was in the mouth of every one, as often as they thought of it. Our Second Lieut. Marshall, in breaking a prisoner's gun, shot himself so badly that he died in a few hours. "This was the most unkindest cut of all." True bravery, which not only deserves but compels respect, had elevated him in the estimation of the company and the regiment, and his cruel, unfortunate death cast a shadow athwart the glories of the day.

Capt. Cook, than whom none truer can be found, was all shot to pieces, but his usual fortitude remained with him. The ghastly smile with which he endeavored to make light of his wounds, to cheer his boys, betrayed his agony.

We lost three men—Martin Dutro, Jude W. Johnson and George Thompson. Mart was shot down obliquely through the head, and again through the chest, and lived till near morning. He was a noble hearted, generous fellow, and the boys loved him. As we lowered his remains to their last resting place, all the stoicism I could muster was unsufficient to suppress some bitter tears at his early and cruel death. The other boys died instantly, one shot through the head, the other through the heart. They were among our very best men. Bristol, Pratt, Keel, Hall, Logan and Patterson were wounded, and left in the hospital at Pigeon's Ranche.

After burying our dead, some teams went out and brought in a lot of Texan flour and corn, stored at a short distance. As there was only a well at Pigeon's from which to water our stock, we fell back to our camp at Coslosky's. The prisoners were sent to Union under guard of Lord's company of dragoons.

As near as we could learn, the Texan loss yesterday was 16 killed, 30 to 40 wounded, and 75 prisoners, including 7 commissioned officers.

BATTLE OF PIGEON'S RANCHE.

MARCH TWENTY-EIGHTH.

Late last evening Col. Slough arrived with the reserve, from Vernal Spring. They had heard of the engagement yesterday, and could not be restrained. Companies A, B, E and H, of the First, Jim Ford's of the Second, and A and G of the Fifth Infantry, were detached from the command and sent across the mountains, under Major Chivington, to harass the enemies' rear. Lieut. Falvey, of the dragoons, with forty mounted men, went on a scout towards Galisteo. The balance of the regiment, with two batteries and two small companies of regular cavalry, numbering about six hundred, moved forward again towards Santa Fe, not doubting but that every inch of ground would be stubbornly contested by the Rangers. We knew nothing certainly of their force, either as to strength, disposition or intentions, and consequently were slightly surprised when at Pigeon's our pickets came in somewhat hurriedly and reported the Texans advancing in force, and less than half a mile distant. The men were resting—some visiting the wounded in the hospital, others filling their water canteens. Suddenly the bugles sounded assembly, we seized our arms, fell in and hastened forward perhaps five hundred yards, when their artillery commenced cutting the tree tops over our heads.

The cavalry halted, dismounted and formed to the front, under shelter of a small hill. Both batteries, the large one consisting of two twelve-pound howitzers and two six-pound shot-guns, Capt. Ritter, the small one of four twelve-pound mountain howitzers, Capt. Claflin, were run forward and opened with great spirit. Col. Slough came up, and in a hoarse voice gave his orders. Companies K and C were stationed in the road, sheltered by the brow of the hill, as a support to the batteries; D and I were advanced on either hand as skirmishers; G was on guard perhaps a mile in the rear.

The battle was opened and seemed going well enough, judging from the deafening roar of artillery, the unceasing rattle of small arms, accompanied by all kinds of cheering and yelling from the men, when the Colonel, to draw them out, ordered the cavalry to fall back on Pigeon's. The artillery followed; Claflin's battery took position on a hill on the left, while Ritter's remained in the road near the house. The Texan battery soon slackened its fire till it almost ceased. Companies D and I had picked off all the gunners and one piece was dismounted by our guns. If there had been anybody to support Capt. Downing they never would have taken their artillery from the field.

But these brave boys paid dearly for their temerity. Advancing without support they combated the whole Texan force alone for a few minutes. Having lost one half their men and seen Lieut. Baker fall, severely wounded, they reluctantly gave ground.

Our company was posted on a rocky point opposite Claflin's battery and near the ranche, behind which our horses were sheltered.

Owing to the nature of the ground, rough, hilly, rocky and timbered, cavalry and artillery were almost useless, and it became evident that rifles must decide the contest. We were obliged to remain near our horses, yet many of the boys thought our Sharpes inspired more terror, even at five hundred yards distance, than the battery opposite.

The regular cavalry was of no account at all, for whenever the Texans came in sight they would mount and fall back out of range. Walker's company never discharged a single rifle during the day.

Company G, hearing the rumpus, came up on double-quick. The first platoon, Capt. Wilder, hurried to the support of Downing; the second, Lieut. Hardin, was assigned to Ritter's battery, which had retired three or four hundred yards.

The Texan artillery was again playing a lively tune, and as the thunder reverberated from mountain to mountain we could scarcely tell our guns from theirs—both about equidistant.

The hard breast to breast fighting was mostly confined to the flanks. Outnumbering us three to one they made the preponderance still greater by flocking thither to avoid our artillery, which was well served throughout the day. In this unequal struggle Lieut. Chambers, of C, a brave soldier and a gentleman, was severely wounded in the shoulder and thigh, while electrifying his men by his voice and example.

Downing, Wilder, Baker, Davidson, Kerber and others stubbornly held their ground, only yielding, inch by inch, to an overwhelmingly superior fire. When they were outflanked and nearly surrounded they would deliver a stunning volley and fall back a piece. Thus they were nearly always covered, an advantage which their sparse numbers rendered inestimable.

If the Texans had known how weak we were doubtless they would have ruined us, but the lesson of the day before made them cautious. They would creep along up from tree to tree, and from rock to rock, but as sure as one rose in fair view a dozen balls gave his soul choice in the way of departure.

Doubtless other officers performed their duty gallantly— but not coming under my immediate observation it is not so particularly noticed. Report says, however, that Lieuts.

Cobb and Anderson, on the Colonel's staff, were fearless and prompt in the discharge of their arduous duties.

About noon we were forced to retire our whole line half a mile, as they had discovered our weakness and were endeavoring to surround us. At this juncture about three hundred fresh troops came to their assistance, and with this for a charging column they designed to corral our whole command.

Claflin's battery was posted in the road, some portions of the wings called to its support, the cavalry formed on the left in line of battle, and we were ready for them. Col. Slough came to the front and assisted in the disposition of our handful of men. Robbins, Soule and Hardin were there, every one of them as cool and collected as if on parade. Lieut. Col. Tappan sat on his horse during the charge, leisurely loading and firing his pistols as if rabbit hunting.

The bullets came from every point but the rear, showing that this was an effort to close in and capture us. It was right, of course, if they had the "sand" to do it.

Soon they appeared in front, encouraged and shouted on by as brave officers as live; some in squads, others singly, taking advantage of the timber as much as possible in their approach. Waiting till they came within fifty yards, Claflin's battery opened on them like a regiment of Mexican dogs roused by the stranger at midnight. One man shoved in a charge with his arm, another fired her off, and the four pieces played the liveliest Yankee doodle ever heard—and all the time thud, thud, thud, the bullets coming down off the mountains on each side into the ground.

Claflin's salute appeared to astonish them, but when that ceased and the support fired volley after volley into their faces they concluded they were going the wrong way and turned back. We followed them a ways to see how well they could run.

The time gained by this repulse enabled us to extricate ourselves from our perilous position, move back, and take a new stand. This was immediately done. They closed in, and where they expected to wipe us out they found a few dead and wounded.

We took a new position beyond a large open space; our guns thundered as defiantly as ever, but their firing soon ceased. They had no inclination to come out of the woods and fight on open ground, and we slowly retired to camp.

Though we were obliged to give ground from the commencement yet considering the disparity of our forces (by their own admission they had 1800) we were well satisfied. The Colorados are willing to fight them, man for man, every day in the year.

A flag of truce, which seems to be their best hold, arrived in camp as soon as we did, requesting an armistice of eighteen hours duration, ostensibly to bury their dead and take care of their wounded; really to gain time to return to Santa Fe, which they immediately commenced doing in the greatest confusion.

The cause of this remains to be noticed. Though we had crippled them severely, yet they would undoubtedly have tried us on again whenever we were so disposed had not the Major succeeded in striking a blow which pierced to their vitals and drew from thence the life blood. He left camp in the morning with a force of 450 men, crossed the mountains with no regard to obstacles, routes, or ought else save direction and gained their rear. Scattering their rearguard to the winds, he blew up and destroyed their supply train of seventy wagons, containing all the ammunition, provisions, clothing and other war supplies they had in the

Territory; spiked one six-pounder with a ram-rod and tumbled it down the mountain, and then, every man taking his own course, regained our camp soon after dark without any loss whatever.

On arriving in sight of our camp-fires, the Major, ignorant of the events of the day, characteristically called a halt, and as he gave the command, "Fall in, every man in his place;" "Fix bayonets," only replied to the murmur of inquiry as to whose camp it was, "I don't know whose it is, but if it a'nt ours we'll soon make it so." "Forward," "Keep close," and they started for the camp. On coming within hailing distance of the guard they found it was the Colorados, and reserved their hostility for other occasions.

This was the irreparable blow that compelled the Texans to evacuate the Territory. Its audacity was the principal cause of its success.

Had we known the extent of the injury inflicted, we might have advanced to Santa Fe without firing a gun. Caution, however, seemed to be in the ascendant, and perhaps it will win oftener than it will lose.

Tardy George

THE COUNTRY CHAFED at General George B. McClellan's slowness to move his army into action.

President Lincoln exercised his prerogative as commander in chief to question in early February McClellan's plans:

"*My dear Sir*—You and I have distinct and different
plans for a movement of the Army of the Potomac—
yours to be down the Chesapeake, up the Rappahannock to Urbanna, and across land to the terminus of the
railroad on York River; mine to move directly to a point
on the railroad southwest of Manassas. If you will give
me satisfactory answers to the following questions I
shall gladly yield my plan to yours:

"1. Does not your plan involve a greatly larger ex-
penditure of *time* and *money* than mine?

"2. Wherein is a victory more certain by your plan
than mine?

"3. Wherein is a victory *more valuable* by your plan
than mine?

"4. In fact, would it not be *less* valuable in this, that

96

it would break no great line of the enemy's communication, while mine would?

"5. In case of disaster, would not a safe retreat be more difficult by your plan than by mine? Yours truly,

A. LINCOLN"

George H. Boker expressed the feeling of the people generally in a satirical poem, "Tardy George."

McClellan secured approval for *his* plan, however, and spoke to his army with confidence and pride in an address to his soldiers in March.

TARDY GEORGE.

WHAT are you waiting for, George, I pray?—
To scour your cross-belts with fresh pipe-clay?
To burnish your buttons, to brighten your guns;
Or wait you for May-day and warm Spring suns?
Are you blowing your fingers because they are cold,
Or catching your breath ere you take a hold?
Is the mud knee-deep in valley and gorge?
What are you waiting for, tardy George?

Want you a thousand more cannon made,
To add to the thousand now arrayed?
Want you more men, more money to pay?
Are not two millions enough per day?
Wait you for gold and credit to go,
Before we shall see your martial show;
Till Treasury Notes will not pay to forge?
What are you waiting for, tardy George?

Are you waiting for your hair to turn,
Your heart to soften, your bowels to yearn
A little more towards "our Southern friends,"
As at home and abroad they work their ends?
"Our Southern friends!" whom you hold so dear
That you do no harm and give no fear,
As you tenderly take them by the gorge?
What are you waiting for, tardy George?

Now that you've marshaled your whole command,
Planned what you would, and changed what you
    planned;
Practiced with shot and practiced with shell,
Know to a hair where every one fell,
Made signs by day and signals by night;
Was it all done to keep out of a fight?
Is the whole matter too heavy a charge?
What are you waiting for, tardy George?

Shall we have more speeches, more reviews?
Or are you waiting to hear the news;
To hold up your hands in mute surprise
When France and England shall "recognize"?
Are you too grand to fight traitors small?
Must you have a Nation to cope withal?
Well, hammer the anvil and blow the forge:
You'll soon have a dozen, tardy George!

Suppose for a moment, George, my friend—
Just for a moment—you condescend
To use the means that are in your hands,
The eager muskets, and guns, and brands;

Take one bold step on the Southern sod,
And leave the issue to watchful God!
For now the Nation raises its gorge,
Waiting and watching you, tardy George!

I should not much wonder, George, my boy,
If Stanton get in his head a toy,
And some fine morning, ere you are out,
He send you all "to the right about"—
You and Jomini, and all the crew
Who think that war is nothing to do
But drill, and cipher, and hammer, and forge—
What are you waiting for, tardy George?
    JANUARY, 1862.

————

HEADQUARTERS ARMY OF THE POTOMAC,

FAIRFAX COURT HOUSE, VA., *March* 14, 1862.

SOLDIERS OF THE ARMY OF THE POTOMAC!

For a long time I have kept you inactive, but not without a purpose; you were to be disciplined, armed and instructed; the formidable artillery you now have, had to be created; other armies were to move and accomplish certain results. I have held you back that you might give the death-blow to the rebellion that has distracted our once happy country. The patience you have shown, and your confidence in your General, are worth a dozen victories. These preliminary results are now accomplished. I feel that the patient labors of many months have produced their fruit; the Army of the Potomac is now a real Army,—magnificent in material, admirable in discipline and instruction, excellently equipped and armed;—your commanders are all that I could wish. The

moment for action has arrived, and I know that I can trust
in you to save our country. As I ride through your ranks, I
see in your faces the sure presage of victory; I feel that you
will do whatever I ask of you. The period of inaction has
passed. I will bring you now face to face with the rebels,
and only pray that God may defend the right. In whatever
direction you may move, however strange my actions may
appear to you, ever bear in mind that my fate is linked with
yours, and that all I do is to bring you, where I know you
wish to be,—on the decisive battlefield. It is my business to
place you there. I am to watch over you as a parent over his
children; and you know that your General loves you from
the depths of his heart. It shall be my care, as it has ever
been, to gain success with the least possible loss; but I know
that, if it is necessary, you will willingly follow me to our
graves, for our righteous cause. God smiles upon us, victory
attends us, yet I would not have you think that our aim is to
be attained without a manly struggle. I will not disguise it
from you: you have brave foes to encounter, foemen well
worthy of the steel that you will use so well. I shall demand
of you great, heroic exertions, rapid and long marches, desperate combats, privations, perhaps. We will share all these
together; and when this sad war is over we will all return
to our homes, and feel that we can ask no higher honor than
the proud consciousness that we belonged to the ARMY OF
THE POTOMAC.

GEO. B. McCLELLAN,
Major General Commanding.

One of the Strangest Naval Combats

THE GREAT NAVAL BATTLE at Hampton Roads between the Federal *Monitor* and the Confederate *Virginia* (the renamed *Merrimac*) was, in the words of Swiss observer Ferdinand LeComte, "one of the strangest naval combats." It was also one of the most important. It was the test in an actual military situation of the iron vessels whose adoption would soon revolutionize the navies of the world.

LeComte was most interested in the uses of new tools of war in the army. But the chance to report on such an important military development as these new ships, even to the navy-less Swiss, was one he could not overlook.

His report on the American war was sound and interesting throughout, and it was soon translated and published in New York for the American audience.

⚜

Since I am to speak of machinery utilized for the war, I shall be pardoned for saying, also, a few words of one of the most remarkable facts of this war, viz.: the transformation in naval constructions.

101

We may well wait for what the mechanical genius of this people may realize, having reference to the means of the struggle, as well as the remarkable innovations in other more pacific domains. The results have still surpassed the anticipations. The old wooden navy, those collossi of 120 guns, which made the pride of England and of France, are now only decayed powers in the presence of the heavy calibres and the armored vessels created by the Americans.

The two belligerent parties had from the commencement of the war constructed vessels covered with iron, of various forms, and on each side they hoped to surprise one another. On both sides they found themselves gradually entering the lists with equal arms.

The 6th of March, in Hampton Roads, near Fortress Monroe, one of the strangest naval combats took place—one with which the whole world has resounded. The secession frigate, the *Merrimac*, proceeding from Norfolk, had just attacked, and disabled in a few hours, two powerful frigates of war of the United States, the *Cumberland* and the *Congress*. The next day a vessel equally singular in construction, the *Monitor*, in its turn entered the contest on the side of the Federals, and forced the terrible vanquisher to a retreat.

Having had the advantage of seeing these two vessels, and of visiting the *Monitor* in the very roadstead of the combat, I shall endeavor to give here a brief description of it.

The *Merrimac* has nothing particularly remarkable in fact, except her iron armor and ram. She is an old frigate of the first class, of the United States. She was of very small cost, and made in 1857 her first voyage to England. Anchored at Southampton, she was then remarked upon by critics for her proportions and for the cut of her hull, and provoked controversy amongst seamen and builders.

Sunk by the Federals at the time that they were engaged

in evacuating their maritime arsenal at Norfolk, where she was, she was afterwards put afloat again by the Secessionists. They razed her, and covered her with iron plating, rising by plates superposed one upon the other, in the form of a roof above the deck. They furnished her with ten Armstrong guns: four at each side, one on the prow, and one on the poop. In front was fixed an enormous iron ram; by the port, and by two openings near the chimney, were arranged pipes for throwing boiling water and steam, as a defence against attempts at boarding.

When the *Merrimac* wished to go out, thus armed, for the first time, she could not float, and was obliged to be lightened; but she remained always slow in her movements. Only once was she able to use her ram at pleasure; this was on the occasion of her demonstration against the *Cumberland,* which once experienced her destructive power. Since then, her adversaries have always been able to avoid her blows.

The strength of this vessel, as the engagements at Hampton have demonstrated, consisted chiefly in the resistance which her armor opposed to the enemy's fire, and which permitted her, without fear, to moor herself with broadside presented, at short range. She confronted thus three complete broadsides of the *Cumberland,* a sustained fire from the *Congress* at short distance, and another of the *Monitor.* This last succeeded only in inflicting upon her an injury in front, which caused her to abandon the struggle. To supply the rapidity of movement which she lacked, the *Merrimac* went escorted by two or three steamers and gunboats, performing about her the service of scouts and sharp-shooters.

At a distance, the heavy-looking *Merrimac,* without mast, and with her low chimney, gliding slowly over the sea, had a strange and monstrous aspect, which struck the inhabitants of the coast with superstitious terror.

It is known that this vessel was destroyed the 18th of May, at the time of the capture of Norfolk by the Federals. The Secessionists not being willing to let her fall into the hands of her former proprietors, and not being able to carry her away, inasmuch as she was then receiving repairs, blew her up while evacuating the place. On the other hand, they towed to Richmond the carcass of another *Merrimac,* whose early appearance on the James River has been announced.

The *Monitor,* created by Captain Ericcson [Ericsson], is of a wholly different character. It was constructed after a plan well considered, and with the idea of offering the least possible surface to the blows of the enemy; of giving to this exposed surface a solidity proof against every thing; and of causing the density of the water to operate as a shield for the most delicate parts.

Entirely answering to this plan, the *Monitor* makes but little show, and it was some time before I was able to discover her at Hampton Roads, in the midst of the vessels of every dimension confided to her protection.

Upon the whole, this vessel is a raft, like a body on a level with the water, under which is found a hull, less long and less wide, enclosing the machinery, and with the spiral line of the hull, the anchor, and the helm all below. On the raft is raised a tower, sheltering two Dahlgren cannon of two hundred pounds each. The tower can be moved on a circular framework, and this movement is directed from the interior of the tower. By this means the cannon, while remaining all the while under cover, can be brought to bear in every direction of the horizon.

The raft has a length of about one hundred and seventy feet by a width of forty, and a depth of five, of which three and a half are under water. Her waterline is elliptical.

The lower hull is about one hundred and twenty feet in length, thirty-five in width, and seven in depth. It is perceived then that she is curtailed at the points of the ellipse by fifty feet, and on the sides by five feet, on the full length of the raft. These two parts are of oak, covered with sheets and plates of iron. The tower, wholly of iron, is nine feet high by twenty in diameter, and presents a thickness of metal of nine inches, in eight concentric walls. The two ports are three feet above the deck. Her mechanism for effecting the rotation of the tower is very ingenious, but would demand, in order to give a complete idea of it, a detailed description with drawings, which I have not the means of presenting here. Two men alone suffice to handle the guns. The smoke escapes by traps in the roof of the tower, and also by means of a ventilating apparatus which conducts it to other grated traps under the deck. Apart from the tower, the raft offers no other prominent point except the pilot-house, also of iron, which rises twelve inches above the deck, and has inclined sides. Holes, covered with glass, allow the pilot to direct the vessel, while being fully under cover.

It is thus seen that this battery is theoretically adapted to its object; its delicate portions are covered by a great thickness of water, and its exterior portions, of small surface, strongly protected, and circular, offer little hold for the action of the projectiles. Practical experiment corroborated these calculations of theory. In the combat of the 7th of March the two guns of the *Monitor* contended for two hours against the ten of the *Merrimac*, without other damage than a blow at the look-out of the pilot-house. Several times did the *Monitor*, manœuvring with ease, avoid, without ceasing her fire, the charges of the ram of her antagonist.

Since then the *Monitor* has not been engaged but once, against Fort Darling, below Richmond, and it was admitted that she required still some improvements, among others the following:

1st. The arrangement of the guns in the tower does not permit a sufficient inclination of range;

2d. Her slight elevation above the water-line causes it to be doubted whether she can bear the open sea. Room would also fail her for supplies for a long voyage;

3d. The tower has the ordinary inconvenience of casemates; the smoke, and especially the heat, are not dissipated there with sufficient readiness, and soon become very annoying to the gunners.

These observations, the first two in particular, will appear the better founded, as Captain Ericsson had not had the intention of making the *Monitor* any thing else than a coast battery, designed originally, during the incident of the *Trent*, to defend the entrance to the harbor of New York. The constructor having afterwards solicited the opportunity of proving his battery against the enemy, she was sent in haste to Fortress Monroe, when the real existence and the approaching sortie of the *Merrimac* were learned. The guns which were used in the fight were not of the intended calibre; and Commodore Dahlgren thinks that if his gun, of large calibre, had been in action, the *Merrimac* would have been pierced and sunk.

The fight of the 7th of March produced a great sensation in the United States. The two vessels engaged in the tilt, which until then had been considered as chimerical constructions, and on which many a jester had exercised his wit, were surrounded with respect, and on all sides mechanicians, ship-owners, and engineers put themselves to work to create and improve vessels of this kind. They used old vessels which they improved; they constructed new ones; they invented others, of forms more and more odd; and to-day the navy of the United States possesses a whole fleet of these formidable engines. The *Naugatuck* and the *Galena* were the first to join the *Monitor* in the James River. The waters of the Mississippi bear also a fleet of them, and, very recently, the Secessionists have put one afloat, the *Arkansas,* which made her *début* in passing by force the Federal gunboats, in order to strengthen the defences of Vicksburg.

It is necessary, however, to recognize, that these so improved products of the mechanic arts bear in them defects, arising from their very excellencies. The smallest error in time, a slight accident to the machinery, is sufficient, sometimes, to paralyze the action of an immense force, and to cause disappointments which are so much the more lively as the hopes excited have been great. It is thus that, at the attack on Fort Darling, the 15th of May, the Federal flotilla was unable to obtain any result. The *Galena,* which had been grounded in ascending the James River, had to be lightened, and was soon deficient in munitions. The *Naugatuck* saw her hundred-pound gun burst at the first fire; and the *Monitor* had to remain at long range to get her angle of aim.

At the same time that it was sought to appropriate these new means of destruction, each party aimed with not less eagerness at obtaining the corresponding means of preservation. After the poison, the antidote, after the projectile, the plate: thus is the career of invention pursued. This second search is also not less interesting than the other.

I give below the facts of the contest which I have heard the most appreciated, in view of new combats between the *Merrimac* and the *Monitor.*

Against the *Merrimac,* the North proposed to employ the shock, as being the most effectual mode of action. Certain enormous steamers, of great swiftness, and heavily ballasted, amongst others the *Vanderbilt* and the *Constitution,* were to rush, under a full head of steam, upon the *Merrimac*. The latter, less capable of moving, could not avoid the shock of one of these steamers, and, according to the calculations and the laws of dynamics, would necessarily be sunk. With this object, a flotilla of this naval cavalry was for a long while in station below Fortress Monroe, always under steam. While it should have prepared and executed its charges, the *Merrimac* would have been entertained by the fire of the *Monitor* and other armored vessels.

Great success was not expected from boarding, considering the difficulty of throwing men on the inclined sides of the armor, who, besides, could be driven back by jets of boiling water and steam.

Against the *Monitor*, I have heard it said that the seamen of the South thought, amongst others, of three means, which appear in fact susceptible of some efficiency.

They would attempt to board her, and bold men would throw shell into the tower through the ports. But the *Monitor* put herself on guard against this danger by the arrangement of pumps of boiling water discharging at the ports.

Or, they would open the deck and sink her, by a bomb-shot of heavy calibre, and as vertical as possible. But such a shot it is difficult to make.

Or, to capture her with a chain,—to throw it in the manner of a *lasso* around the tower, and to ground her on the coast.

It is unfortunate that these different means, sufficiently curious, of contest, cannot, perhaps, be put to the proof, in new actions between these same two vessels. But they will be so, without doubt, in others, under conditions very similar.

Upon the whole, the navy of the United States, whether it be by its creations or by its operations, has acquired, and is acquiring still, the greatest honor in this war. It may well console her for the disappointments which the land army has experienced.

The blockade of so great an extent of coast, a blockade which, whatever may be said of it, is as real and as effective as a blockade has ever been, testifies the power and the vigilance of the Federal fleet.

The actions of Fort Pulaski, of Forts Donelson and Henry, of Port Royal, of Hampton, of Vicksburg, of New Orleans, and of other points of the Mississippi; also of Pittsburg Landing, and of Harrison's Landing, show what resources of energy, of precision, and of intrepidity, there are among these brave seamen.

In fine, the frequent transportation of troops, successfully effected at the distance of hundreds of leagues along the coast, the embarkation and disembarkation of the Army of the Potomac, of those of Burnside, Butler, and Sherman, with all their supplies and *matériel* of the heaviest calibre, prove that the most difficult and extensive operations can be seriously undertaken by an army, as well as seconded on all the navigable waters.

At this time an entire fleet of vessels, identical with the *Monitor*, is in course of construction in the various shipyards of the North, without reckoning a great number of others on different models.* When these different vessels shall have taken the sea, that is to say, in a few months only, the United States will possess, for the moment, the greatest military naval force in the world, and will be able to exercise sovereign control over their waters. I have it from a very

---

* Amongst other variations from the system of Capt. Ericsson, is mentioned the system of Whitney, of which a specimen, the *Keokuk*, is at this time being built at New York. As capable of resistance as the Monitors, it will be lighter, inasmuch as wood enters, for a great part, into its construction, and be more manageable. It will have a speed of ten knots an hour.

experienced and impartial seaman, that the famous *Warrior*, or her rival *La Gloire*, would find themselves at a disadvantage against a single Monitor. In return, those vessels are more suitable, it is true, for distant navigation.

In the course of this year, nine new Monitors, constructed under the direction of Capt. Ericsson, ought to be launched, to wit: the *Montauk*, the *Catskill*, and the *Passaic*, in course of construction at Green Point, New York; the *Sangamon* and *Lehigh*, in construction at Chester, Pennsylvania; the *Nantucket* and the *Nahant*, in construction at Boston; the *Weehawken*, in construction at Jersey City; and the *Patapsco*, in construction at Wilmington, Delaware.

At the commencement of the year 1863, the military marine of the North should reckon fifty mailed vessels, on different systems and of different strength.

The South, really very inferior in this respect, and everywhere closely blockaded in her ports, is also making great efforts to establish for herself a navy. It is said that two new Merrimacs are already in advanced construction at Richmond, and that they ought soon to make their appearance in the waters of the James River. Another is expected to contribute to the defence of Vicksburg, on the Mississippi. Others are in construction at Charleston, and still others are receiving their armament in England, designed to give chase to the commercial vessels of the North.

Shiloh

THERE WAS STILL no movement of the army in Virginia, but the army in the West was pressing deep into Confederate territory. Nashville fell in February. Early in April one of the great battles of the war took place, forever changing the meaning of "Shiloh" from "place of peace."

Here is the account of that battle written by a private soldier only a week after the event. It is signed only "W." but, according to John Page Nicholson, the author was W. W. Worthington.

FIELD OF SHILOH, TENNESSEE, APRIL 14th, 1862.

DEAR KING:—I commence writing you a letter, which, I know, you will be glad to get; for I mean to tell you what our battalion did on the 6th and 7th inst., whilst the great battle at this place was progressing. * * * Leaving Columbia, we took up the line of march for Savannah, a distance of eighty-two miles through a country almost uninhabited and barren to the last degree. On Saturday night we en-

111

camped at a place seventeen miles from the latter town. Starting again the next morning, we had proceeded but a little way when the noise of the battle of that disastrous day broke upon our ears. As we advanced the cannonading became each moment more distinct. It was plain that a desperate fight was going on somewhere: but not one of our number dreamed that Grant had been attacked and was at that instant slowly losing ground before the enemy. Indeed the general belief was created by reports brought from the front that our gunboats were attacking some batteries at a place called Hamburg. About noon, however, we began to think it possible that in some way or other our aid might be needed; for we were halted in an old cotton field, our arms were inspected, and rations and ammunition were issued. Still we were ignorant of the terrible conflict then going on, though by this time the ground fairly trembled under our feet with the rapid discharge of artillery. Again pushing on, sweltering in the hot southern sun, travelling over roads almost impassable and fording several streams, about dark we halted for a few hours at a creek three miles inland from Savannah. There we learned for the first time, that instead of a gunboat bombardment, that day had been fought at Pittsburg Landing, the bloodiest battle in which American troops were ever engaged. The accounts of the conflict were most cheering. They represented that Grant had that morning attacked the immense army under Albert Sidney Johnston and Beauregard, completely defeating and routing it after a desperate fight of fifteen hours duration. The cannon we continued to hear at intervals were said to be those hurried forward in pursuit of the flying enemy. You may be sure we were jubilant at this news; although we declaimed somewhat against the selfishness that precipitated the engagement and won the victory before Buell's column had an opportunity to take a part. Little did we dream that so far from having gained a triumph, Grant's force was then defeated and panic-stricken, with an insolent foe occupying most of his camps, and that the morrow would introduce us to scenes of carnage the mere imagination of which sickens the heart.

It was quite dark, though still early in the night, when we moved on again. The men were in the best of spirits, rude witticisms, laughter and snatches of song ran along the whole line. Here and there some fellow boasted of the gallant deeds he would have performed had he been in the day's engagement. The officers, on the other hand, were more quiet than usual. They marched in silence or gathered in little knots and conversed in whispers. At length, the town of Savannah was entered. Every house in the place seemed to be illuminated; for each had been converted into an hospital and was packed from attic to basement with the dying and wounded who had been conveyed thither by the steamer.

Groans and cries of pain saluted our ears from all the buildings we passed. Through the windows, the sash of which were removed to give air to the injured, we could see the surgeons plying their horrid profession. The atmosphere was that of a vast dissecting room. The streets were crowded with ambulances, baggage trains, parties bearing the victims of the fight on stretchers, on rails, on rude litters of muskets and on their shoulders, and with batteries of artillery and long lines of infantry waiting to be taken to the scene of the struggle. The confusion everywhere visible, the shouting, cursing, quarrelling, beggars descriptions. Teams of mules, abandoned by their drivers, ran away trampling down every thing in their course. Quartermasters rode about at furious pace trying to extricate their transportation from the general mass. Doctors, one hand full of instruments, the other of bandages, and covered with blood, wildly rushed through the immense crowd in search of additional subjects of their art. Still, from all that could be gathered, the idea appeared to be that we had achieved a great victory. No one could exactly tell the events of the day; but the fact of our decisive triumph was unquestioned. The falsity of this common opinion every reader of the newspapers already knows.

Getting on board the "Hiawatha," by midnight we were ploughing the turbid Tennessee river *en route* for Pittsburg Landing, by water a distance of fourteen miles. From the officers of the steamer we got other accounts of the battle, which we afterwards ascertained to be correct. Their statements were, that Johnston and Beauregard, hoping to destroy Grant before he was joined by Buell, then close at hand, made a furious attack upon him, in great strength, that Sunday morning immediately after daylight. There is some dispute whether or not we had outposts; those who maintain we had, admit that they were playing cards at the time of the assault. At all events our troops were completely and criminally surprised. Unable to form to resist the onslaught, hundreds of them were mercilessly shot down in their tents and company streets. Those who escaped fled in the greatest terror through the camps in their rear, spreading the panic and closely followed by the successful foe. At least two miles of the ground occupied by our forces was thus abandoned before the regiments near the river could be brought to present a front to the rebels. A temporary check was then given to the enemy's impetuous advance, but being strongly reinforced they pushed our army slowly and surely towards the landing. During the whole day the battle raged with violence. Several corps of our volunteers behaved with great gallantry; but others ran at the first fire, and with those surprised in the morning (at least 10,000 men) could not again be brought into action. But the Secessionists steadily gained upon us. Seven batteries of our light artillery and a large number of our soldiers fell into their hands, as well as thousands of tents, and immense quantities of Commissary and Quartermaster's stores. When night closed upon the struggle we were driven within three hundred yards of the river, and would have been pushed into it had not the spiteful little gunboats then been enabled to come to our relief. Our loss in the engagement was terrible; but it was not all we suffered. At times when the fortune of war was most decidedly against us, the skulkers under the bluff, would rush in crowds to reach the steamers moored in the Tennessee, and by jostling and pushing each other into and struggling together in the water, hundreds of them were drowned. Little pity is felt for their fate, of course; but still these help to swell the casualties of that disastrous day.

Regaled, as we were, during the entire passage from Savannah to Pittsburg Landing, with stories of defeat and forebodings of what would occur the next day, you may be certain that we were not as comfortable as if we were in the old barracks. It was plain to the dullest comprehension that McCook's, Nelson's and Crittenden's divisions of Buell's army, then arrived at the scene of action, would have work enough to do early in the morning, and that too against an enemy flushed with recent victory. It seemed like folly to hope for success; for our strength did not exceed thirty thousand. From Grant's badly beaten and demoralized force we expected nothing, unless it was a mere show of numbers. On the other hand, the rebels were estimated at from 60,000 to 80,000. These considerations did not do much to inspirit, whilst throughout the night our anxiety was kept alive and our consciousness of the immediate presence of the foe not permitted to slumber by the regular firing from the gunboats upon the camps of the enemy close beside those of our own.

At daybreak on Monday the 7th inst. our battalion was disembarked. Forcing its way with difficulty through the vast crowd of fugitives from the previous day's fight gathered on the river bank, we scrambled up the bluff in the best way we could and formed in the camp of the Missouri Artillery. Here there were more refugees, their officers riding among them and urging them to rally, but without the least success. I never witnessed such abject fear as these fellows exhibited. Without a single avenue of escape in the event of defeat, they were unable, even, to muster up the desperation of cornered cowards. It is said that several in high command set them the example of pusillanimity. As we moved among them they inquired "what regiment is that?" "15th Regulars," replied some of our men. "Well, you'll catch regular hell to-day," was their rejoinder. Others said "Boys, it's of no use; we were beaten yesterday and you'll be beaten now." But still our men got into line well, and were marched by the right flank a few hundred yards to the place where the action of the previous day had ended. Here Capt. Swaine and Major King joined us, knapsacks were unslung, and we made the final preparations for the conflict we knew to be imminent. Being informed that we were the reserve of Rousseau's Brigade, we were slowly moved forward in column at half distance, through camps our troops had abandoned in the fight of the 6th inst. Other corps, all the while, were passing us on either side, and disappearing from view in a dip of ground in front, but as yet the engagement had not begun.

Let me try, at this point, to give you as good an idea of the field of battle as I am able. The Tennessee river at Pittsburg Landing describes a considerable curve; in the neck formed by this bend and some distance outside of it were

the camps of Gen. Grant's command. On the morning of the
7th, the rebels were posted some distance inside of the
ground formerly occupied by us, so that the line of conflict
was pretty nearly straight between the two points of the
semi-circle. Nelson's division was on our extreme left, resting
on the river; Crittenden was next to him on his right, then
came McCook in the centre, and joined to him was McCler-
nand, who had other of Grant's generals beyond him. This
order continued unbroken until the struggle was over.

Nelson and Crittenden's commands having passed the left
flank of our battalion speedily became engaged. A few scattering shots were heard from their direction, which were
soon followed by such a heavy firing of small arms that it
was plain our men had found the enemy. The field artillery
also broke in with its thunder, increasing the din already so
great that it was difficult to hear one's self speak. As further
evidence that the battle had begun in earnest, a mounted
officer dashed by, crying, "bring on the ambulances," and
those vehicles were at once taken to the front, to return in a
few minutes laden with mangled freight. Other wounded
men, some on foot, others carried by their comrades, likewise
now came to the rear. From these we learned that Nelson
and Crittenden, although suffering severely, were steadily
pushing the rebels back, a story attested by the frequent
cheers that arose from their gallant fellows.

A sharp firing that now took place almost immediately in
our front, showed that the left and centre of our (McCook's)
division had got into action, and that the battle was rapidly
becoming general. Our battalion was instantly deployed into
line to receive the foe should the troops in advance give way.
While in this position, Generals Buell and Rousseau rode up,
ordered us to proceed to the right of the brigade, which was
the right of the division, and be ready for any emergency,

and to send out at the same time a company of skirmishers to provoke an attack. This converted us from a reserve into an assaulting party.

Forming in column by division on the first, we marched by the right flank to the position we were to occupy, Captain Haughey with his command, being thrown forward to feel the enemy. (I will state here that battalions of the 16th and 19th regiments U. S. Infantry, the whole under Major John H. King, were with us and shared in all our operations.) At this place we again deployed, then moved by the right of companies to the front, until a little hill between us and the rebels was surmounted, when we were again brought into line. Rapid discharges of small arms forward of our left flank, now showed that our skirmishers were successful in their search. Again we were advanced, until having gained some distance, we were ordered to lie close to the ground. Immediately we were exposed to a cannonade and fire of musketry, whose severity defies description. From three batteries and their strong support of infantry just before us, masked by the underbrush, came a shower of grape, canister, spherical case, rifle balls, &c., that would have swept every one of us away had we been standing on our feet. An examination I have since made of the ground exhibits the fact that every tree and sapling bears the marks of shot. Protecting ourselves as we did, our loss was still severe. Among the injured were Capt. Acker of the 16th, killed, and Capt. Peterson of the 15th, wounded in the head. As yet, as I have said before, the foe was concealed in the thick woods so that we could not see them; but now emboldened, perhaps, by what they supposed their irresistible attack, they emerged from their cover. Never did they commit a more fatal mistake. Our men, restrained by their officers, had not discharged a piece up to this time. But now each coolly marked his man; and when

Capt. Swaine, in a voice that could be heard along the whole line, gave the command to fire, our Springfield rifles dealt a destruction that was awful. After pelting the rebels a little while longer, we again moved forward to the sound of the bugle, taking to the earth once more when the enemy opened upon us. Here Lieut. Mitchell of the 16th was killed, and Lieut. Lyster of the 19th, and 1st Sergeants Williams and Kiggins of the 15th dangerously wounded. Halting a few moments to reply, we moved down upon the traitors a third time, subjected the while to a fearful storm of missiles, by which Capt. Curtiss and Lieut. Wykoff of the 15th were very severely hurt, and 1st Sergeant Killink of the same corps instantly killed. But at length the artillery of the enemy, that had been playing upon us so long, came in sight. Hastily fixing bayonets, we charged upon it at a double-quick. Capt. Keteltas of the 15th being then shot through the body. Unable to withstand our desperate assault, the rebel cannoneers abandoned their guns, and with the infantry supports fled across an open space into the woods beyond. An opportunity offered at this point to ascertain the havoc we had done. Every horse in each piece and caisson lay dead in his harness, and the ground was covered with the killed and dying. Among the latter was the Chief of the Artillery. As we came up he said, "You have slain all my men and cattle, and you may take the battery and be damned." But we had not leisure to stop and talk with him or any other person; for we were already being fired upon from the new covert of the foe. Pushing forward amid great danger across the field, we gained the edge of the timber and continued the fight in which we had then been engaged for more than five hours.

The foregoing was the state of affairs at high noon. Let us pause a moment to see what was the condition of the battle field at that hour. There was no fighting on the right of the

centre; indeed it had not been severe in that quarter during
the day. On the left, Nelson and Crittenden having repulsed
the enemy, were resting on their arms; for the foe in their
front had mysteriously disappeared. Our three battalions
were our only troops then hotly engaged. You inquire,
"where were the rest of the rebels?" That is just what I propose telling you. Leaving only enough of men before the
other divisions to mask their purpose, they were engaged
massing their troops, those that had been engaged as well
as their reserves, for an overwhelming onslaught upon the
right of our centre, where we had contested all morning
without support. I think it possible that Gen. Rousseau suspected their scheme; for whilst we strove in the edge of the
timber, two regiments of volunteers took position on our
right, and a section of a battery quietly unlimbered on our
left. Scarcely were these dispositions completed, when down
upon us came the enemy, pouring in a withering, staggering
fire, that compelled the regiments just mentioned to break
and fly, in such confusion that they could not be rallied
again. This panic not only left us alone to sustain the dreaded
onset, but in addition, put us in extraordinary peril by the
total exposure of our left flank. The occasion was indeed
critical. But before the enemy could take any advantage of
the condition of things, Capt. Swaine averted the danger by
causing our battalion to charge front, thus giving the 15th,
16th and 19th the form of two sides of a triangle. Here we
fought for a time that seemed interminable, holding the
rebel force in check, until Col. Gibson's brigade, hastily
brought up to our relief, assisted by a flanking attack from
Nelson and Crittenden's divisions started the foe in the retreat, that shortly became a rout. Falling back, then, only
long enough to replenish our ammunition, we joined in the
pursuit, keeping it up, notwithstanding our exhausted condi-

tion, until we got beyond the line of the camps captured from our troops the day before.

I do not undertake to say what body of troops engaged in the battle of Shiloh, is entitled to the most honor. But I unhesitatingly assert that the 1st Battalion of the 15th U. S. Infantry did its whole duty. For seven hours it fought without ceasing, that, too, after it had marched seventeen miles the day before, and been deprived of sleep the night previous. And when the dreadful attack upon our centre was made, which caused Willich's German veterans to scatter like cattle upon a thousand hills, it still stood up to its work as though there was no such word as defeat in its lexicon. Throughout the struggle, Major King, Capt. Swaine and the company officers conducted themselves with great gallantry. In our company, nine men are killed and wounded. The loss of the command is sixty-three. Curtenius escaped without a scratch.

Dr. Parry informs me that our loss in killed and wounded, will not fall short of nine thousand men, and may exceed that number. From what I have seen myself, I give the fullest credence to his statement. On the evening of the engagement, the dead were everywhere. There never has been such carnage on this continent. I trust I may never again see anything of the kind.

The battle was fought in the woods, which were as serviceable to the enemy as fortifications. You may travel for a day around here and you will scarcely find a tree, sapling or twig, that has not been struck by a bullet. How any of us escaped is more than I can imagine.

W.

But You Must Act

IN HIS REPORT praising the army for its efficient use of printing presses Ferdinand LeComte commented also on the telegraph as an efficient method of conducting military business. But he added a caveat. "In many circumstances," he wrote, "it would have been very desirable for the army to have fewer telegrams at its command, and to be more independent of the political fluctuations of Washington."

With victory at Shiloh flushing Union ambitions, there was more reason than ever for the President to be impatient at General McClellan's continued inactivity. His letter of April 9 expressed that impatience unequivocally.

WASHINGTON, *April* 9, 1862.

To MAJOR-GENERAL McCLELLAN:

My Dear Sir—Your dispatches, complaining that you are not properly sustained, while they do not offend me, pain me very much. Blenker's Division was withdrawn before you left here, and you know the pressure under which I did it, and, as I thought, acquiesced in it, certainly not without reluctance. After you left, I ascertained that less than 20,-000 unorganized men, without a field battery, were all you designed should be left for the defence of Washington and Manassas Junction, and part of this even was to go to Gen. Hooker's old position. Gen. Banks's corps, once designed for Manassas Junction, was divided and tied up on the line of Winchester and Strasburg, and could not leave that position without again exposing the Upper Potomac and the Baltimore and Ohio Railroad.

This presented, or would present, when McDowell and Sumner should be gone, a great temptation for the enemy to turn back from the Rappahannock and sack Washington. My explicit directions that Washington, sustained by the judgment of all the commanders of corps, should be left secure, had been entirely neglected. It was precisely this that drove me to detain McDowell. I do not forget that I was satisfied with your arrangement to leave Banks at Manassas Junction. But when that arrangement was broken up, and nothing was substituted for it, of course I was not satisfied. I was constrained to substitute something for it myself. And now allow me to ask you, do you really think I could permit the line from Richmond, via Manassas Junction, to this city, to be entirely open, except what resistance could be presented by less than 20,000 unorganized troops? This is a question which the country will not allow me to evade.

There is a curious mystery about the number of troops now with you. I telegraphed you on the 6th, saying that you had over 100,000 with you. I had just obtained from the Secretary of War a statement taken, as he said, from your own returns, making 108,000 then with you and en route to you. You now say you will have but 85,000 when all en route to you shall have reached you. How can this discrepancy of

35,000 be accounted for? As to Gen. Wool's command, I understand that it is doing precisely what a like number of your own would have to do if that command was away. I suppose the whole force which has gone forward to you is with you by this time; and if so, I think it is the precise time for you to strike a blow.

By delay, the enemy will readily gain on you; that is, he will gain faster by fortifications and re-enforcements than you can by re-enforcements alone. And once more let me tell you, it is indispensable to you that you strike a blow. I am powerless to help. This you will do me the justice to re-member—I was always opposed to going down the Bay in search of a field, instead of fighting at or near Manassas, as only shifting and not surmounting a difficulty; that we would find the same enemy and the same or equal entrenchments at either place. The country will not fail to note—is noting now—that the present hesitation to move upon an intrenched enemy is but the story of Manassas repeated.

I beg leave to assure you that I have never written or spoken to you in greater kindness of feeling than now, nor with a fuller purpose to sustain you so far as in my most anxious judgment I consistently can. But you must act.

Yours, very truly,

A. LINCOLN.

Unfit for Human Beings

THERE IS A MULTITUDE of accounts of prison life behind Confederate lines. One of the best is one of the least known, Chaplain F. F. Kiner's narrative of his experiences in the prison pen at Macon, Georgia.

Food is always an item near the surface of a soldier's thinking. Prison fare was guaranteed not to be good, but the utter badness of it is a fact that is remarked again and again in the accounts of Federal soldiers. Kiner was no exception. It is worthy of note that he mentions that the prisoners' fare was not too different from that of their guards and that the Confederate citizens were so short of food that the prisoners sold to them food they rejected as inedible.

The forenoon of May 4th, 1862, found us in Macon, Georgia. We were taken from the cars and marched to a fairground, called Camp Oglethorpe, which was about fifteen or twenty acres in extent, enclosed by a picket fence. In the north-west corner was a very nice grove of pine trees which formed a most beautiful shade, and served as an excellent retreat in the hot summer days; without this I know not how we could have lived, under the burning sun. In connection with the grove were three large frame buildings, being nothing more than the frames weather-boarded; one of the three, I think, was ceiled, or partly so at least; besides these were two small frame buildings, one of which we used for a doctor shop, the other for a cook house for the hospital; the best of the three large buildings was the hospital. Excepting a row of stalls made for horses in time of fairs, there were no other buildings. There was also, an ever running spring in the camp but the water was not of the best quality. In addition to this was a well of water, about the centre of the grove, and a stronger stream in a well I never saw; fourteen hundred men supplied themselves from it daily and never exhausted it. Sometimes it got very low and muddy, but in a short time gained its usual depth. Here was the first place since our imprisonment that we had an opportunity to wash our bodies and clothes, and you may be sure we were anything but tidy in appearance. When we first went into this camp we had something over eight hundred men, but many of these soon took sick, and a number died.

For the first two months we did not seem to fare so badly, and the food we got was reasonably good. The ration during the month of May was one pound of flour or meal per day; three quarters of a pound of pork; some rice, sugar, molasses, rye for coffee, a small portion of hard soap, &c. So we got along pretty well and began to feel as though we had made a very lucky change. Another advantage was that we had a good chance to exercise, such as walking, playing ball and moving around in various ways, which was very beneficial to our health, and gave relief to our minds by drawing them away from our condition as prisoners, and from the anxious hearts at home. Nothing of any particular note occurred until about the 22nd of June, when orders were received to parole all the privates belonging to the Shiloh prisoners, but to retain the commissioned and non-commissioned officers. This was truly good news to the privates.

On the 24th, they were called into line and took the oath not to take up arms until they were exchanged or otherwise discharged. Thus they bid adieu to us who ranked just enough above them to stay in prison, and took their journey northward by way of Atlanta and Chattanooga, and joined our forces in Gen. Mitchel's command. All that left our camp were accepted; but for some reason, there were five hundred that had been kept at Montgomery, Ala., rejected, and sent back into prison. I presume, however, that Mitchell was acting under proper authority from the War Department. But it looked very hard to see these poor soldiers sent back again; some died upon the way, who had hoped to live long enough to see the Union lines once more; but such is the uncertainty of human expectations. In connection with these five hundred, they kept bringing in prisoners during the summer, until our number increased to twelve or fourteen hundred. We had prisoners from over one hundred and forty different regiments, representing almost every loyal state in the Union. Quite a number of these were captured while hunting blackberries and whisky, and prowling around away from their commands and duty; this they told us themselves. Such persons, I think, are to a certain extent censurable for such conduct.

But let us now notice more particularly our life in this camp during the balance of the summer. After they had paroled the privates, we had only about one hundred left. At this time the guards came and took all the cooking utensils from us, except what were sufficient for this number of

men. These were the same that we had got in Mobile, and
we never got them back again. When our number was increased to fourteen hundred, we had but the same amount
of cooking implements, and we never could get any more for
either love or money. Things became worse and worse with
us; the nights were always cold, and having no covering, the
poor soldiers began to get sicker, and diseases got more fatal.
Our flour was now changed to corn or rice meal. The corn
meal was of the coarsest kind, having often pieces of cob in
it, and whole grains of corn, and this unsifted. This meal we
had to bake as best we could, there being but few skillets
or ovens. Many, yes very many, had to gather up any old
piece of tin or sheet iron, or any piece of flat iron they could
find, and make plates and pans. We would stir the meal up
in any old thing we could get to hold it. Sometimes we could
buy a little saleratus at two dollars and a half per pound,
and scarce at that. As for salt, they issued us about a table-
spoonful to the man for seven days; sometimes we bought
it at the rate of ten cents per spoonful. At these rates our
cakes had often neither salt nor soda, and baked in every
kind of shape. You could see men baking at almost all hours
of the day or night; this was because of the scarcity of things
to bake in. It really looked pitiable to see hungry men, young
and old, holding an old piece of tin or iron over a smoking
fire, with a batch of coarse corn dough upon it, trying to
bake it, and perhaps when done, it was so sad, or burnt and
smoked, that it was not fit for a dog to eat. But what could
we do? we had no better. For plates we used any old scrap
of tin we could find, while some made them out of a pine
board or shingle. A few of us however, had good tin plates.
As for knives and forks the fingers answered all purposes.
The bread however, was the best part of our living com-
pared to the meat. They would call us all into line and give

us printed tickets good for seven days' rations, which were gathered up by our quartermaster, who drew rations for the number of tickets; these they hauled into the yard under the trees. The meal was brought in barrels, or old sugar hogsheads; the meat was thrown out upon the ground and literally crawled with maggots. They put guards around these rations till they were issued, and we often told them it was necessary to guard it to keep it from crawling off. Some of these hams and sides of meat were so badly spoiled that we could push a finger through and through them, as if they were mince meat. In fact, that was what was the matter with it, the worms had minced it too much. It had spoiled mostly from want of salt, for the grease we got from it was not salt enough to use for gravy. Of this rotten stuff, we got one half pound to the man per day, The maggots upon it were of the largest kind; perhaps I should call them skippers, for they could skip about and jump several feet at one leap; from their size I judged the climate agreed with them. There was, however, a kind much smaller, which worked into the meat, though it looked middling good, similar to those in cheese, and we could not see them until the meat was cooked, when they made their appearance on the top of the water in the pot, and floated around like clever sized grains of rice.

After thus describing our cookery ware, bread and meat, let us see what kind of dinner we could get up, and just such a dinner as this I have eaten many a time: When the cook pronounced dinner ready, we arranged our plates upon boards stuck up on four sticks, or perhaps on the ground just as the case might be; some plates were made by the tinner, some of wood, &c., while our spoons, knives and forks were of the same material and manufacture. This was all well so far, but when the soup came round was the time to talk of delicacies; it was immaterial whether you called it rice or maggot soup. Dear reader, I have seen men almost starving, refuse to eat it, while others with myself, took our spoons and lifted these poor unfortunate victims from the dish, and with the remainder tried to satisfy our craving appetites; and this was not only once, but an every day occurrence with some. I have taken my meat and fried it, when there would be a dozen maggots in the pan, and in trying to get them out many would go to pieces, when, to avoid the sight, I would stir in corn meal and eat the whole mess together. Thus have we spent our time in prison, living upon what any decent man or woman in the North would feel ashamed to offer to a dog. This was not my case alone, it was the case of hundreds with me, who to-day are living witnesses to this fact. A few days ago, while conversing with one of my own regiment who was in prison with me, he stated that he saw a joint of ham or shoulder, cooked while there in prison and the soup from it eaten; when they went to divide the meat, in the joint connecting the bones was a small spoonful of these maggots. I am aware that many will not feel inclined to believe this story, thinking I am taking the extreme side of the matter, and making it the excuse for this history. All I have to say is, that these are facts I wish I had never experienced; and I further say, that there is no writer's pen can do justice to this matter, in describing our wants and sufferings while in this camp of Tophet.

It is not pretended that all of our pork was of this description, but I am certain that I am in the bounds of reason when I say that at least one-third of it was unfit for use. This percentage was too much to lose from our scanty allowance, and as a matter of necessity we had to make use of some of the rancid article. During the latter part of our stay in this camp, we were allowed to sell our pork to the citizens, or as much of it as we did not wish to use ourselves, or could not use on account of its spoiled condition. For this meat they would give us at first twenty, and at last as high as forty cents per pound; and so eager were they to get it that they would come beforehand and try to engage it, and upon the day of issuing rations sent buyers to come and gather it up; sometimes they furnished money to one of our men to buy it for them, and often there was quite a competition in this branch of our trade. The money we got from the sale of the bacon we invested in yams, sweet potatoes, tomatoes, onions, peaches, or anything of the vegetable kind we could get hold of; but everything seemed very scarce among them except sweet potatoes. Irish potatoes were exceedingly scarce. I do not think we had over five bushels during the whole summer, and what few we did get, cost from twenty to twenty-five cents a quart, making about eight dollars a bushel. After we commenced selling our unhealthy meat and used sweet potatoes, we got along much better. They became the principal article of our food during the remainder of our stay in prison. Sometimes beef was brought in to sell to us; this was generally second rate, and what did not sell well among the citizens. They usually brought in the head, horns and all, and the leg below the knee, containing the hoof—in fact, every part that could be used as soup pieces or in any other way. Once in a while we could get a good piece that eat very well; for this we paid about fifteen cents per pound; the head and hoofs we bought by the piece. I have every reason to believe that food was scarce among them, and in fact they told us frequently that they hardly knew how to keep us for want of food. Their own soldiers that guarded us lived as we did, except that they had a better article, while we of course, got the second rate. I am convinced that these mountain arabs in the South can live on food that Northern laboring men would consider unfit

for use. Flour was then forty dollars a barrel; meat forty to
fifty cents per pound; sugar from thirty-five to fifty cents per
pound; salt one hundred and ten to one hundred and forty
dollars per sack; coffee and tea not to be had at any price,
and other things in proportion. Clothing was also very high.
A good wool hat, eight dollars; coarse shoes, eight to twelve
dollars a pair; calf skin boots, from twenty-five to forty dollars a pair. As a matter of course, the clothes we had on were
worn out, and we had none to take their place, or to wear
while we washed our filthy rags. There was a small stream
of water running through one side of the camp, in which we
bathed and washed; some would strip off their clothes and
wash them, then hang them on the picket fence and pass the
time in the water till they were dry enough to put on again.
When the clothes needed boiling, they borrowed from each
other if they could, till their own were done, or tied an old
blanket around them while they washed and boiled their
proper dress. We managed every style we could think of to
get along, yet very many towards the last, had nothing but
a piece of an old shirt and an old pair of drawers, or pants
with the knees and seats worn out, and torn in shreds every
way. Our patching and mending was very limited, having
nothing to do it with. Muslin, woolen, tarpaulin, oil cloth,
linen, and all kinds were sewed together to hide nakedness and
stop the rents in worn out clothing. During the six months'
imprisonment we never received from the Southern Confederacy over three hundred coarse, cotton shirts, for all the
men that were in camp, and this was all we got of any kind
except a few old clothes brought in to the hospital for the
sick by the citizens. So there will be no wonder that we were
bad off for something to put upon our bodies. This part of
our destitution was the cause of much suffering among us,
resulting in sickness and death. We used all the vacant build-

ings, sheds and stalls to sleep in, but they were too small to contain all, and the balance had to lie out under the trees; this brought disease and speedy death on many of the soldiers—it could not be otherwise. It was a pitiable sight to see so many of our brave boys lying out under the trees, with nothing but shirt and drawers, bare headed and bare footed, shivering in every nerve. Though it may be properly said that we were in the sunny South, yet I never passed one night in it but that I needed at least one good blanket, to get which was out of the question with many.

Our hospital contained about one hundred sick, who for the greater part of the time had to lay upon the floor; some were furnished mattresses; a few weeks before we left they got bunks made to lay the sick on. But for want of a proper change of clothing, their beds soon became filthy, as well as their bodies. There were two young doctors in attendance every day, who were, I think, fine young men, and did the best they could, but often had no medicine. We generally had a quantity of medicine sent to us to last a certain time, and if it was exhausted before that time expired, we had to do without. Under these circumstances, many of the sick would sell their scanty rations of food and send out and buy some from the druggist in the town, and we also would get leave to go with an escort of guards into the woods and get such barks as we thought contained medical properties and tonics, for ourselves; every man to a certain extent had to be his own doctor, and as a matter of course there were very many quite strange prescriptions given; some were recommended with miraculous faith. Many were afflicted with swelled feet and legs, having the appearance of dropsy, caused by weakness and diseased constitutions. I have known them to dig holes in the ground and bury their feet and legs knee deep for hours, hoping that the application of fresh ground might do them good; and it occurs to me that numbers had some faith in the operation. There were four or five hundred men for medicine every morning, and often none to be had. Towards the latter part of the summer the mortality among us became great, and with few exceptions we had every day from one to seven of our men to bury. I have known them to get so poor that their thighs were no larger than a man's arm, and they were really nothing more than living skeletons, yet they would try to keep about until in many cases they would drop dead from their feet. Others would die sitting against a tree, or anywhere, while many would die so easily upon their beds, without a groan or a sigh, that even the nurses were not aware of it. . . .

While in prison, we furnished nurses of our own men to wait upon the sick; every morning a fresh set of nurses would relieve the ones that went on duty the day before. All our hospital duties were unpleasant; not because we cared nothing for the sick, nor felt it our duty to do all in our power for them, but because our feelings were so mortified to see the poor beings suffering for the want of something to nourish or make them comfortable which we were unable to furnish. Often there was but one candle in the entire building by which to give medicine. But let us leave these sad reflections for a short time, (for our lives were a continued scene of misery), and notice our various occupations. Even in this place of confinement Yankee ingenuity and industry must be engaged. Many of the younger would play marbles; others, benefit themselves by exercising in playing ball, pitching horse shoes, &c., but the most popular as well as the most profitable employment was the manufacture of bone jewelry, which was carried on very extensively by nearly all classes in prison, the only exceptions being those who had no taste or tact for the business. We managed to get files of different sizes and styles, and made saws out of common table knives, with which we sawed beef bones into whatever shape we desired to have them—either for finger rings, breastpins, slides, watch seals, or, in fact, anything almost that could be thought of. These pieces of bone we filed off very smooth, and to the exact shape desired, and then polished them off with sand paper, after which we drew with a pencil, all kinds of letters, flowers, figures, &c.; these marks we carved out with the sharp pointed blade of a pocket knife, and filled the crevices with sealing wax of different colors; by this means we got up some most beautiful jewelry, for which we found ready sale, or at least for a great deal of it. The citizens, both ladies and gentlemen, from far and near, came to purchase relics from the Yankees. I think I can safely say, that we sold several thousand dollars worth of it. This money helped us to increase our diet of vegetables and improved our living very much; indeed very many did not live on anything else than what they bought in this way. The Confederates were very much astonished at our ingenuity, and gave us credit for being a go-ahead kind of people, and for turning everything into some use. Old bones got to be quite in demand among us, and we used to give little boys a ring for bringing us in an armful; sometimes we paid the money for them. These articles sold for various prices, according to the style in which they were gotten up; generally the rings brought from twenty-five cents to one dollar; the other articles, such as breastpins and seals, several dollars. They paid us altogether in Southern money, some of which was issued by states, others by various associations, or companies, and some by individuals. They were very scrupulous about using the bills issued by different companies, associations, or individuals of any other state, because these parties were liable to be dissolved, or perhaps broken up at any time, and could not be considered as permanent. Another of our daily duties was to see to our personal comfort. I have already spoken of washing and boiling our clothes, but now we had another enemy to combat with, which our boys knew by the name of "graybacks." They were very troublesome and with all the care we could take, made inroads upon our peace, and increased in numbers so rapidly that our buildings and camp soon became full of them. They seemed as numerous as when they paid Pharaoh a visit in Egypt, and all the execution we could do did not seem to diminish their number. It became one of our regular daily duties, mostly in the morning, to hunt a shady place and make a general search for these intruders, and seldom failed to secure a large number of captives. These we executed upon the spot as guerrillas, and never considered them as entitled to the rights of prisoners of war, although they undoubtedly belong to both the regular and volunteer army.

The Capture and Occupation of New Orleans

THE SPRING OF 1862 brought a great naval victory on the Mississippi when Admiral David G. Farragut's fleet stormed past the forts protecting New Orleans and forced the surrender of the largest Confederate city.

The Confederates had believed the defenses of the lower Mississippi impregnable. They had overestimated the strength of Forts Jackson and St. Philip and, because of pressing needs in other areas, had in fact neglected properly to defend New Orleans.

Farragut bombarded the forts for nearly a week, succeeded in breaking the chain stretched across the river to close the channel, and took his fleet into the unfortified area between the forts and the city. He had brought with him a land army under command of Major General Benjamin F. Butler. These men were successfully landed and Confederate General Mansfield Lovell had no choice but to leave New Orleans and permit its surrender.

Butler became famous as a military despot. He ruled the city with an iron hand, caring little for the opinions of the New Orleanais or of the world. Most famous is his General Orders No. 28, in which he "ordered that hereafter when any female shall, by word, gesture or movement, insult or show contempt for any officer or soldier of the United States, she shall be regarded and held liable to be treated as a woman of the town plying her avocation."

Equally as harsh, and controlling nearly every facet of New Orleans life, was his very first pronouncement, his Proclamation of May 1, 1862, which established military rule in the city.

PROCLAMATION.

HEADQUARTERS DEPARTMENT OF THE GULF,⎫
New-Orleans, May 1, 1862. ⎬

The City of New-Orleans and its environs, with all its interior and exterior defenses, having been surrendered to the combined naval and land forces of the United States, and having been evacuated by the rebel forces in whose possession they lately were, and being now in occupation of the forces of the United States, who have come to restore order, maintain public tranquility, enforce peace and quiet under the Laws and Constitution of the United States, the Major-General commanding the forces of the United States in the Department of the Gulf, hereby makes known and proclaims the object and purposes of the Government of the United States in thus taking possession of the City of New-Orleans and the State of Louisiana, and the rules and regulations by which the laws of the United States will be for the present and during a state of war enforced and maintained, for the plain guidance of all good citizens of the United States, as well as others who may heretofore have been in rebellion against their authority.

Thrice before has the City of New-Orleans been rescued from the hand of a foreign government, and still more calamitous domestic insurrection, by the money and arms of the United States. It has of late been under the military control of the rebel forces, claiming to be the peculiar friends of its citizens, and at each time, in the judgment of the Commander of the military forces holding it, it has been found necessary to preserve order and maintain quiet by the administration of Law Martial. Even during the *interim* from its evacuation by the rebel soldiers and its actual possession by the soldiers of the United States, the civil authorities of the city have found it necessary to call for the intervention of an armed body known as the "European Legion," to preserve public tranquility. The Commanding General, therefore, will cause the city to be governed until the restoration of Municipal Authority, and his further orders, by the Law Martial, a measure for which it would seem the previous recital furnishes sufficient precedents.

All persons in arms against the United States are required to surrender themselves, with their arms, equipments and munitions of war. The body known as the "European Legion," not being understood to be in arms against the United States, but organized to protect the lives and property of the citizens, are invited still to co-operate with the forces of the United States to that end, and, so acting, will not be included in the terms of this order, but will report to these Headquarters.

All flags, ensigns and devices, tending to uphold any authority whatever, save the flag of the United States and the flags of foreign Consulates, must not be exhibited, but suppressed. The American Ensign, the emblem of the United States, must be treated with the utmost deference and respect by all persons, under pain of severe punishment.

All persons well disposed towards the Government of the United States, who shall renew their oath of allegiance, will receive the safeguard and protection, in their persons and property, of the armies of the United States, the violation of which, by any person, is punishable with death.

All persons still holding allegiance to the Confederate States will be deemed rebels against the Government of the United States, and regarded and treated as enemies thereof.

All foreigners not naturalized and claiming allegiance to their respective Governments, and not having made oath of allegiance to the supposed Government of the Confederate States, will be protected in their persons and property as heretofore under the laws of the United States.

All persons who may heretofore have given their adherence to the supposed Government of the Confederate States, or have been in their service, who shall lay down and deliver up their arms and return to peaceful occupations and preserve quiet and order, holding no further correspondence nor giving aid and comfort to the enemies of the United States, will not be disturbed either in person or property, except so far, under the orders of the Commanding General, as the exigencies of the public service may render necessary.

The keepers of all public property, whether State, National or Confederate, such as collections of art, libraries, museums, as well as all public buildings, all munitions of war, and armed vessels, will at once make full returns thereof to these Headquarters; all manufacturers of arms and munitions of war, will report to these Headquarters their kind and places of business.

All rights of property, of whatever kind, will be held inviolate, subject only to the laws of the United States.

All inhabitants are enjoined to pursue their usual avocations; all shops and places of business are to be kept open in the accustomed manner, and services to be had in the churches and religious houses as in times of profound peace.

Keepers of all public houses, coffee houses and drinking saloons, are to report their names and numbers to the office of the Provost Marshal; will there receive license, and be held responsible for all disorders and disturbances of the peace arising in their respective places.

A sufficient force will be kept in the city to preserve order and maintain the laws.

The killing of an American soldier by any disorderly person or mob, is simply assassination and murder, and not war, and will be so regarded and punished.

The owner of any house or building in or from which such murder shall be committed, will be held responsible therefor, and the house will be liable to be destroyed by the military authority.

All disorders and disturbances of the peace done by combinations and numbers, and crimes of an aggravated nature, interfering with forces or laws of the United States, will be referred to a military court for trial and punishment; other misdemeanors will be subject to the municipal authority, if it chooses to act. Civil causes between party and party will be referred to the ordinary tribunals. The levy and collection of all taxes, save those imposed by the laws of the United States, are suppressed, except those for keeping in repair and lighting the streets, and for sanitary purposes. Those are to be collected in the usual manner.

The circulation of Confederate bonds, evidences of debt, except notes in the similitude of bank notes issued by the

Confederate States, or scrip, or any trade, in the same, is strictly forbidden. It having been represented to the Commanding General by the city authorities that these Confederate notes, in the form of bank notes, are, in a great measure, the only substitute for money which the people have been allowed to have, and that great distress would ensue among the poorer classes if the circulation of such notes were suppressed, such circulation will be permitted so long as any one may be inconsiderate enough to receive them, till further orders.

No publication, either by newspaper, pamphlet or handbill, giving accounts of the movements of soldiers of the United States within this Department, reflecting in any way upon the United States or its officers, or tending in any way to influence the public mind against the Government of the United States, will be permitted; and all articles of war news, or editorial comments, or correspondence, making comments upon the movements of the armies of the United States, or the rebels, must be submitted to the examination of an officer who will be detailed for that purpose from these Headquarters.

The transmission of all communications by telegraph will be under the charge of an officer from these Headquarters.

The armies of the United States came here not to destroy but to make good, to restore order out of chaos, and the government of laws in place of the passions of men, to this end, therefore, the efforts of all well-disposed persons are invited to have every species of disorder quelled, and if any soldier of the United States should so far forget his duty or his flag as to commit any outrage upon any person or property, the Commanding General requests that his name be instantly reported to the Provost Guard, so that he may be punished and his wrongful act redressed.

The municipal authority, so far as the police of the city and crimes are concerned, to the extent before indicated, is hereby suspended.

All assemblages of persons in the streets, either by day or by night, tend to disorder, and are forbidden.

The various companies composing the Fire Department in New-Orleans, will be permitted to retain their organization, and are to report to the office of the Provost Marshal, so that they may be known and not interfered with in their duties.

And, finally, it may be sufficient to add, without further enumeration, that all the requirements of martial law will be imposed so long as, in the judgment of the United States authorities, it may be necessary. And while it is the desire of these authorities to exercise this government mildly, and after the usages of the past, it must not be supposed that it will not be vigorously and firmly administered as occasion calls.

By command of   MAJOR-GENERAL BUTLER.

GEO. C. STRONG, A. A. G., Chief of Staff.

A Change in Virginia

PRESIDENT LINCOLN had called for action in Virginia. He now got it.

"Stonewall" Jackson conducted a whirlwind campaign in the Valley of Virginia that secured his military fame forever. The Confederates withdrew up the Peninsula, relinquishing Yorktown and being defeated at Williamsburg early in May. By the end of May McClellan had crossed the Chickahominy and was threatening Richmond. In a bloody action near Fair Oaks Station May 31 and June 1 each side lost over forty thousand men. Confederate General Joseph E. Johnston was wounded on the first day of the battle, and, on the next, General R. E. Lee was appointed to command the Confederate troops facing McClellan. Costly as it was, Fair Oaks was indecisive. A little over two weeks later Confederate General J. E. B. Stuart rode around McClellan's army in his famous Chickahominy Raid. There was no further major action till the end of the month, when the great Seven Days' Battles began June 26. Repulsed with heavy loss after battles at Mechanicsville, Gaines' Mill, Allen's Farm, Savage's Station, Glendale, and Malvern Hill,

McClellan nevertheless succeeded in withdrawing to a new base at Harrison's Landing on the banks of the James River. Though Confederate losses had exceeded Federal, the Union Army had failed in its grand attempt on the Confederate capital. General Henry W. Halleck was appointed to the command of all United States land forces on July 11, and withdrawal of the Army of the Potomac from the Peninsula was begun. On July 14 General John Pope took command of the Federal Army of Virginia.

Three army circulars are milestones in the progress of the campaign, General McClellan's addresses to his army on June 2 and July 4 and General Pope's message on his assumption of command.

HEAD-QUARTERS, ARMY OF THE POTOMAC.

CAMP NEAR NEW BRIDGE, VA., *June 2d*, 1862.
SOLDIERS OF THE ARMY OF THE POTOMAC!

I have fulfilled at least a part of my promise to you; you are now face to face with the rebels, who are at bay in front of their Capital. The final and decisive battle is at hand. Unless you belie your past history, the result cannot be for a moment doubtful. If the troops who labored so patiently, and fought so gallantly at Yorktown, and who so bravely won the hard fights at Williamsburg, West Point, Hanover Court House and Fair Oaks, now prove worthy of their antecedents, the victory is surely ours. The events of every day prove your superiority; wherever you have met the enemy you have beaten him; wherever you have used the bayonet he has given way in panic and disorder. I ask of you now one last crowning effort. The enemy has staked his all on the issue of the coming battle. Let us meet and crush him here in the very centre of the rebellion.

Soldiers! I will be with you in this battle, and share its dangers with you. Our confidence in each other is now founded upon the past. Let us strike the blow which is to restore peace and union to this distracted land. Upon your valor, discipline and mutual confidence that result depends.

GEO. B. McCLELLAN,

Major General Commanding.

HEAD-QUARTERS, ARMY OF THE POTOMAC.

CAMP NEAR HARRISON'S LANDING, VA., *July 4th.* 1862

SOLDIERS OF THE ARMY OF THE POTOMAC!

Your achievements of the last ten days have illustrated the valor and endurance of the American Soldier! Attacked by vastly superior forces, and without hope of reinforcements, you have succeeded in changing your base of operations by a flank movement, always regarded as the most hazardous of military expedients. You have saved all your material, all your trains, and all your guns, except a few lost in battle, taking in return guns and colors from the enemy. Upon your march you have been assailed day after day with desperate fury by men of the same race and nation, skillfully massed and led; and under every disadvantage of numbers, and necessarily of position also, you have in every conflict beaten back your foes with enormous slaughter. Your conduct ranks you among the celebrated armies of history. No one will now question that each of you may always say with pride: "I belonged to the Army of the Potomac!" You have reached this new base, complete in organization and unimpaired in spirit. The enemy may at any moment attack you. We are prepared to receive them. I have personally established your lines. Let them come, and we will convert their repulse into a final defeat. Your Government is strengthening you with the resources of a great people.

On this our Nation's Birthday we declare to our foes, who are rebels against the best interests of mankind, that this Army shall enter the Capital of their so-called Confederacy; that our National Constitution shall prevail; and that the Union which can alone insure internal peace and external security to each State must and shall be preserved, cost what it may in time, treasure and blood.

GEO. B. McCLELLAN,
Major General Commanding.

HEADQUARTERS, ARMY OF VIRGINIA,

WASHINGTON, D. C., *July* 14, 1862.

To the Officers and Soldiers
of the Army of Virginia:

By special assignment of the President of the United States, I have assumed the command of this Army. I have spent two weeks in learning your whereabouts, your condition, and your wants; in preparing you for active operations, and in placing you in positions from which you can act promptly and to the purpose. These labors are nearly completed, and I am about to join you in the field.

Let us understand each other. I have come to you from the West, where we have always seen the backs of our enemies; from an Army whose business it has been to seek the adversary and to beat him when he was found; whose policy has been attack and not defence. In but one instance has the enemy been able to place our western armies in defensive attitude. I presume that I have been called here to pursue the same system, and to lead you against the enemy. It is my purpose to do so, and that speedily. I am sure you long for an opportunity to win the distinction you are capable of achieving. That opportunity I shall endeavor to give you. Meantime I desire you to dismiss from your minds certain phrases which I am sorry to find much in vogue amongst you. I hear constantly of taking "strong positions and holding them," of "lines of retreat," and of "bases of supplies." Let us discard such ideas. The strongest position a soldier should desire to occupy is one from which he can most easily advance against the enemy. Let us study the probable lines of retreat of our opponents, and leave our own to take care of themselves. Let us look before us, and not behind. Success and glory are in the advance; disaster and shame lurk in the rear. Let us act on this understanding, and it is safe to predict that your banners shall be inscribed with many a glorious deed, and that your names will be dear to your countrymen forever.

JNO. POPE,
Major General Commanding.

We Must Learn Righteousness

THE EXTENT to which slavery was a cause of the Civil War has been debated ever since the war began. If it was not a principal cause, agitation over slavery was certainly the catalyst that precipitated war.

By the fall of 1862 the moral issue of slavery had achieved greater importance than ever. From many sides there was pressure on President Lincoln to promulgate a proclamation which would end slavery. Typical of such pressure is the Memorial issued by a meeting of citizens in Chicago, September 7. Prominent citizens had been called together "to take measures to memorialize the President to issue a Proclamation of National Emancipation."

A delegation was appointed to carry the Memorial to Washington and present it to the President. It was published and circulated widely with the admonition:

"Read it! read it carefully! Call your Christian fellow citizens together without distinction of sect, and adopt it or something like it, and send it to the President. The united voice of the Christians of this whole land should go up to the Executive Mansion, calling for justice to

149

the oppressed. We must as a Nation learn righteousness, or our poor bleeding, imperiled Country is undone! Religious men everywhere, at such a time as this, should act and speak fearlessly and promptly. They should also pray unceasingly that God would incline our President to do that great act of justice and mercy, which this Memorial implores."

There follows the "Memorial of the Christian Men of Chicago. To His Excellency, Abraham Lincoln, President of the United States."

MEMORIAL
OF THE
PUBLIC MEETING OF THE CHRISTIAN MEN OF CHICAGO.

To His Excellency, Abraham Lincoln, President of the United States:

Your memorialists of all Christian denominations in the city of Chicago, assembled in solemn meeting to consider the moral aspects of the war now waging, would utter their deepest convictions as to the present relation of our country and its rulers to the government and providence of Almighty God; and would respectfully ask a hearing for the principles and facts deemed fundamental to a right judgment of this appalling crisis. And to this we are encouraged by the frequency with which, on various public occasions, you have officially recognized the dependence of the country and its chief magistrate upon the Divine favor.

We claim, then, that the war is a Divine retribution upon our land for its manifold sins, and especially for the crime of oppression, against which the denunciations of God's Word are so numerous and pointed.

The American nation, in this its judgment-hour, must acknowledge that the cry of the slave, unheeded by man, has been heard by God and answered in this terrible visitation. The time has at length come of which Jefferson solemnly warned his countrymen, as he declared that the slaves of America were enduring "a bondage, one hour of which is fraught with more misery than ages of that which occasioned the war of the Revolution," and added, "When the measure of their tears shall be full, when their tears shall have involved heaven itself in darkness, doubtless a God of justice will awaken to their distress, by diffusing a light and liberality among their oppressors, or at length by his exterminating thunder, manifest his attention to things of this world, and that they are not left to the guidance of blind fatality."

The slave oligarchy has organized the most unnatural, perfidious and formidable rebellion known to history. It has professedly established an independent government on the avowed basis of slavery, admitting that the Federal Union was constituted to conserve and promote liberty. All but four of the slave states have seceded from the Union, and those four (with the exception of Delaware, in which slavery but nominally exists) have been kept in subjection only by overwhelming military force. Can we doubt that this is a Divine retribution for national sin, in which our crime has justly shaped our punishment?

Proceeding upon this belief, which recent events have made it almost atheism to deny, your memorialists avow their solemn conviction, deepening every hour, that there can be no deliverance from Divine judgments *till slavery ceases in the land.* We cannot expect God to save a nation that clings to its sin. This is too fearful an hour to insult

God, or to deceive ourselves. National existence is in peril: our sons and brothers are falling by tens of thousands on the battle-field: the war becomes daily more determined and destructive. While we speak the enemy thunders at the gates of the capital. Our acknowledged superiority of resources has thus far availed little or nothing in the conflict. As Christian patriots we dare not conceal the truth, that these judgments mean what the divine judgments meant in Egypt. They are God's stern command—"LET MY PEOPLE GO!"

This work of national repentance has been inaugurated by the abolition of slavery in the District of Columbia, and its prohibition in the territories, as also by encouragement to emancipation in the border slave states, offered by Congress at the suggestion of the President.

But these measures do not meet the crisis as regards either the danger of the country or the national guilt. We urge you, therefore, as the head of this Christian nation, from considerations of moral principle, and, as the only means of preserving the Union, to proclaim, *without delay*, NATIONAL EMANCIPATION.

However void of authority in this respect you might have been in time of peace, you are well aware, as a statesman, that the exigences of war are the only limits of its powers, especially in a war to preserve the very life of the nation. And these exigences are not to be restricted to what may avail at the last gasp prior to national death, but are to be interpreted to include all measures that may most readily and thoroughly subdue the enemy. The rebels have brought slavery under your control by their desperate attack upon the life of the republic. They have created a moral, political and military necessity, which warrants the deed, and now God and a waiting world demand that the opportunity be used. And surely the fact that they have placed in our power a system which, while it exposes them, is itself the grossest wickedness, adds infinitely to the obligation to strike the blow.

In this view of a change of power involving an equal change in duty, we will not conceal the fact that gloom has filled our hearts at every indication that the war was regarded as simply an issue between the Federal authorities and the rebel states; and that therefore slavery was to be touched only to the extent that the pressure of rebel success might absolutely necessitate. Have we not reason to *expect* rebel success on that policy? Are we to omit from our calculations the necessary conditions of Divine favor? Has the fact no moral force, that the war has suddenly placed within the power of the President, the system that has provoked God's wrath? Is there not danger that while we are waiting till the last terrible exigency shall force us to liberate the slave, God may decide the contest against us, and the measure that we would not adopt on principle, prove too late for our salvation? We claim that justice, here as everywhere, is the highest expediency.

At the time of the national peril of the Jews under Ahasuerus, Mordecai spake in their name to Queen Esther, who hesitated to take the step necessary to their preservation, in these solemn words: "Think not with thyself that thou shalt escape in the king's house, more than all the Jews. For if thou altogether holdest thy peace at this time, then shall there enlargement and deliverance arise to the Jews from another place; but thou and thy father's house shall be destroyed; and who knoweth whether thou art come to the kingdom for such a time as this?" And your memorialists believe that in Divine Providence you have been called to the Presidency to speak the word of justice and authority which shall free the bondman and save the nation. Our prayer to God is, that by such an act the name of ABRAHAM LINCOLN may go down to posterity with that of GEORGE WASHINGTON, as the second SAVIOR OF OUR COUNTRY.

RESOLUTIONS.

Resolved, That universal emancipation seems pointed out by Providence as the most effectual, if not the only means of saving our country.

That in the appalling loss of blood and treasure, and re- peated reverses to our arms, pressing the nation to the verge of destruction should be heard the voice that sounded above the wail of desolated Egypt—"Let my people go."

That universal emancipation as a mere act of *political* jus- tice would be without a parallel in the annals of the world.

That it would be the abandonment of a wrong long per- petuated against the oppressed race, to the contravention of impartial liberty, the reproach of free institutions and the dishonor of our country.

That it would be a consummation of the expectations of the founders of the republic, who, deploring while tolerating slavery, anticipated its early disappearance from the conti- nent.

That it would accord with the world's convictions of jus- tice, and the higher teachings of Christianity.

That we should not expect national deliverance till we rise at least to the moral judgment of Jefferson who, in view of slavery exclaimed: "I tremble for my country when I reflect that God is just; that his justice cannot sleep forever; that considering numbers, nature, and natural means only, a revolution of the wheel of fortune, an exchange of situation, is among possible events, that it may become probable by supernatural interference! The Almighty has no attribute which can take side with us in such a contest."

That all assumed right to slavery under the Constitution is forfeited by open and persistent rebellion; and therefore, emancipation, to preserve the republic, would only vindicate and honor the Constitution.

That, as slavery is a principal reliance of the rebellion, conserving its property, tilling its plantations, feeding and clothing its armies, freeing the slaves would take away its support, recall its armies from the field, demoralize its conspiracy, and organize in its midst a power for its overthrow.

That, putting down this rebellion is as obvious a Christian duty as prayer, preaching, charity to the poor, or missions to heathen.

That the postponement of emancipation jeopards countless treasure, the best blood and the *existence* of the nation.

That no evils apprehended from emancipation are comparable to those that would arise from the overthrow of the republic, and they would fall upon those madly provoking the catastrophe.

That as the perpetuation and extension of slavery were a primary aim of this rebellion, its overthrow would seem a fitting and signal retribution upon its authors—like hanging Haman upon the gallows he erected for Mordecai.

That it were better for this generation to perish than that the American Union should be dissolved; and it is a delusion that those disloyal and belligerent under the Constitution and traditions of their fathers, would become peaceable citizens, observant of treaties and oaths in rival states.

L. B. OTIS, *Chairman,*

E. W. BLATCHFORD, *Secretary.*

Maryland Invaded

A SECOND FEDERAL DEFEAT at Bull Run had ended General John Pope's career as a field commander and paved the way for Confederate invasion of Maryland. General McClellan resumed command and prepared to face his old enemies again.

Dr. Lewis H. Steiner, an inspector for the Sanitary Commission, was a native of Frederick, Maryland. He was thus qualified by both duty and natural interest as a particularly appropriate reporter of the occupation of that town.

The occupation of Frederick is famous out of proportion to its importance because it inspired one of the best loved of American poems, John Greenleaf Whittier's "Barbara Frietchie." As it may well be that Steiner's account was the source of Whittier's inspiration (the story was relayed to him, possibly already embellished by the popular novelist, Mrs. E. D. E. N. Southworth), it is appropriate to point out here how history and myth become interwoven and how the reality of history can disappear in the stronger truth of fiction.

Steiner's factual version appears as a single paragraph

in his report. Whittier's poem was published the next
year. In a perceptive article, "The Yankee Muse in History," in the fall of 1863 the Richmond *Examiner*
(quoted in *The Record of News, History and Literature*
for November 26, 1863) prophesied the future of the
piece.

"Verse is stronger than prose," wrote the anonymous
Richmond reporter, "and history is powerless in competition with the popular ballad. . . . Late Yankee
papers bring us a ballad fresh from the mint, which is
so remarkable in itself, and destined to play such havoc
with Southern histories of the war, that we cannot re-
frain from inserting it entire. . . .

"A likely story, truly. Frederick City, fair as a garden
of the Lord to famished rebels; Jackson at the head of
his columns, ordering his men to fire on a Dutch dame,
ninety years old, because she hung a flag out of the
garret window, and then blushing for shame because
the bullets cut the flag clean away from the staff, and
the nimble old harridan catches it as it fell, leans far out
the window sill and shakes it forth with a royal will,
careless of the danger of losing her center of gravity and
pitching headlong into the street. See the noble nature
within him stirred at Dame Barbara's deed and word,
and hear him thunder

'Who touches a hair of yon gray head,
Dies like a dog! March on!' he said.

"Think, too, of the loyal winds upholding the flag
they loved so well. The sunset light, bidding the flag
good night, in pure Yankee accents, and drop a tear on

Stonewall's bier for old Frietchie's sake, if you can; and if you cannot, employ a loyal onion to aid you in the pathetic task.

"The uncultivated may pronounce the poem so much unadulterated and self-evident nonsense, but the wise, the gifted, the good, know that it will outlive and disprove all histories, however well authenticated."

REPORT.

FREDERICK L. OLMSTED, Esq.,
>   *Secretary U. S. Sanitary Commission:*

IN accordance with your request, I have the honor to transmit an account of my operations as Sanitary Inspector during the last month. The engagements which crowd so thickly upon me just now, prevent that careful preparation which a report, including incidents of such deep interest to every American, should receive from the reporter. The best that I can do is to give you as faithful an account as my diary and recollections, and the reports of other officers of the Commission, will enable me, in as few words as possible, deprecating all criticism of its style and finish. . . .

Friday, September 5.—Left Washington at 6 o'clock, under the impression that the Confederate army had crossed the Potomac the preceding evening and were then in Frederick. Anxiety as to the fate of my friends, as well as to the general treatment my native place would receive at rebel hands, made the trip by no means a pleasant one.

Along the road, at different stopping-places, reports reached us as to the numbers of the Confederates that had crossed into Maryland. The passengers began to entertain fears that the train would not be able to reach Frederick. These were, however, quieted by a telegram received at a station near Monrovia, which announced the road open. Arriving at 12 o'clock, M., I found the town full of surmises and rumors. Such information had been received by the Post Quarter Master and the Surgeon in charge of Hospital, that they were busy all the afternoon making arrangements to move off their valuable stores. The citizens were in the greatest trepidation. Invasion by the Southern army was considered equivalent to destruction. Impressment into the ranks as common soldiers, or immurement in a *Southern* prison— these were not attractive prospects for quiet, Union-loving citizens!

Towards nightfall it became pretty certain that a force had crossed somewhere about the mouth of the Monocacy. Telegrams were crowding rapidly on the army officers located here, directing that what stores could not be removed should be burned, and that the sick should as far as possible be sent on to Pennsylvania. Here began a scene of terror seldom witnessed in this region. Lieut. Castle, A. Q. M., burned a large quantity of his stores at the depot. Assist. Surg. Weir fired his store-house on the Hospital grounds and burned the most valuable of his surplus bedding contained in Kemp Hall, in Church street near Market. Many of our prominent citizens, fearing impressment, left their families and started for Pennsylvania in carriages, on horseback, and on foot. All the convalescents at the Hospital that could bear the fatigue, were started also for Pennsylvania, in charge of Hospital Steward Cox. The citizens removed their trunks containing private papers and other valuables from the bank-vaults, under the firm belief that an attack would be made on these buildings for the sake of the specie contained in them.

About 1½ o'clock, A.M., it was ascertained that Jackson's force—the advance guard of the Southern army—was encamped on Moffat's farm, near Buckeystown, and that this force would enter Frederick after daylight; for what purpose no one knew. Having possession of this amount of information, I retired about two o'clock, being willing to wait the sequel, whatever it might be.

Saturday, September 6.—Found, on visiting the market in the morning, that a very large number of our citizens had *"skedaddled"* (i. e. retired rapidly in good order) last night. Every mouth was full of rumors as to the numbers, whereabouts, and whatabouts of the Confederate force. One old gentleman, whose attachment to McClellan has become proverbial, declared that it was an impossibility for the rebels to cross the Potomac; and another, who looks upon Banks as the greatest of generals, declared that Banks' force had been taken for Confederates, and that the supposed enemies were friends.

At length uncertainty was changed into certainty. About nine o'clock two seedy-looking individuals rode up Market street as fast as their jaded animals could carry them. Their dress was a dirty, faded gray, their arms rusty and seemingly uncared for, their general appearance raffish or vagabondish. They shouted for Jeff. Davis at the intersection of Patrick and Market street, and then riding to the intersection of Church and Market, repeated the same *strange* jubilant shout. No one expressing an opinion as to the propriety or impropriety of this proceeding, they countermarched and trotted down the street. Then followed some fifty or a hundred horsemen, having among them Bradley T. Johnson, *soi-disant* Colonel C.S.A. These were received with feeble shouts from some secession-sympathizers. They said, "the time of your deliverance has come." It was plain that the deliverance they meant was from the rule of law and order. The sidewalks were filled with Union-loving citizens, who felt keenly that their humiliation was at hand, and that they had no course but submission, at least for a time.

As this force of cavalry entered the town from the south, Capt. Yellot's company retreated west from the town, and disappeared no one knew whither. One ruffian cavalry soldier rode up to Sergt. Crocker (in charge of hospital stores in Kemp Hall) and accosted him with "Sa-ay, are you a Yankee?" "No, I am a Marylander." "What are you doing in the Yankee army?" "I belong to the United States army," said the old man, proudly. "If you don't come along with me, I'll cut your head off." Having waved his sabre over the *unarmed* old man's head, he demanded his keys, and rode off with the sergeant as a prisoner. This display of chivalry did not infuse great admiration of the Southern army into the hearts of the bystanders.

A force of cavalry entered the hospital grounds and took possession of hospital and contents. All the sick were carefully paroled, not excepting one poor fellow then in a moribund condition. After some hours, the medical officers and hospital stewards were allowed to go about town on passes.

At ten o'clock Jackson's advance force, consisting of some five thousand men, marched up Market street and encamped north of the town. They had but little music; what there was gave us "My Maryland" and Dixie in execrable style. Each regiment had a square red flag, with a cross, made of diagonal blue stripes extending from opposite corners: on these blue stripes were placed thirteen white stars. A dirtier, filthier, more unsavory set of human beings never *strolled* through a town—marching it could not be called without doing violence to the word. The distinctions of rank were recognized on the coat collars of officers; but all were alike

dirty and repulsive. Their arms were rusty and in an unsol-
dierly condition. Their uniforms, or rather multiforms, corre-
sponded only in a slight predominance of gray over butter-
nut, and in the prevalence of filth. Faces looked as if they
had not been acquainted with water for weeks; hair, shaggy
and unkempt, seemed entirely a stranger to the operations
of brush or comb. A motlier group was never herded
together. But *these* were the chivalry—the deliverers of
Maryland from Lincoln's oppressive yoke.

During the afternoon a Provost Marshal was appointed
for the town, and he occupied the same office which had
been the headquarters of the U. S. Provost Marshal. Guards
were posted along our streets, and pickets on the roads leading from Frederick. Our stores were soon thronged with
crowds. The shoe stores were most patronized, as many of
their men were shoeless and stockingless. The only money
most of them had was Confederate scrip, or shinplasters
issued by banks, corporations, individuals, etc.—all of equal
value. To use the expression of an old citizen "the notes de-
preciated the paper on which they were printed." The
crowded condition of the stores enabled some of the chivalry
to *take* what they wanted, (confiscate is the technical expression,) without going through the formality of even
handing over Confederate rags in exchange. But guards
were placed at the stores wherever requested, and only a
few men allowed to enter at a time. Even this arrangement
proved inadequate, and the stores were soon necessarily
closed. The most intense hatred seems to have been encouraged and fostered in the men's hearts towards Union people,
or *Yankees* as they style them; and this word *Yankee* is employed with any and every manner of emphasis possible to
indicate contempt and bitterness. The men have been made
to believe that "to kill a Yankee" is to do a duty imperatively

imposed on them. The following incident will illustrate this:
A gentleman was called aside, while talking with some
ladies, by an officer who wished information as to shoes. He
said he was in want of shoes for his men, that he had United
States money if the dealers were so foolish as to prefer it,
or he would procure them gold; but if they wouldn't sell he
was satisfied to wait until they reached Baltimore, where
he had no doubt but that shoes in quantity could be procured. No reply was made. Changing the subject, he inquired how the men were behaving. The answer was *very
well;* there was no complaint, although some few had been
seen intoxicated on the street. "Who gave them the liquor,"
said the officer. "Townsmen who sympathize with you and
desire to show their love for you." "The only way to do that,"
said the officer, "is to kill a Yankee: kill a Yankee, sir, if you
want to please a Southerner." This was uttered with all imag-
inable expression of vindictiveness and venom.

Our houses were besieged by hungry soldiers and officers.
They ate everything offered them with a greediness that
fully sustained the truth of their statement, that their entire
subsistence lately had been *green corn, uncooked, and eaten
directly from the stalk.* Union families freely gave such food
as they had. "If thine enemy hunger, feed him," seemed the
principle acted on by our good people. But few of our secession citizens aided them. They seemed ashamed of their
Southern brethren. The Union people stood out for their
principles, and took care to remind them that they were getting their food from those they had come to destroy. A gentleman relates the following: "In the evening, after having
had one of their officers to tea—one whom I had known in
former days—two officers came to the door and begged that
something might be given them for which they wished to
pay. On giving them the last biscuits in the house, one of

them offered *pay*. The reply was, 'No, sir, whenever you meet a Federal soldier wanting food, recollect that a Union man in Frederick gave you the last morsel of food in his house when *you* were famishing.' The officer's face flushed up, and he replied, 'You are right, sir, I am very, very much obliged to you.' The coals of fire had been heaped on his head."

Outrages were committed on the National flag whenever one fell into the hands of the soldiers. These simply strengthened the Union feeling, and made the men and women of Frederick more attached than ever to the National cause for which their fathers had fought and died. Stauncher, stouter, stronger did Unionism in Frederick grow with each passing hour. We were conquered, not enslaved,—humiliated greatly with the thought that rebel feet were pressing on our soil, but not disposed to bow the knee to Baal.

An attack on the *Examiner* Printing Office being anticipated, a small guard was placed at the door. About nine o'clock, P.M., a rush was made on the guard by some of the Southern soldiers, the door was driven in and the contents of the office thrown into the street. W. G. Ross, Esq., a prominent lawyer of Frederick, called on the Provost Marshal, who soon arrived with a strong force, suppressed the riot, and, having obliged the rioters to return every thing belonging to the office, put them in the guard-house. During the continuance of this disturbance, the oaths and imprecations were terrific. Every one in the neighborhood expected that a general attack would be made on the Union houses. Fortunately, a quiet night ensued.

Sunday, September 7.—The rebels obliged most of our shoe-stores to be kept open during the day so that their men could obtain shoes. The reign of terror continued, although no personal violence was done to any citizen. Pickets are posted miles out of town. The main body of rebel troops is said to be encamped about Urbana. General Robert E. Lee is in command, and there are three divisions or, it may be, four, commanded by Jackson, Longstreet, D. H. Hill, and some one else. Forage is obtained by taking it and offering Confederate notes in payment.

At the Evangelical Reformed Church, the pastor, Rev. Dr. Daniel Zacharias, offered up prayers for the President of the United States, notwithstanding the presence of a number of Confederate officers. In the evening General Jackson was seen *asleep* in the same church.

The Commissioner for the Enrolment of the State Militia was seized to-day and made to hand over the enrolment-books. No further requirement was made of him, except that he should report himself daily at the office of the Provost-Marshal.

During the afternoon one of those incredible incidents occurred, which have been occasionally reported in our papers, but have always been disbelieved by those who have faith in the humanity of rebels. Several young ladies were standing in front of the house of one of our prominent citizens, when a rebel officer rode up and, halting his horse, said, "Ladies, allow me to make you a present. This is a ring made from *the bone of a dead Yankee.*" A gentleman, near the curb, seized the article before the officer had finished speaking and handed it to the ladies, who quickly answered, "Keep your present for those who appreciate *such* presents." The only reply of the chivalry was, "Ah! I supposed you were *Southern* ladies!" This incident is instructive.

Monday, September 8.—General Robert E. Lee issues a proclamation, announcing that the Southern Army enters Maryland to restore her to freedom, that she has been down-trodden for a long time, and that her Sister States of the

Southern Confederacy have sworn to set her free from the influence of Northern bayonets,—free to decide for herself whether she will go with the South or no,—and promising protection to all of whatever opinion. Colonel B. T. Johnson, emulating the example of his superior officer, calls upon the citizens to unite in forming companies and regiments to join the Confederate States Army. Captain E. V. White announces that he is empowered to raise a regiment of cavalry. Mr. Heard (former Editor of the *Frederick Herald*—a secession paper) issues a card calling for recruits to a company he is forming. Thus we are flooded with proclamations. . . .

The supplies in our stores having nearly given out, some of the Union merchants resolutely closed their stores to the soldiers, and sending for their customers asked them to take what they required at the usual rates. The wealthiest grocer in the town raised the price of coffee to seventy-five cents, and brown sugar to forty cents per pound, to be paid in gold or in our own currency. This outrageous attempt to take advantage of the troublous condition of the community has excited considerable indignation in a quiet way all around.

We are still importuned by the rebels for food. It is furnished whenever asked, but the Union citizens take care to inform them that they are fed by their opponents. How the rebels manage to get along no one can tell. They are badly clad. Many of them without shoes. Uncleanliness and vermin are universal. The odor of clothes worn for months, saturated with perspiration and dirt, is intense and all-pervading. They look stout and sturdy, able to endure fatigue, and anxious to fight in the cause they have espoused, willingly or unwillingly. The movement they have now made is believed by them to be a desperate one, and they must "see it through." They all believe in *themselves* as well as in their generals, and are terribly in earnest. They assert that they have never been whipped, but have driven the Yankees before them whenever they could find them. They have killed so many Yankees and have gloried therein to such an extent that one would almost think them veritable Thugs. Bragging is a favorite game with them, and they do it well. Their army is plainly intended for an advance into Pennsylvania, and they speak freely of their intention to treat Pennsylvania very differently from Maryland. I fear there will be great destruction of property as they move forwards. Many a citizen will lose his all of this world's goods in this raid, for devastation is meant to be the order or disorder of their march when they cross the border.

Tuesday, September 9.—Recruiting goes on slowly in the town. We are told that three companies are to be raised here. It may be so, but one "can't see it." If ever suicide were contemplated by any one it must be by those civilians who propose to attach themselves to Jackson's corps. His men have become inured to hardships by long training, and are now on one of their most difficult undertakings. New recruits, taken from the comforts of social life, altogether unused to hardships, will readily sink under the fatigue of camp and field life.

A clergyman tells me that he saw an aged crone come out of her house as certain rebels passed by trailing the American flag in the dust. She shook her long, skinny hands at the traitors and screamed at the top of her voice, "My curses be upon you and your officers for degrading your country's flag." Her expression and gesture as described to me were worthy of Meg Merilies.

The Confederates have been seizing horses from our farmers, tendering Confederate scrip in payments. They allege military necessity in justification of this seizure. Military necessity is a convenient cloak for any outrage whatever.

As an offset to these operations of the rebels may be mentioned the sale of a horse to a Confederate by a *smart* Frederick boy. He had purchased a condemned Government horse for thirteen dollars, with the hope that by careful feeding he might so improve the animal's condition that he would command a profit. Food and care, however, proved vain. The horse refused to eat for two days, and was manifestly "sinking." A rebel asked the youth if he had a horse to sell. "Well, yes; I have a very fine horse, worth two hundred dollars to any man who can prize a good horse."

The rebel proposed entering the stable to examine the horse. "No sir! he is a spirited animal and might do a stranger some injury. Let me bring him out for you." By some special stimulus the horse was induced to come out, and the proprietor stated that on reflection he would let his valuable animal go for eighty dollars in *money*—not Confederate scrip. The rebel remarked that the horse held one foot off the ground, resting the weight of his body on three legs. He inquired as to the cause of this phenomenon. "Why, Lord bless you! don't you understand that? He is a *natural racker; all* natural rackers stand on three legs that way—always." The enunciation of this physiological law settled the question. The money was paid over. The rebel mounted his newly-purchased steed and rode away, somewhat to the seller's astonishment. He remarked to the by-standers, "I pledge you my word, gentlemen, he will last about three quarters of an hour at least. Any other gentleman wanting a natural racker can be accommodated at the shortest notice, if he will only call on me."

Wednesday, September 10.—At four o'clock this morning the rebel army began to move from our town, Jackson's force taking the advance. The movement continued until eight o'clock P.M., occupying sixteen hours. The most liberal calculations could not give them more than 64,000 men. Over 3,000 negroes must be included in this number. These were clad in all kinds of uniforms, not only in cast-off or captured United States uniforms, but in coats with Southern buttons, State buttons, etc. These were shabby, but not shabbier or seedier than those worn by white men in the rebel ranks. Most of the negroes had arms, rifles, muskets, sabres, bowie-knives, dirks, etc. They were supplied, in many instances, with knapsacks, haversacks, canteens, etc., and were manifestly an integral portion of the Southern Confederacy Army. They were seen riding on horses and mules, driving wagons, riding on caissons, in ambulances, with the staff of Generals, and promiscuously mixed up with all the rebel horde. The fact was patent, and rather interesting when considered in connection with the horror rebels express at the suggestion of black soldiers being employed for the National defence.

Some of the rebel regiments have been reduced to 150 men; none number over 500. The men are stout and ragged, anxious to "kill a Yankee," and firm in their belief that *Confederate notes* are as good as gold. Their marching is generally very loose. They marched by the flank through the streets of Frederick. Some few houses had rebel flags, to which one enthusiastic admirer of secession had added a white cross on a red ground. Some handkerchiefs waved, but all felt there was no genuine enthusiasm. The movement to Frederick had proved a failure. Their friends were anxious to get rid of them and of the penetrating ammoniacal smell they brought with them. Union citizens had become stronger in their faith. Rebel officers were unanimous in declaring that "Frederick was a d——d Union hole." The ill-suppressed expressions of delight on the countenances of the citizens could not be interpreted into indication of sympathy with Secession. They manifested only profound delight at the prospect of its speedy departure.

This force had about 150 guns with the letters U. S. This rebel army seemed to have been largely supplied with transportation by some United States Quartermaster. Uncle Sam's initials were on many of its wagons, ambulances, and horses. One neat spring-wagon was lettered *"General Casey's Headquarters."* Each regiment was supplied with but one or two wagons. The men were mostly without knapsacks; some few carried blankets, and a *tooth-brush* was occasionally seen pendant from the button-hole of a private soldier, whose reminiscences of home-life were not entirely eradicated.

Their apologies for regimental bands were vile and excruciating. The only real music in their column to-day was from a bugle blown by a negro. Drummers and fifers of the same color abounded in their ranks. The men seemed generally disinclined to insult our citizens. But there were conspicuous exceptions. A drunken, bloated blackguard on horseback, for instance, with the badge of a Major-General on his collar, understood to be one *Howell Cobb,* formerly Secretary of the United States Treasury, on passing the house of a prominent sympathizer with the rebellion, removed his hat in answer to the waving of handkerchiefs, and reining his horse up, called on "his boys" to give three cheers. "Three more, my boys" and "three more!" Then, looking at the silent crowd of Union men on the pavement, he shook his fist at them, saying, "Oh you d——d long-faced Yankees! Ladies, take down their names and I will attend to them personally when I return." In view of the fact that this was addressed to a crowd of unarmed citizens, in the presence of a large body of armed soldiery flushed with success, the prudence—to say nothing of the bravery—of these remarks, may be judged of by any man of common sense.

Some of the citizens have been encouraging the Confederate soldiers by assuring them of the sympathy of Maryland, and urging them to push on northward with their offensive operations. One gray-haired man, who had escaped from the military authorities twelve months since by taking the oath of allegiance, was overheard saying to a rebel Colonel, "Make them feel the war when you reach Philadelphia."

Thursday, September 11.—General Hill's division, numbering about eight thousand men, marched through the streets, on their route westward, this morning. This division showed more of military discipline than either of its predecessors; the men marched in better order, had better music and were fairly clothed and equipped. This division moves more rapidly than either of the others. This was held to indicate the approach of the National army.

Three of the buildings on the hospital grounds were taken possession of by the Confederates for the accommodation of their sick. These soon threw themselves on the beds, with their filthy clothing and boots. In a few hours a marked contrast could be noticed between the neatness of the wards containing the Union soldiers and those occupied by the rebels. The secessionists collected the ladies of their order of thinking, and, for the first time since the breaking out of the rebellion, the fair forms of female secessionists were seen within the walls of the Frederick hospital, ministering to the wants of suffering humanity. I must confess that they seemed to work with a will. The Union ladies, whenever they found their supplies more than sufficient for our own sick, freely gave them to sick rebels. Charity knows neither party nor religious creed as a limit to its blessed work.

Rumors of a strong Federal force moving towards Frederick prevailed during the evening. Old and young prayed with fervor that these rumors might be based on truth. The

Union citizens were not harboring vindictive feelings towards their secession neighbors, but they longed for the old flag. Bright eyes were growing dim and rosy cheeks pale from anxious watching, day and night, for the coming of our National army. Hope deferred had made the heart sick, but still it was clung to with wondrous tenacity. Dreams of "blue-coats" were the attendants of such sleep as met their eyelids —dreams of a happy restoration to the rights of the old Union. Would they never be realized!

Friday, September 12.—Stewart's [Stuart's] cavalry passed through town to-day, on their way towards Hagerstown. It is said to be composed of Ashby's Cavalry and the Hampton Legion. The men are more neat and cleanly than the infantry that preceded them, and their horses, of good stock, are well-groomed and fed. Bragging is the order of the day with the cavalry. They boast that they never met more than one Federal regiment that dared to cross sabres with them, and that was the First Michigan Cavalry. Stewart has been visiting some of our sympathizers with the rebellion. Meeting Hospital Steward Fitzgerald, he asked him to state to the commanding officer of the Federal troops that might come to Frederick, that he would inflict severe punishment on Union men, wherever he could find them, if any punishment was meted out to the Southern sympathizers in Frederick by such officer. The steward answered that he, as a warrant-officer of the United States Army, could carry no such message, and suggested that General Stewart should remain to deliver it himself. The General did *not* act on this suggestion.

The joyous news at last reached town that the Federal troops were near at hand. Union people looked up their National flags. Two companies of Stewart's men, still in town, were stationed at the intersection of Market and Patrick streets. Cannonading was heard in the distance. Hearts were beating with joyous expectation. Our Union citizens were assembling at different points, discussing the probable results of the skirmish then taking place. It was evident that nothing more than a skirmish would take place, for the enemy, notwithstanding his boast that our troops would not meet him in a fair fight, was retreating westward towards the mountains. The advance cavalry of our National Army charged into our streets, driving the rebels before them. They were met by a counter-charge of Stewart's men, made in grand style. Saddles were emptied on both sides. Stewart's men fell back, carrying with them seven of our men as prisoners, and leaving many of their own men wounded on the ground. The accidental discharge of a cannon caused the death of seven horses and the wounding of a few men. Martial music is heard in the distance; a regiment of Ohio volunteers makes its appearance and is hailed with most enthusiastic demonstrations of joy. Handkerchiefs are waved, flags are thrown from Union houses, and a new life appears infused into the people. Burnside enters amid vociferous plaudits from every one, and the citizens, with enthusiastic eagerness, devote themselves to feeding the troops and welcoming them to their houses, as their *true* deliverers from a bondage more debasing than that of the African slave.

A little incident connected with the charge referred to is worthy of note. The wife of one of our prominent Union men threw out the National flag from her window just as Stewart's men dashed by the house. It seemed peculiarly fitting that a member of the *Washington* family should first unfurl her country's banner as our victorious troops entered a place which had been infested with the armed supporters of treason.

Saturday, September 13.—The town was effervescent with

joy at the arrival of the Union troops,—no business was done. Every one felt jubilant, and congratulated himself and neighbor that the United States troops were once more in possession. General McClellan with his staff rode through, about nine o'clock, and was received on all sides with the most unlimited expressions of delight. Old and young shouted with joy; matrons held their babes towards him as their deliverer from the rule of a foreign army, and fair young ladies rushed to meet him on the streets, some even throwing their arms around his horse's neck. It was a scene difficult to realize in this matter-of-fact age, but deep-seated feelings of gratitude found expression in every possible form. The reality of the joy constituted the poetry of the reception. Years of obloquy and reproach might have been considered compensated for by such a reception. The army, as well as its loved general, was welcomed with enthusiasm. To Frederick belongs the high honor of having given the *first* decided, enthusiastic, whole-souled reception which the Army had met since its officers and men had left their families and homes to fight the battles of their country. It is true that companies and regiments on their way to join the Army had been received with shouts of approval in the towns through which they passed, but the Army, as such, had always trudged along its accustomed line of duty without one word from the people in the way of satisfaction or commendation. But in Frederick it was received as a band of brothers, fighting for the welfare of the whole country and, whether successful or unsuccessful, entitled to the warmest demonstrations of good feeling possible.

I Think He Should Be Engaged

O NCE AGAIN General McClellan did not move with the
alacrity and forcefulness President Lincoln felt he
should. Success in turning back the Confederates at
Antietam was not enough. It had enabled Mr. Lincoln
to announce the Emancipation Proclamation on the
heels of Federal victory, but the country clamored for
greater victories still. First there was a letter of admonition, then another change of command. Here are the
President's letter and addresses to the troops by Generals
George B. McClellan and Ambrose E. Burnside respectively.

EXECUTIVE MANSION, WASHINGTON, *Oct. 13, 1862.*
My dear Sir—You remember my speaking to you of what
I called your overcautiousness. Are you not overcautious
when you assume that you can not do what the enemy is
constantly doing? Should you not claim to be at least his
equal in prowess, and act upon the claim?
As I understand, you telegraphed Gen. Halleck that you

175

can not subsist your army at Winchester, unless the railroad
from Harper's Ferry to that point be put in working order.
But the enemy does now subsist his army at Winchester at
a distance nearly twice as great from railroad transportation
as you would have to do without the railroad last named.
He now wagons from Culpepper [Culpeper] Court House,
which is just about twice as far as you would have to do
from Harper's Ferry. He is certainly not more than half as
well provided with wagons as you are. I certainly should
be pleased for you to have the advantage of the railroad
from Harper's Ferry to Winchester; but it wastes all the remainder of the autumn to give it to you, and in fact ignores
the question of *time*, which can not and must not be ignored.

Again, one of the standard maxims of war, as you know,
is, "to operate upon the enemy's communications as much
as possible, without exposing your own." You seem to act
as if this applies *against* you, but can not apply in your *favor*.
Change positions with the enemy, and think you not he
would break your communication with Richmond within
the next twenty-four hours? You dread his going into Pennsylvania. But if he does so in full force, he gives up his communications to you absolutely, and you have nothing to do but
to follow and ruin him; if he does so with less than full
force, fall upon and beat what is left behind all the easier.

Exclusive of the water line, you are now nearer Richmond
than the enemy is by the route that you *can* and he *must*
take. Why can you not reach there before him, unless you
admit that he is more than your equal on a march? His route
is the arc of a circle, while yours is the chord. The roads
are as good on yours as on his.

You know I desired, but did not order, you to cross the
Potomac below instead of above the Shenandoah and Blue
Ridge. My idea was, that this would at once menace the

enemy's communications, which I would seize if he would permit. If he should move northward, I would follow him closely, holding his communications. If he should prevent our seizing his communications, and move toward Richmond, I would press closely to him, fight him if a favorable opportunity should present, and at least try to beat him to Richmond on the inside track. I say, "try"; if we never try, we shall never succeed. If he make a stand at Winchester, moving neither north nor south, I would fight him there, on the idea that if we can not beat him when he bears the wastage of coming to us, we never can when we bear the wastage of going to him. This proposition is a simple truth, and is too important to be lost sight of for a moment. In coming to us, he tenders us an advantage which we should not waive. We should not so operate as to merely drive him away. As we must beat him somewhere, or fail finally, we can do it, if at all, easier near to us than far away. If we can not beat the enemy where he now is, we never can, he again being within the intrenchments of Richmond. Recurring to the idea of going to Richmond on the inside track, the facility of supplying from the side, away from the enemy, is remarkable, as it were by the different spokes of a wheel, extending from the hub toward the rim, and this whether you move directly by the chord or on the inside arc, hugging the Blue Ridge more closely. The chord-line, as you see, carries you by Aldie, Haymarket, and Fredericksburg, and you see how turnpikes, railroads, and finally the Potomac, by Aquia Creek, meet you at all points from Washington. The same, only the lines lengthened a little, you press closer to the Blue Ridge part of the way. The gaps through the Blue Ridge I understand to be about the following distances from Harper's Ferry, to wit: Vestal's, five miles; Gregory's, thirteen; Snicker's, eighteen; Ashby's, twenty-eight; Manassas, thirty-eight; Chester, forty-five; and Thornton's, fifty-three. I should think it preferable to take the route nearest the enemy, disabling him to make an important move without your knowledge, and compelling him to keep his forces together for dread of you. The gaps would enable you to attack if you should wish. For a great part of the way you would be practically between the enemy and both Washington and Richmond, enabling us to spare you the greatest number of troops from here. When, at length, running to Richmond ahead of him enables him to move this way; if he does so, turn and attack him in the rear. But I think he should be engaged long before such point is reached. It is all easy if our troops march as well as the enemy, and it is unmanly to say they can not do it. This letter is in no sense an order. Yours, truly,   A. LINCOLN.

Major-Gen. McCLELLAN.

HEAD-QUARTERS, ARMY OF THE POTOMAC,

CAMP NEAR RECTORTOWN, VA., *Nov.* 7, 1862.
OFFICERS AND SOLDIERS OF THE
ARMY OF THE POTOMAC:

An order of the President devolves upon Major General BURNSIDE the command of this Army.

In parting from you I cannot express the love and gratitude I bear to you. As an army you have grown up under my care. In you I have never found doubt or coldness. The battles you have fought under my command will proudly live in our nation's history. The glory you have achieved, our mutual perils and fatigues, the graves of our comrades fallen in battle and by disease, the broken forms of those whom wounds and sickness have disabled,—the strongest associations which can exist among men,—unite us still by an indissoluble tie. We shall ever be comrades in supporting the Constitution of our country and the nationality of its people.

GEO. B. McCLELLAN,

Major General U. S. A.

HEAD-QUARTERS, ARMY OF THE POTOMAC,

WARRENTON, VA., *November* 9, 1862.

General Orders, ⎫
   No. 1.   ⎬

In accordance with General Orders, No. 182, issued by the President of the United States, I hereby assume command of the Army of the Potomac.

Patriotism and the exercise of my every energy in the direction of this army, aided by the full and hearty co-operation of its officers and men, will, I hope, under the blessing of God, ensure its success.

Having been a sharer of the privations and a witness of the bravery of the old Army of the Potomac in the Maryland campaign, and fully identified with them in their feeling of respect and esteem for General McCLELLAN, entertained through a long and most friendly association with him, I feel that it is not as a stranger that I assume their command.

To the 9th Corps, so long and intimately associated with me, I need say nothing; our histories are identical.

With diffidence for myself, but with a proud confidence in the unswerving loyalty and determination of the gallant army now entrusted to my care, I accept its control with the steadfast assurance that the just cause must prevail.

A. E. BURNSIDE,

Major General Commanding.

Battle of Fredericksburg

HUMORISTS OF THE DAY, both Yankee and Confederate, parodied Dan Emmett's "Jordan Is a Hard Road to Travel" as "Richmond Is a Hard Road to Travel." General Burnside learned that lesson quickly. On December 13 he threw his troops against the Confederates across the natural breastwork of a sunken road at the base of Marye's Hill. The Federal loss of over ten thousand nearly doubled Confederate losses, and the attack was not renewed. Burnside retired, soon to be relieved by General Joe Hooker.

The letter following relates the story of the Battle of Fredericksburg as it concerned one New York regiment. It was written by an unidentified private and quoted in William P. Maxson's *Camp Fires of the Twenty-Third.*

⁓

CAMP "PAUL" (NOWHERE), *December 21st, 1862.*
Dear M——: On the night before the bombardment we bivouacked in a dense thicket of pines near the old campground known as "Rufus King." We were not long in gather-

ing the cedar boughs, always abundant, and spreading this bed of down over the floor of our little tents. As darkness came on, the huge camp-fires gave a charming outline and feature to this little fairy city of white roofs. Their bright light in long diverging rays beat back the dark, and showed in relief the graceful tapering trunks of the pines, gray and dusky. Their boughs arch and form deep, dark aisles of nature's grand old cathedral filled with dim and spectral shadows. Around the fires groups of hardy soldiers were telling stories.

Aside from the deep, wild interest of battle, the shock of armies, when death is wantonly swooping into the gulf of ruin so many precious lives, there is a peculiar something in camp-life that may challenge comparison in interest to any other. . . . This noble band of men have come together to defend liberty with their lives, and a cord of sympathy ties the knot around the cheerful camp-fires. The rude jostling of these great hearts together, as they talk of their mutual dangers, hair-breadth escapes, noble deeds of comrades and the sacred cause, unites them one in purpose, one in action. To be sure, there is a lack of polish of manner and speech about all this (camp dialect is blunt), but it has the plain outspoken manhood, a smack of truth and honor, that atones for much of refinement. We are compelled to look upon it in this light. Such thoughts are born of such a life, no matter how uncultivated the soldier or rude the thought.

The pontoon bridges had been pushed nearly to the opposite shore under cover of darkness, and ere the faintest ray of dawn had streaked the east, the quick, sharp rattle of musketry broke the stillness. The engineers laying the last plank were charged upon, and a bloody struggle followed. Ought not that blood to doom that proud and ancient city? It certainly cries to Heaven for vengeance. A shaft of flame leaps out from the opposite shore, the earth trembles, the air breaks with a deafening roar, and a huge shell, with a shriek like a demon, speeds out upon its errand of destruction. Another followed, and another, till the storm of iron crushed through the walls and set the town on fire. All day long the incessant thunder of the bombardment shook the hills and rent the air. Our brigade moved down near to the river during the day and awaited orders. When the sun sunk darkly into the smoke of burning, the rebels on the opposite hills looked down upon the wreck of their proud city.

On the following morning the sun strove in vain to dispel the mountains of fog that covered the two armies like a shroud, and the mist held the river till after noon. Under this kindly cover we crossed the river. As we reached the level of the plain, a rebel battery opened upon the division while *en masse*, and with surprising accuracy dropped the shell in our midst, but to very little effect. One man in the regiment was slightly wounded. The advance was thrown briskly forward and a footing for the army obtained. Night now closed in upon the opposing armies, and they await the morrow.

The morrow came, and with it the conflict. It was evident that the enemy must be driven from the plain to his stronghold on the heights, and these heights must be stormed. The forces were disposed in order of battle before the mists of morning had been dispersed by the rising sun. Our brigade, now commanded by Colonel Rogers, of the Twenty-first New York Volunteers, held the extreme left, and had the supreme satisfaction of driving the vanguard of the enemy from that part of the field. Batteries B and L made it decidedly too warm for them.

The fight opened fiercely. The great wave of battle surged across the plain and up the rugged heights, swallowing up in its bloody tide regiments, brigades, divisions of brave and heroic men who went down before that death-storm to bite the dust. Great men, men of promise, the sturdy oaks of society as well as the brushwood, were swept by its fury into a soldier's grave. Fortune seemed to favor us, the rebel lines gave way, and our forces drove them up the slope of the heights. But an avalanche awaited them. A flame of fire leaped from the now uncovered supports, and our columns melted before it like dew before the morning sun. The tide of battle changed and rolled back upon the plain.

It was at this point that Lieutenant-Colonel N. M. Crane, as inspector-general of General Reynolds' staff, seeing the Pennsylvania reserves in full retreat, rode up to General Reynolds and said:

"See yonder, General! the 'reserves' have broken."

"My God! Colonel," said the General, "can't you go and stop them!"

Colonel Crane dashed into the midst of the flying mob, and by threats, persuasion, and praise of their former deeds of valor, succeeded in rallying a small battalion of them in the face of the storm of lead that followed them.

It was here also that General Reynolds, failing to get immediate support from the right, sent in haste to General Doubleday for a brigade. Colonel Rogers was ordered up, and with cheerfulness and spirit the entire brigade moved forward double quick, and in perfect line, though the field was continually raked by cannon-shot. Files of men were swept away without a waver in the lines. The expected support arrived before we reached the ground, and the brigade returned to its post. The day had been almost lost, but the veteran regiments were thrown heavily against the triumphant host, and quivering under the awful blow it was beaten back with equal loss. Night at last approached. The sunset was gorgeously beautiful. Nature seemed to laugh at the great calamity. Fighting did not cease till late, and when at last we thought of sleep, we were kept awake by grape and canister.

Sunday morning dawned bright and beautiful, and as calm as though the earth had not groaned and the heavens been rent by a scene of carnage seldom equaled in history. Slight cannonading and skirmishing occupied the day, and as we lay down at night with the sky for our cover, Aurora flung out the grand banner of the heavens, "red, white, and blue," bespangled by the everlasting stars. Its beautiful folds floated up and covered one half of the arch. As we gazed upon it with delight, we felt that the national emblem had not been dishonored by act of ours, and we worshiped in silence the starry banner.

Another day of anxious expectation, of skirmishing, and it became evident that our position was untenable. With masterly skill of plan and execution General Burnside placed his army on the east side of the Rappahannock during the night of the 15th, much to the chagrin and disappointment of the foe.

In this engagement the Twenty-third lost two killed and sixteen wounded. There were instances of especial coolness and courage, but to point out these in a regiment where a want of courage is the exception and not the rule, would be unjust to others. Each man, in whatever capacity, did his duty nobly. You will of course guess by this letter that your friend came off whole, not damaged. Yours,

P—— S——.

A Day in a Hospital

EVERY BATTLE produced more work for already over-
loaded hospitals. Here is Louisa May Alcott's
sprightly account of a day of hospital service shortly
after the Battle of Fredericksburg.

"THEY'VE come! they've come! hurry up, ladies—you're
wanted."

"Who have come? the rebels?"

This sudden summons in the gray dawn was somewhat
startling to a three days' nurse like myself, and, as the thundering knock came at our door, I sprang up in my bed, prepared

"To gird my woman's form,
And on the ramparts die,"

if necessary, but my room-mate took it more coolly, and, as
she began a rapid toilet, answered my bewildered question.—

"Bless you, no, child; it's the wounded from Fredericksburg; forty ambulances are at the door, and we shall have
our hands full in fifteen minutes."

"What shall we have to do?"

185

"Wash, dress, feed, warm and nurse them for the next three months, I dare say. Eighty beds are ready, and we were getting impatient for the men to come. Now you will begin to see hospital life in earnest, for you won't probably find time to sit down all day, and may think yourself fortunate if you get to bed by midnight. Come to me in the ball-room when you are ready; the worst cases are always carried there, and I shall need your help."

So saying, the energetic little woman twirled her hair into a button at the back of her head, in a "cleared for action" sort of style, and vanished, wrestling her way into a feminine kind of pea-jacket as she went.

I am free to confess that I had a realizing sense of the fact that my hospital bed was not a bed of roses just then, or the prospect before me one of unmingled rapture. My three days' experiences had begun with a death, and, owing to the defalcation of another nurse, a somewhat abrupt plunge into the superintendence of a ward containing forty beds, where I spent my shining hours washing faces, serving rations, giving medicine, and sitting in a very hard chair, with pneumonia on one side, diphtheria on the other, five typhoids on the opposite, and a dozen dilapidated patriots, hopping, lying, and lounging about, all staring more or less at the new "nuss," who suffered untold agonies, but concealed them under as matronly an aspect as a spinster could assume, and blundered through her trying labors with a Spartan firmness, which I hope they appreciated, but am afraid they didn't. Having a taste for "ghastliness," I had rather longed for the wounded to arrive, for rheumatism wasn't heroic, neither was liver complaint, or measles; even fever had lost its charms since "bathing burning brows" had been used up in romances, real and ideal; but when I peeped into the dusky street lined with what I at first had innocently called market carts, now unloading their sad freight at our door, I recalled sundry reminiscences I had heard from nurses of longer standing, my ardor experienced a sudden chill, and I indulged in a most unpatriotic wish that I was safe at home again, with a quiet day before me, and no necessity for being hustled up, as if I were a hen and had only to hop off my roost, give my plumage a peck, and be ready for action. A second bang at the door sent this recreant desire to the right about, as the little woolly head popped in, and Joey, (a six years' old contraband,) announced—

"Miss Blank is jes' wild fer ye, and says fly round right away. They's comin' in, I tell yer, heaps on 'em—one was took out dead, and I see him,—ky! warn't he a goner!"

With which cheerful intelligence the imp scuttled away, singing like a blackbird, and I followed, feeling that Richard was *not* himself again, and wouldn't be for a long time to come.

The first thing I met was a regiment of the vilest odors that ever assaulted the human nose, and took it by storm. Cologne, with its seven and seventy evil savors, was a posy-bed to it; and the worst of this affliction was, every one had assured me that it was a chronic weakness of all hospitals, and I must bear it. I did, armed with lavender water, with which I so besprinkled myself and premises, that, like my friend, Sairy, I was soon known among my patients as "the nurse with the bottle." Having been run over by three excited surgeons, bumped against by migratory coal-hods, water-pails, and small boys; nearly scalded by an avalanche of newly-filled tea-pots, and hopelessly entangled in a knot of colored sisters coming to wash, I progressed by slow stages up stairs and down, till the main hall was reached, and I paused to take breath and a survey. There they were! "our brave boys," as the papers justly call them, for cowards could hardly have been so riddled with shot and shell, so torn and shattered, nor have borne suffering for which we have no name, with an uncomplaining fortitude, which made one glad to cherish each as a brother. In they came, some on stretchers, some in men's arms, some feebly staggering along propped on rude crutches, and one lay stark and still with covered face, as a comrade gave his name to be recorded before they carried him away to the dead house. All was hurry and confusion; the hall was full of these wrecks of humanity, for the most exhausted could not reach a bed till duly ticketed and registered; the walls were lined with rows of such as could sit, the floor covered with the more disabled, the steps and doorways filled with helpers and lookers on; the sound of many feet and voices made that usually quiet hour as noisy as noon; and, in the midst of it all, the matron's motherly face brought more comfort to many a poor soul, than the cordial draughts she administered, or the cheery words that welcomed all, making of the hospital a home.

The sight of several stretchers, each with its legless, armless, or desperately wounded occupant, entering my ward, admonished me that I was there to work, not to wonder or weep; so I corked up my feelings, and returned to the path of duty, which was rather "a hard road to travel" just then. The house had been a hotel before hospitals were needed, and many of the doors still bore their old names; some not so inappropriate as might be imagined, for my ward was in truth a *ball-room,* if gun-shot wounds could christen it. Forty beds were prepared, many already tenanted by tired men who fell down anywhere, and drowsed till the smell of food roused them. Round the great stove was gathered the dreariest group I ever saw—ragged, gaunt and pale, mud to the knees, with bloody bandages untouched since put on days before; many bundled up in blankets, coats being lost or useless; and all wearing that disheartened look which proclaimed defeat, more plainly than any telegram of the Burnside blunder. I pitied them so much, I dared not speak to them, though, remembering all they had been through since the rout at Fredericksburg, I yearned to serve the dreariest of them all. Presently, Miss Blank tore me from my refuge behind piles of one-sleeved shirts, odd socks, bandages and lint; put basin, sponge, towels, and a block of brown soap into my hands, with these appalling directions:

"Come, my dear, begin to wash as fast as you can. Tell them to take off socks, coats, and shirts, scrub them well, put on clean shirts, and the attendants will finish them off, and lay them in bed."

If she had requested me to shave them all, or dance a hornpipe on the stove funnel, I should have been less staggered; but to scrub some dozen lords of creation at a moment's notice, was really—really——. However, there was no time for nonsense, and, having resolved when I came to do everything I was bid, I drowned my scruples in my washbowl, clutched my soap manfully, and, assuming a businesslike air, made a dab at the first dirty specimen I saw, bent on performing my task *vi et armis* if necessary. I chanced to light on a withered old Irishman, wounded in the head, which caused that portion of his frame to be tastefully laid out like a garden, the bandages being the walks, his hair the shrubbery. He was so overpowered by the honor of having a lady wash him, as he expressed it, that he did nothing but roll up his eyes, and bless me, in an irresistible style which was too much for my sense of the ludicrous; so we laughed together, and when I knelt down to take off his shoes, he "flopped" also and wouldn't hear of my touching "them dirty craters. May your bed above be aisy, darlin', for the day's work ye are doon!—Whoosh! there ye are, and bedad, it's hard tellin' which is the dirtiest, the fut or the shoe." It was; and if he hadn't been to the fore, I should have gone on pulling, under the impression that the "fut" was a boot, for trousers, socks, shoes and legs were a mass of mud. This comical tableau produced a general grin, at which propitious beginning I took heart and scrubbed away like any tidy parent on a Saturday night. Some of them took the performance like sleepy children, leaning their tired heads against me as I worked, others looked grimly scandalized, and several of the roughest colored like bashful girls. One wore a soiled little bag about his neck, and, as I moved it, to bathe his wounded breast, I said,

"Your talisman didn't save you, did it?"

"Well, I reckon it did, marm, for that shot would a gone a couple a inches deeper but for my old mammy's camphor bag," answered the cheerful philosopher.

Another, with a gun-shot wound through the cheek, asked for a looking-glass, and when I brought one, regarded his swollen face with a dolorous expression, as he muttered—

"I vow to gosh, that's too bad! I warn't a bad looking chap before, and now I'm done for; won't there be a thunderin' scar? and what on earth will Josephine Skinner say?"

He looked up at me with his one eye so appealingly, that I controlled my risibles, and assured him that if Josephine was a girl of sense, she would admire the honorable scar, as a lasting proof that he had faced the enemy, for all women thought a wound the best decoration a brave soldier could wear. I hope Miss Skinner verified the good opinion I so rashly expressed of her, but I shall never know.

The next scrubbee was a nice looking lad, with a curly brown mane, and a budding trace of gingerbread over the lip, which he called his beard, and defended stoutly, when the barber jocosely suggested its immolation. He lay on a bed, with one leg gone, and the right arm so shattered that it must evidently follow; yet the little Sergeant was as merry as if his affliction were not worth lamenting over, and when a drop or two of salt water mingled with my suds at the sight of this strong young body, so marred and maimed, the boy looked up, with a brave smile, though there was a little quiver of the lips, as he said,

"Now don't you fret yourself about me, miss; I'm first rate here, for it's nuts to lie still on this bed, after knocking about in those confounded ambulances, that shake what there is left of a fellow to jelly. I never was in one of these places before, and think this cleaning up a jolly thing for us, though I'm afraid it isn't for you ladies."

"Is this your first battle, Sergeant?"

"No, miss; I've been in six scrimmages, and never got a scratch till this last one; but it's done the business pretty thoroughly for me, I should say. Lord! what a scramble there'll be for arms and legs, when we old boys come out of our graves, on the Judgment Day: wonder if we shall get our own again? If we do, my leg will have to tramp from Fredericksburg, my arm from here, I suppose, and meet my body, wherever it may be."

The fancy seemed to tickle him mightily, for he laughed blithely, and so did I; which, no doubt, caused the new nurse to be regarded as a light-minded sinner by the Chaplain, who roamed vaguely about, informing the men that they were all worms, corrupt of heart, with perishable bodies, and souls only to be saved by a diligent perusal of certain tracts, and other equally cheering bits of spiritual consolation, when spirituous ditto would have been preferred.

"I say, Mrs.!" called a voice behind me; and, turning, I saw a rough Michigander, with an arm blown off at the shoulder, and two or three bullets still in him—as he afterwards mentioned, as carelessly as if gentlemen were in the habit of carrying such trifles about with them. I went to him, and, while administering a dose of soap and water, he whispered, irefully:

"That red-headed devil, over yonder, is a reb, damn him! You'll agree to that, I'll bet? He's got shet of a foot, or he'd a cut like the rest of the lot. Don't you wash him, nor feed him, but just let him holler till he's tired. It's a blasted shame to fetch them fellers in here, along side of us; and so I'll tell the chap that bosses this concern; cuss me if I don't."

I regret to say that I did not deliver a moral sermon upon the duty of forgiving our enemies, and the sin of profanity, then and there; but, being a red-hot Abolitionist, stared fixedly at the tall rebel, who was a copperhead, in every sense of the word, and privately resolved to put soap in his eyes, rub his nose the wrong way, and excoriate his cuticle generally, if I had the washing of him.

My amiable intentions, however, were frustrated; for, when I approached with as Christian an expression as my principles would allow, and asked the question— "Shall I try to make you more comfortable, sir?" all I got for my pains was a gruff—

"No; I'll do it myself."

"Here's your Southern chivalry, with a witness," thought I, dumping the basin down before him, thereby quenching a strong desire to give him a summary baptism, in return for his ungraciousness; for my angry passions rose, at this rebuff, in a way that would have scandalized good Dr. Watts. He was a disappointment in all respects, (the rebel, not the blessed Doctor,) for he was neither fiendish, romantic, pathetic, or anything interesting; but a long, fat man, with a head like a burning-bush, and a perfectly expressionless face: so I could hate him without the slightest drawback, and ig-

nored his existence from that day forth. One redeeming trait
he certainly did possess, as the floor speedily testified; for
his ablutions were so vigorously performed, that his bed soon
stood like an isolated island, in a sea of soap suds, and he
resembled a dripping merman, suffering from the loss of a
fin. If cleanliness is a near neighbor to godliness, then was
the big rebel the godliest man in my ward that day.

Having done up our human wash, and laid it out to dry,
the second syllable of our version of the word war-fare was
enacted with much success. Great trays of bread, meat, soup
and coffee appeared; and both nurses and attendants turned
waiters, serving bountiful rations to all who could eat. I can
call my pinafore to testify to my good will in the work, for in
ten minutes it was reduced to a perambulating bill of fare,
presenting samples of all the refreshments going or gone. It
was a lively scene; the long room lined with rows of beds,
each filled by an occupant, whom water, shears, and clean
raiment, had transformed from a dismal ragamuffin into a
recumbent hero, with a cropped head. To and fro rushed
matrons, maids, and convalescent "boys," skirmishing with
knives and forks; retreating with empty plates; marching
and counter-marching, with unvaried success, while the
clash of busy spoons made most inspiring music for the
charge of our Light Brigade:

> "Beds to the front of them,
>   Beds to right of them,
>   Beds to the left of them,
>   Nobody blundered.
>   Beamed at by hungry souls,
>   Screamed at with brimming bowls,
>   Steamed at by army rolls,
>   Buttered and sundered.

With coffee not cannon plied,
Each must be satisfied,
Whether they lived or died;
All the men wondered."

Very welcome seemed the generous meal, after a week of
suffering, exposure, and short commons; soon the brown
faces began to smile, as food, warmth, and rest, did their
pleasant work; and the grateful "Thankee's" were followed
by more graphic accounts of the battle and retreat, than any
paid reporter could have given us. Curious contrasts of the
tragic and comic met one everywhere; and some touching
as well as ludicrous episodes, might have been recorded that
day. A six foot New Hampshire man, with a leg broken and
perforated by a piece of shell, so large that, had I not seen
the wound, I should have regarded the story as a Munchau-
senism, beckoned me to come and help him, as he could not
sit up, and both his bed and beard were getting plentifully
anointed with soup. As I fed my big nestling with corresponding mouthfuls, I asked him how he felt during the
battle.

"Well, 'twas my fust, you see, so I aint ashamed to say I
was a trifle flustered in the beginnin', there was such an all-
fired racket; for ef there's anything I do spleen agin, it's
noise. But when my mate, Eph Sylvester, caved, with a bullet through his head, I got mad, and pitched in, licketty cut.
Our part of the fight didn't last long; so a lot of us larked
round Fredericksburg, and give some of them houses a
pretty consid'able of a rummage, till we was ordered out of
the mess. Some of our fellows cut like time; but I warn't
a-goin to run for nobody; and, fust thing I knew, a shell
bust, right in front of us, and I keeled over, feelin' as if I
was blowed higher'n a kite. I sung out, and the boys come

back for me, double-quick; but the way they chucked me over them fences was a caution, I tell you. Next day I was most as black as the darkey yonder, lickin' plates on the sly. This is bully coffee, ain't it? Give us another pull at it, and I'll be obleeged to you."

I did; and, as the last gulp subsided, he said, with a rub of his old handkerchief over eyes as well as mouth:

"Look a here; I've got a pair of earbobs and a handkercher pin I'm a goin' to give you, if you'll have them; for you're the very moral o' Lizy Sylvester, poor Eph's wife: that's why I signalled you to come over here. They aint much, I guess, but they'll do to memorize the rebs by."

Burrowing under his pillow, he produced a little bundle of what he called "truck," and gallantly presented me with a pair of earrings, each representing a cluster of corpulent grapes, and the pin a basket of astonishing fruit, the whole large and coppery enough for a small warming-pan. Feeling delicate about depriving him of such valuable relics, I accepted the earrings alone, and was obliged to depart, somewhat abruptly, when my friend stuck the warming-pan in the bosom of his night-gown, viewing it with much complacency, and, perhaps, some tender memory, in that rough heart of his, for the comrade he had lost.

Observing that the man next him had left his meal untouched, I offered the same service I had performed for his neighbor, but he shook his head.

"Thank you, ma'am; I don't think I'll ever eat again, for I'm shot in the stomach. But I'd like a drink of water, if you aint too busy."

I rushed away, but the water-pails were gone to be refilled, and it was some time before they reappeared. I did not forget my patient patient, meanwhile, and, with the first mugful, hurried back to him. He seemed asleep; but something

in the tired white face caused me to listen at his lips for a
breath. None came. I touched his forehead; it was cold: and
then I knew that, while he waited, a better nurse than I had
given him a cooler draught, and healed him with a touch. I
laid the sheet over the quiet sleeper, whom no noise could
now disturb; and, half an hour later, the bed was empty. It
seemed a poor requital for all he had sacrificed and suffered,
—that hospital bed, lonely even in a crowd; for there was
no familiar face for him to look his last upon; no friendly
voice to say, Good bye: no hand to lead him gently down
into the Valley of the Shadow; and he vanished, like a drop
in that red sea upon whose shores so many women stand
lamenting. For a moment I felt bitterly indignant at this
seeming carelessness of the value of life, the sanctity of
death; then consoled myself with the thought that, when the
great muster roll was called, these nameless men might be
promoted above many whose tall monuments record the
barren honors they have won.

All having eaten, drank, and rested, the surgeons began
their rounds; and I took my first lesson in the art of dressing
wounds. It wasn't a festive scene, by any means; for Dr. P.,
whose Aid I constituted myself, fell to work with a vigor
which soon convinced me that I was a weaker vessel, though
nothing would have induced me to confess it then. He had
served in the Crimea, and seemed to regard a dilapidated
body very much as I should have regarded a damaged gar-
ment; and, turning up his cuffs, whipped out a very unpleasant looking housewife, cutting, sawing, patching and piecing,
with the enthusiasm of an accomplished surgical seamstress;
explaining the process, in scientific terms, to the patient,
meantime; which, of course, was immensely cheering and
comfortable. There was an uncanny sort of fascination in
watching him, as he peered and probed into the mechanism

of those wonderful bodies, whose mysteries he understood so well. The more intricate the wound, the better he liked it. A poor private, with both legs off, and shot through the lungs, possessed more attractions for him than a dozen generals, slightly scratched in some "masterly retreat;" and had any one appeared in small pieces, requesting to be put together again, he would have considered it a special dispensation.

The amputations were reserved till the morrow, and the merciful magic of ether was not thought necessary that day, so the poor souls had to bear their pains as best they might. It is all very well to talk of the patience of woman; and far be it from me to pluck that feather from her cap, for, heaven knows, she isn't allowed to wear many; but the patient endurance of these men, under trials of the flesh, was truly wonderful; their fortitude seemed contagious, and scarcely a cry escaped them, though I often longed to groan for them, when pride kept their white lips shut, while great drops stood upon their foreheads, and the bed shook with the irrepressible tremor of their tortured bodies. One or two Irishmen anathematized the doctors with the frankness of their nation, and ordered the Virgin to stand by them, as if she had been the wedded Biddy to whom they could administer the poker, if she didn't; but, as a general thing, the work went on in silence, broken only by some quiet request for roller, instruments, or plaster, a sigh from the patient, or a sympathizing murmur from the nurse.

It was long past noon before these repairs were even partially made; and, having got the bodies of my boys into something like order, the next task was to minister to their minds, by writing letters to the anxious souls at home; answering questions, reading papers, taking possession of money and valuables; for the eighth commandment was reduced to a very fragmentary condition, both by the blacks and whites, who ornamented our hospital with their presence. Pocket books, purses, miniatures, and watches, were sealed up, labelled, and handed over to the matron, till such times as the owners thereof were ready to depart homeward or campward again. The letters dictated to me, and revised by me, that afternoon, would have made an excellent chapter for some future history of the war; for, like that which Thackeray's "Ensign Spooney" wrote his mother just before Waterloo, they were "full of affection, pluck, and bad spelling;" nearly all giving lively accounts of the battle, and ending with a somewhat sudden plunge from patriotism to provender, desiring "Marm," "Mary Ann," or "Aunt Peters," to send along some pies, pickles, sweet stuff, and apples, "to yourn in haste," Joe, Sam, or Ned, as the case might be.

My little Sergeant insisted on trying to scribble something with his left hand, and patiently accomplished some half dozen lines of hieroglyphics, which he gave me to fold and direct, with a boyish blush, that rendered a glimpse of "My Dearest Jane," unnecessary, to assure me that the heroic lad had been more successful in the service of Commander-in-Chief Cupid than that of Gen. Mars; and a charming little romance blossomed instanter in Nurse Periwinkle's romantic fancy, though no further confidences were made that day, for Sergeant fell asleep, and, judging from his tranquil face, visited his absent sweetheart in the pleasant land of dreams.

At five o'clock a great bell rang, and the attendants flew, not to arms, but to their trays, to bring up supper, when a second uproar announced that it was ready. The new comers woke at the sound; and I presently discovered that it took a very bad wound to incapacitate the defenders of the faith for the consumption of their rations; the amount that some of them sequestered was amazing; but when I suggested the probability of a famine hereafter, to the matron, that motherly lady cried out: "Bless their hearts, why shouldn't they eat? It's their only amusement; so fill every one, and, if there's not enough ready to-night, I'll lend my share to the Lord by giving it to the boys." And, whipping up her coffee-pot and plate of toast, she gladdened the eyes and stomachs of two or three dissatisfied heroes, by serving them with a liberal hand; and I haven't the slightest doubt that, having cast her bread upon the waters, it came back buttered, as another large-hearted old lady was wont to say.

Then came the doctor's evening visit; the administration of medicines; washing feverish faces; smoothing tumbled beds; wetting wounds; singing lullabies; and preparations for the night. By eleven, the last labor of love was done; the last "good night" spoken; and, if any needed a reward for that day's work, they surely received it, in the silent eloquence of those long lines of faces, showing pale and peaceful in the shaded rooms, as we quitted them, followed by grateful glances that lighted us to bed, where rest, the sweetest, made our pillows soft, while Night and Nature took our places, filling that great house of pain with the healing miracles of Sleep, and his diviner brother, Death.

1863

The Grand Terpsichorean Festival

Early in 1862 General Burnside had led an expedition which secured a Federal beachhead at Roanoke Island, North Carolina. From there Federal control was extended over much of the coastal plain of the state, and a major command centered around the old Carolina town of New Bern. There was sporadic activity between these occupation troops and the Confederates, marked chiefly by battles at Kinston, Whitehall, and Goldsboro in December, 1862. But the soldiers' chief enemy when their principal duty is that of occupation is boredom.

To help relieve the boredom in eastern North Carolina the soldiers of the Forty-fourth Massachusetts Regiment got up their own entertainments. In the winter of 1863 they amused themselves with improvised dances. To one they announced that none but those in costume would be admitted, but "the restriction was of little avail. Those who failed to pass the door keepers entered at the ventilators." Here is Zenas T. Haines's account of the "grand Terpsichorean Festival" of January 20, 1863.

NEWBERN, N. C., JAN. 23, 1863.

The first grand Terpsichorean festival of the New Year in our regiment transpired on the evening of the 20th instant, in the barracks of Co. D. The much lamented absence of the feminine element was in part atoned for by female apparel donned for the occasion by a number of young men with smooth faces and an eye to artistic effect. If Jenkins had been present his pencil would have waxed eloquent over the superb attire and tasteful colors of the magnificent blonde, Miss C. D. N. His page would have glowed with lover-like panegyrics of the tall and peerless, white-robed queen of the night, Miss G. F. B. Good taste, however, might have suggested that the former was a little too *en bon point,* as well as too demonstrative in her personal decorations, and that the latter was a trifle tall for the breadth of her raiment. But when Jenkins came to the Misses C. F. W., J. H. W., W. G. R. and especially to Miss C. W. S., of East Boston, he would assuredly have "slopped over" in his characteristic manner. Not, however, because these Hebes were less faulty in toilet than the others, for a critical eye might have suggested dresses higher in the neck, longer in skirt, and less protuberant in the rear; less suggestive, in short, of those gay and festive occasions which have rendered Joe Clash and North street immortal the world over. Some of the gallants of the young women were scarcely less stunning in their make up. The insignia of military office, from that of Major Generals to Lieutenants, extensively prevailed. Dancing, of course, was the order of the night; a fiddler was engaged, and

> "When music arose with its voluptuous swell,
> Soft eyes looked love to eyes which spake again,
> And all went merry as a marriage bell."

The following is the

ORDER OF DANCES.

1. SICILIAN CIRCLE, ... March to Tarboro'.
2. QUADRILLE, ... New England Guards.
3. POLKA QUADRILLE, ... Kinston Gallop.
4. QUADRILLE, ... Yankee Doodle.

INTERMISSION.
Waltz, Polka Redowa, Schottische.

5. QUADRILLE, ... Bloody 44th Quickstep.
6. LES LANCIERS, ... Connecticut 10th March.
7. QUADRILLE, ... Lee's March.
8. CONTRA (*Virginia Reel*), ... Rebels' Last Skedaddle.

In this connection I will introduce the managerial card, which was as follows:

GRAND BALL.

SIR:—The pleasure of your company, with ladies, is respectfully solicited at a Grand Ball, to be held in the Grand Parlor of the FIFTH AVENUE HOTEL, (No. 4 Newbern.) on TUESDAY EVENING, January 20th, 1863.

The Management beg leave to state that nothing will be left undone on their part to make it *the* party of the season.

MANAGERS.
C. H. DEMERITT,   W. HOWARD,   J. E. LEIGHTON.

COMMITTEE OF ARRANGEMENTS.

Benj. F. Burchsted,   W. G. Reed,
W. E. Savery,   F. M. Flanders,
J. B. Gardner,   Charles Adams,
C. D. Newell,   H. D. Stanwood,
F. A. Sayer,   H. Howard,
Joe Simonds,   G. W. Hight.

MUSIC.

Quintzelbottom's Grand Quadrille and Serenade Band,
(*One Violin.*)
TICKETS $00.03 EACH, TO BE HAD OF THE MANAGERS.
☞ *No Postage Stamps or Sutler's Checks taken*
in payment.
N. B. LADIES will be allowed to smoke.

Persons wishing carriages will please apply to LIEUT.
WHITE, of the Ambulance Corpse.

Persons wishing anything stronger than Water are referred
to the "Sanitary."

The managers were decorated with official rosettes, a solid
square of hard tack forming the centre of each. Even some
of the belles of the evening were resplendent with pendant
jewels cut from the same tenacious mineral.

That nothing might be wanting to revive the memories
of Clash's Hall, a bar was improvised inside the sliding door
where we get our rations, and here the cooks busily regaled
the dancers with water, and molasses and water, from a
bottle and a single tumbler, while announcing, by means
of placards over the window, "Splendid New Drinks," in the
shape of quinine and diarrhœa mixture No. 3, names forever
associated with and articulate in the surgeon's matutinal
bugle-call. The bar soon began to show its effects in the
shape of cocked hats, awry toilets, loud-mouthed contro-
versies, and, at last, fighting. The intervention of an active
but diminutive policeman was invoked. He was a little man,
but chewed tobacco with a serious determination, which
boded danger to evil doers. His services in keeping back the
crowd and quelling disturbances in the vicinity of the bar
were in constant requisition. Not unfrequently his badge was
seen tossing in the midst of a riotous crowd, and he was re-

ported to be once seen skedaddling before a slightly superior force. He was noticed as being very familiar with your reporter, whom he furnished with considerable doubtful information about his own operations.

At the proper hour refreshments were served. "A beautiful slave," in the person of Mr. West Williams . . . entered with two trays containing severally hard tack and salt horse. His advent was hailed with the same shouts and swaying of the crowd as usually attend the administration of our rations. The tack and horse vanished, and the dance proceeded with various divertisements to the end.

We had many visitors, including Colonel Lee and staff, all of whom evinced their intense satisfaction with what they heard and saw.

It is expected that other balls, including a masquerade, will succeed this affair.

A soldier's life is one of curious contrasts. Although *not* always gay, it has the jolliest kind of episodes. It affords the two emotional extremes. One day finds him in the midst of hilarity and social enjoyment, the next in the blood and carnage of battle, with friends falling all about him

"Thick as autumnal leaves in Valambrosa."

But an hour or two before the festivities recounted above, a slow-moving procession with muffled drum and reversed arms, moved from our lines with the remains of a much-loved comrade suddenly stricken down with the malarious fever. His name was Boynton, of Company G. A day or two previously, Corporal Upham of the same company died of the same disease.

Chancellorsville

THE THIRD SPRING of the war brought renewed activity on the front in Virginia. General Hooker moved the Federal troops once more south of the Rappahannock in an "on to Richmond" campaign. In the great battle of his career as commander of the Army of the Potomac, Federals and Confederates met at Chancellorsville, May 3 and 4.

General orders are notorious for representing the best possible point of view. As Hooker's order points out they are "the guardian of [the army's] own history and its own fame." This order of May 6 describes Chancellorsville as if it might have been an overwhelming victory. Actually it was a severe defeat, the Federals losing 17,287 men and the Confederates 12,423. But it was too costly a victory for the Confederates. They could ill afford to win with such heavy losses, and their loss included General "Stonewall" Jackson, shot down by his own troops on the evening of May 3.

HEAD-QUARTERS, ARMY OF THE POTOMAC,

CAMP NEAR FALMOUTH, VA., *May* 6, 1863.

General Orders,⎱
    No. 49. ⎰

The Major General Commanding tenders to this Army his congratulations on its achievements of the last seven days. If it has not accomplished all that was expected, the reasons are well known to the Army. It is sufficient to say they were of a character not to be foreseen or prevented by human sagacity or resource.

In withdrawing from the south bank of the Rappahannock before delivering a general battle to our adversaries, the Army has given renewed evidence of its confidence in itself and its fidelity to the principles it represents. In fighting at a disadvantage, we would have been recreant to our trust, to ourselves, our cause and our country.

Profoundly loyal, and conscious of its strength, the Army of the Potomac will give or decline battle, whenever its interest or honor may demand. It will also be the guardian of its own history and its own fame.

By our celerity and secrecy of movement, our advance and passage of the rivers were undisputed, and on our withdrawal not a rebel ventured to follow.

The events of the last week may swell with pride the heart of every officer and soldier of this Army. We have added new lustre to its former renown. We have made long marches, crossed rivers, surprised the enemy in his entrenchments, and whenever we have fought, have inflicted heavier blows than we have received.

We have taken from the enemy five thousand prisoners, captured and brought off seven pieces of artillery, fifteen colors, placed *"hors de combat"* eighteen thousand of his chosen troops, destroyed his depots filled with vast amounts of stores, deranged his communications, captured prisoners within the fortifications of his capital, and filled his country with fear and consternation.

We have no other regret than that caused by the loss of our brave companions, and in this we are consoled by the conviction that they have fallen in the holiest cause ever submitted to the arbitrament battle.

BY COMMAND OF MAJOR GENERAL HOOKER:

S. WILLIAMS,
Assistant Adjutant General.

OFFICIAL:

Captain, A D C.

The Second Louisiana

THE USE OF NEGRO TROOPS was questioned in the North and damned in the South. But more and more, as the war grew longer, were colored soldiers accepted into the Federal armies. Not only were Negroes in the North trained as soldiers (under white officers), freed slaves in the South were accepted for military service. Such a unit was the Second Louisiana, a part of the command of General Nathaniel P. Banks.

General Banks had first come to fame as the adversary of "Stonewall" Jackson in the Valley of Virginia. Soundly outgeneraled there, he became known as "Commissary" Banks, from the army stores that Jackson's men captured from his troops. He succeeded General Butler in command at New Orleans and conducted an unsuccessful campaign on the Red River in the spring of 1863. By the end of May he was back on the Mississippi, operating against Port Hudson in part of the campaign which centered on Vicksburg. It was in this campaign that his Second Louisiana Regiment proved its mettle.

Secretary William H. Seward praised the colored soldiers in a pamphlet published as *Secretary Seward's Re-*

view of Recent Military Events. "As the national armies advanced into the insurrectionary territories," he wrote, "slaves in considerable numbers accepted their freedom and came under the protection of the national flag. Amidst the great prejudices and many embarrassments which attend a measure so new and so divergent from the political habits of the country, freedmen with commendable alacrity enlisted in the Federal army. There was in some quarters a painful inquiry about their moral capacity for service. That uncertainty was brought to a sudden end in the siege of Port Hudson. The newly raised regiments exhibited all necessary valor and devotion in the military assaults which were made, with desperate courage, and not without fearful loss, by General Banks."

Here is General Banks's own appraisal of his troops in a letter to General H. W. Halleck. It is reprinted from a propaganda pamphlet, *Washington and Jackson on Negro Soldiers,* compiled by Henry Carey Baird and published in Philadelphia in 1863.

HEADQUARTERS ARMY OF THE GULF,
BEFORE PORT HUDSON, May 30, 1863.
Major-General H. W. Halleck, General-in-Chief,
    Washington.
GENERAL:—Leaving Sommesport on the Atchafalaya, where my command was at the date of my last dispatch, I landed at Bayou Sara at 2 o'clock on the morning of the 21st.

A portion of the infantry were transported in steamers,

and the balance of the infantry, artillery, cavalry, and wagon train moving down on the west bank of the river, and from this to Bayou Sara.

On the 23d a junction was effected with the advance of Major-General AUGUR and Brigadier-General SHERMAN, our line occupying the Bayou Sara road at a distance five miles from Port Hudson.

Major-General AUGUR had an encounter with a portion of the enemy on the Bayou Sara road in the direction of Baton Rouge, which resulted in the repulse of the enemy, with heavy loss.

On the 25th the enemy was compelled to abandon his first line of works.

General WEITZEL's brigade, which had covered our rear in the march from Alexandria, joined us on the 26th, and on the morning of the 27th a general assault was made upon the fortifications.

The artillery opened fire between 5 and 6 o'clock, which was continued with animation during the day. At 10 o'clock WEITZEL's brigade, with the division of General GROVER, reduced to about two brigades, and the division of General EMORY, temporarily reduced by detachments to about a brigade, under command of Colonel PAINE, with two regiments of colored troops, made an assault upon the right of the enemy's works, crossing Sandy Creek, and driving them through the woods to their fortifications.

The fight lasted on this line until 4 o'clock, and was very severely contested. On the left, the infantry did not come up until later in the day; but at 2 o'clock an assault was opened on the centre and left of centre by the divisions under Major-General AUGUR and Brigadier-General SHERMAN.

The enemy was driven into his works, and our troops moved up to the fortifications, holding the opposite sides of the parapet with the enemy on the right. Our troops still hold their position on the left. After dark the main body, being exposed to a flank fire, withdrew to a belt of woods, the skirmishers remaining close upon the fortifications.

In the assault of the 27th, the behavior of the officers and men was most gallant, and left nothing to be desired. Our limited acquaintance of the ground and the character of the works, which were almost hidden from our observation until the moment of approach, alone prevented the capture of the post.

On the extreme right of our line I posted the first and third regiments of negro troops. The First regiment of Louisiana Engineers, composed exclusively of colored men, excepting the officers, was also engaged in the operations of the day. The position occupied by these troops was one of importance, and called for the utmost steadiness and bravery in those to whom it was confided.

It gives me pleasure to report that they answered every expectation. Their conduct was heroic. No troops could be more determined or more daring. They made, during the day, three charges upon the batteries of the enemy, suffering very heavy losses, and holding their position at nightfall with the other troops on the right of our line. The highest commendation is bestowed upon them by all the officers in command on the right. Whatever doubt may have existed before as to the efficiency of organizations of this character, the history of this day proves conclusively to those who were in a condition to observe the conduct of these regiments, that the Government will find in this class of troops effective supporters and defenders.

The severe test to which they were subjected, and the determined manner in which they encountered the enemy, leave upon my mind no doubt of their ultimate success. They require only good officers, commands of limited numbers, and careful discipline, to make them excellent soldiers.

Our losses from the 23d to this date in killed, wounded, and missing, are nearly 1000, including, I deeply regret to say, some of the ablest officers of the corps. I am unable yet to report them in detail.

I have the honor to be, with much respect,
Your obedient servant,
N. P. BANKS, *Major-General Commanding.*

Our Present Duty to Our Country

B<small>Y</small> 1863 <small>THE WAR</small> seemed interminable. Each side had expected a quick victory. Instead, the Confederates had been unable to follow up military victories, and the Federals had been unable to conclude campaigns which struck deep into enemy territory with a definitive defeat of the Southerners.

In the South there was disaffection in East Tennessee, and the western counties of Virginia had early in the war formed themselves into a new state, but the tenor of Confederate opinion and nearly the whole of its man-power supported the war. The North was able (and this should have been an indication of the eventual result) to continue its interests in other affairs—international relations, the development of newly opened areas in the West, the building of a transcontinental railroad. Opposition to the war, therefore, was widely and freely expressed. Antiwar men in the Old Northwest were ready and willing to let the South stay out of the Union, to end the war and turn to business closer to home. The Copperheads and the Knights of the Golden Circle were dangerous to public opinion as enemies of the war. Their

216

spokesman in national circles was Clement L. Vallandigham of Ohio. Vallandigham was arrested and banished outside Union lines. President Lincoln explained: "Mr. Vallandigham avows his hostility to the War on the part of the Union; and his arrest was made because he was laboring, with some effect, to prevent the raising of troops; to encourage desertions from the army; and to leave the Rebellion without an adequate military force to suppress it. He was not arrested because he was damaging the political prospects of the Administration, or the personal interests of the Commanding General, but because he was damaging the Army, upon the existence and vigor of which the life of the Nation depends."

But for every Copperhead there were many more loyal soldiers. Here is the admonition to the soldiers with which Norman Gunnison, of the Second New Hampshire Volunteers, concluded his little book *Our Stars* in the spring of '63.

The war has now reached its culminating point; henceforth its progress must be to the Union cause a course of victory and ultimate triumph, or a course of irretrievable reverse. The indecisive battles of the war have been fought. Victory and defeat have alternated, but whether we have attained victory or suffered defeat, the result has fallen far short of our expectations; were we defeated, our rout was not utter; were we victorious, the fruits of our victory were neither great nor lasting. At this time the rebellion has assumed an entirely new moral phase. The monster is in its

death agonies, but it is only the more deadly. Never is the
leviathan of the deep more dangerous than when in its death
throes. The traitors have collected all their energies for the
final struggle. Treason in the South, treason abroad, and,
worst of all, treason in our own homes, uplifts its hand, red
with fratricidal blood, and braces anew its nerves for the
last despairing effort. As if it were not enough that slavery's
minions in the South should seek to strangle the liberty which
on the American Continent found a fitting birthplace, its
parasites in the North and Northwest—men who were
suckled at the very breast of Freedom—are forming in our
midst secret organizations with the view of aiding and abet-
ting their brother traitors in arms. If the local authorities
have lost the power to suppress and crush out such combinations, will not our soldiers in the field speak out, and emulating the noble soldiery of Illinois, rebuke the monster which,
in their distant homes, by their deserted hearthstones, is now
rearing its hydra-heads? The leaders of these organizations,
using and desecrating the sacred name of Peace, clamor for
a cessation of hostilities; in our Halls of Legislation oppose
and throw stumbling-blocks in the way of the Administration, and embarrass and render of no avail the movements
of our Generals. Soldiers of the Union! when leaving home
and its allurements, you went forth to do battle for our country; you thought not of the vipers you left behind to poison
your own nests. To you I appeal! Men who have passed
through the fire of battle, who have stood in the van at Williamsburg, Yorktown and Manassas, show yourselves equal
to the present emergency! Speak out in the might of your
fire-tried souls, and the reverberations of your voice shall
shake the pillars of the rebellion—whether at the North or
South—from centre to foundation! Remember this: the Administration is struggling to maintain our national existence,

and he who, at this hour, opposes the Administration—be he Democrat or Republican—Seymour or Greeley—stamps his soul forever with the indelible, damning stain of treason! Our duty as men and soldiers is to our present rulers. We do not ask for their political antecedents; we only ask, will they, with the aid of God, save our country? In the past, our army in Virginia has labored under many discouragements: the mismanagement of Generals, the scheming of politicians, the imbecility or covert treason of Quarter Masters, has rendered their bravery and self-sacrifice of no avail. In the Southwest we have experienced a succession of victories, and yet the men have not fought more bravely, the *morale* of the Southwestern army is not better, and no braver hearts lie buried at Donelson or Murfreesboro:, than now lie in their last repose before the walls of Richmond. Never has a more determined, self-sacrificing spirit been evinced than at Gaines' Mills and Fredericksburg. Where, then, does the fault lie? On *you*, base, scheming politician, *you*, General, more anxious for your own personal aggrandizement than for your country's good. *I charge* the sin of our past failures; the blood of our noblest and truest, from the soil of Virginia, cries out against you. Men of the North! men who, unwilling or unable to take the field, have remained in your peaceful homes, I ask of *you* to lay aside for a time your party bickerings, and come forward cordially to the support of our noble ones in the field. How can they fight with traitors in their rear? Knights of the Golden Circle, members of other secret societies in the North and North-west, are you so lost to all sense of honor, to the common dictates of humanity, as to dip your hands in the blood of your fathers, brothers and sons, as you are now doing, and hold them, reeking with kindred gore, to the world? If you cannot aid us, we ask, at least, that you will not impede us. But, rest assured, if you will persist in your course, there is coming a day of retribution when the Arnolds of to-day shall take rank with *the* Arnold of the Revolution. You cry peace, but do you fully understand the meaning of the peace you crave? A peace bought by a nation's dishonor is more dangerous than the sword. A peace with *you* means a division—the giving up of our inalienable rights as freemen—the acknowledgement that the South is too strong for us. True it is that our army of Virginia is in a discontented state at present; but give them but your cordial support, let them know that every heart at home battles for them, and with the prestige of victory resting upon their banners, they will yet go forward, "conquering and to conquer," until this unholy rebellion shall be as the things that were. Allowing, however, that we were to desire peace upon *your* terms, could we divide our Union and mete out an heritage of graves? Will the South give up its share in Bunker Hill? or the North its part in Yorktown's closing fight? Will *you*—breathing the air of Freedom, and calling yourselves men—allow the hallowed shades of Mount Vernon to pass into the hands of traitors, who are fighting against the very principles for which the Father of our Country fought and suffered? The geographical configuration of our country precludes the possibility of disintegration. The hopes of the future, the memories of the past, cry out against it; and did they not, those old bones that, for three-quarters of a century, have whitened at Princeton and Fort Moultrie, would arise from their very graves, and, with out-stretched arms, curse the degenerate sons, who could yield, while life remained, their fathers' dearest birthright. But I do not, *will* not believe that the day will ever come when we shall be willing to accept peace on such terms. With prophetic vision, I look forward to the time when the North and South shall again strike hands. I see our banner waving upon every Southern hill. I see, in the coming day, a vast Republic, stretching from the shores of the Atlantic to the coast of the Pacific—from the frozen regions of Hudson's Bay to the sunny clime of the tropical South, embracing Mexico in its limits, having its centre at New Orleans, and with its power controlling the world, whilst over all, the calm stars of our banner soar triumphant, lighting our Nation's pathway to glory. It needs but a united effort, and this rebellion will be crushed; only let our troops be not trammeled by the traitors of the North, and in the coming campaign they will mark for our country a page of glory.

At the head of our army in Virginia we have now a leader who knows no party where his country is concerned, one who is incapable of forming plans for personal aggrandizement, whose soul is in the cause, and whose valor upon the field, and discretion in council, have been tried and not found wanting. When he moves forward it will be to victory. Let us give to him our entire co-operation. The time to strike is near at hand, and our men in the field—the men who are to bear suffering, wounds, and perhaps death—should have to the utmost, the aid and the sympathy of every man who, in this land of freedom, can raise aloft his hand to Heaven, *and thank God that he is free!* The crisis of the war is now at hand. It is said that propositions of peace have already been made. If we yield to them, we, as a nation, are lost, with our national honor, national pride, everything but life sacrificed, what will remain to us: separated into petty republics, obliged to keep a standing army upon our borders, our form of government will degenerate into a military despotism, and we will present to the world that most pitiable of objects—a nation fallen—a people degenerated. Angels might weep over the picture, but even the tears of the angels would not blot from the records of freedom, the stain of that damning cowardice which would cause our downfall. If, on the other hand, the present contingency is met with the firmness of purpose which becomes a great people whose swords are unsheathed in the sacred cause of freedom, we are saved, and our heritage of liberty will descend to posterity as pure as we received it from the hands of the revolutionary fathers.

Though the ark of our national salvation may only come to us over an ocean of blood, still let us pray—God speed its coming.

Gettysburg

L EE's VICTORY at Chancellorsville cleared the way for an offensive move on the part of the Confederates. A march north into Pennsylvania could threaten Washington and the big cities of the East. It would remove the Confederate Army from a home ground swept clean of supplies to an enemy area of rich farms and towns well stocked with stores. And it would be a vast boost to Confederate morale.

The Confederate campaign reached its climax, and the climax of the war, at Gettysburg. Gettysburg is one of the most fully described battles of all history. It is not necessary to record its military development here. Instead, two general orders and excerpts from a straightforward account by a woman who lived in Gettysburg throughout the invasion are printed here as accurate reflections of the times.

HEAD-QUARTERS, ARMY OF THE POTOMAC,

June 28, 1863.

General Orders,⎱
   No. 67. ⎰

By direction of the President of the United States, I hereby assume command of the Army of the Potomac.

As a soldier, in obeying this order—an order totally unexpected and unsolicited—I have no promises or pledges to make.

The country looks to this Army to relieve it from the devastation and disgrace of a hostile invasion. Whatever fatigues and sacrifices we may be called upon to undergo, let us have in view, constantly, the magnitude of the interests involved, and let each man determine to do his duty, leaving to an all-controlling Providence the decision of the contest.

It is with just diffidence that I relieve in the command of this Army, an eminent and accomplished soldier, whose name must ever appear conspicuous in the history of its achievements; but I rely upon the hearty support of my companions in arms to assist me in the discharge of the duties of the important trust which has been confided to me.

GEORGE G. MEADE,
Major General Commanding.

OFFICIAL:

DIARY.

JUNE 15, 1863.—To-day we heard that the Rebels were crossing the river in heavy force, and advancing on to this State. No alarm was felt until Governor Curtin sent a telegram, directing the people to move their stores as quickly as possible. This made us begin to realize the fact that we were in some danger from the enemy, and some persons, thinking the Rebels were near, became very much frightened, though the report was a mistake.

JUNE 16.—Our town had a great fright last night between 12 and 1 o'clock. I had retired, and was soundly asleep, when my child cried for a drink of water. When I got up to get it, I heard so great a noise in the street that I went to the window, and the first thing I saw was a large fire, seemingly not far off, and the people were hallooing, "The Rebels are coming, and burning as they go." Many left town, but, having waited for the fire to go down a little, I returned to bed and slept till morning. Then I learned that the fire was in Emmettsburg [Emmitsburg], ten miles from here, just over the Maryland line, and that the buildings were fired by one of her townsmen. Twenty-seven houses were burned, and thirty-six families made homeless, all effort to stop the flames being useless, as, owing to everything being so dry, they spread with great rapidity. . . .

JUNE 19.—Another excitement to-day. The 87th Pennsylvania Volunteers is composed of men from this and adjacent counties, one company from our town being of the number. Word came that the captain, both lieutenants, and nearly all the officers and men had been killed or captured. Such a time as we had with those having friends in the regiment! At 10 o'clock it was rumored that some of the men were coming in on the Chambersburg pike, and not long after about one dozen of those who lived in town came in, and their report and presence relieved some and agonized others. Those whose friends were not of the party, were in a heart-rending plight, for these returned ones could not tell of the others; some would say, This one was killed or taken prisoner, and others, We saw him at such a place, and the Rebels may have taken him; and so they were kept in suspense.

JUNE 20.—The report of to-day is that the Rebels are at Chambersburg and are advancing on here, and refugees begin to come in by scores. Some say the Rebels number from twenty to thirty thousand, others that Lee's whole army is advancing this way. All day we have been much excited. . . .

JUNE 22. *Sunday.*—The report now is that a large force is in the mountains about eighteen miles away, and a call is made for a party of men to go out and cut down trees to obstruct the passages of the mountains. About fifty, among them my husband, started. I was very uneasy lest they might be captured, but, they had not gone half way, when the discovery was made that it was too late; that the Rebels were on this side of the mountain, and coming this way. Our men turned back, uninjured, though their advance, composed of a few men, was fired upon. About seventy of the Rebels came within eight miles, and then returned by another road to their main force. They stole all the horses and cattle they could find, and drove them back to their encampment. We did not know but that the whole body would be down upon us, until 11 o'clock, when a man came in and said that he had seen them, and that they had recrossed. I shall now retire, and sleep much better than I had expected an hour since.

JUNE 23.—This has been the most quiet day since the excitement began. I expect news to-morrow, for it has been too quiet to last long.

JUNE 24.—As I expected, the Rebels have, several times, been within two or three miles, but they have not yet reached here. Two cavalry companies are here on scouting duty, but they can be of little use, as they have never seen service.

Deserters come in every little while, who report the enemy near in large force. This morning early a despatch was received, saying that a regiment of infantry was coming from Harrisburg. We do not feel much safer, for they are only raw militia. The train bringing them came within ten miles, when it ran over a cow, which threw the cars off the track. No one was hurt, and they are now encamped near the place of the accident. The town is a little quieter than on yesterday. We are getting used to excitement, and many think the enemy, having been so long in the vicinity without visiting us, will not favor us with their presence. They have carried off many horses. Some, who had taken their stock away, returned, supposing the Rebels had left the neighborhood, and lost their teams.

June 25.—To-day passed much as yesterday did. Every one is asking, Where is our army, that they let the enemy scour the country and do as they please? It is reported that Lee's whole army is this side of the river, and marching on Harrisburg; also, that a large force is coming on here, to destroy the railroad between there and Baltimore. Our militia did not come to town, but remain encamped where they were yesterday.

June 26.—Our militia passed through town this morning about 10 o'clock, and encamped about three miles to the west. Before they had unpacked their baggage, a scout came in with a report, which proved true, that the enemy were quite near. Our men then had to retreat and get off the best way they could. About two hundred were captured. The town was quiet after our men retreated, until about 2 o'clock P.M., when a report spread that the Rebels were only two miles from town. No one believed this, for they had so often been reported as just coming, and had as often failed to appear, and little attention was now paid to the rumor.

When, however, the wagons of the militia came thundering through the streets, and the guard stated that they had been chased back, we began to realize that the report was a fact. In about half an hour the entrance of Jenkins' Rebel cavalry began, and they came with such horrid yells that it was enough to frighten us all to death. They came in on three roads, and we soon were surrounded by them. We all stood in the doors whilst the cavalry passed, but when the infantry came we closed them, for fear they would run into our houses and carry off everything we had, and went up stairs and looked out of the windows. They went along very orderly, only asking every now and then how many Yankee soldiers we had in town. I answered one that I did not know. He replied: "You are a funny woman; if I lived in town I would know that much." The last regiment stacked arms, on both sides of the street in front of our door, and remained for an hour. They were a miserable-looking set. They wore all kinds of hats and caps, even to heavy fur ones, and some were barefooted. The Rebel band were playing Southern tunes in the Diamond. I cannot tell how bad I felt to hear them, and to see the traitors' flag floating overhead. My humiliation was complete when I saw our men marching behind them surrounded by a guard. Last of all came an officer, and behind him a negro on as fine a horse as I ever saw. One, looking up, and noticing my admiration of the animal, said: "We captured this horse from General Milroy, and do you see the wagons up there? we captured them, too. How we did whip the Yankees, and we intend to do it again soon." I hope they may not.

JUNE 27.—I passed the most uncomfortable night of my life. My husband had gone in the cars to Hanover Junction, not thinking the Rebels were so near, or that there was much danger of their coming to town, and I was left entirely alone, surrounded by thousands of ugly, rude, hostile soldiers, from whom violence might be expected. Even if neighbors were at hand, it was not pleasant, and I feared my husband would be taken prisoner before he could return, or whilst trying to reach me. I was not disturbed, however, by anything except my fears, and this morning when I got up I found that the Rebels had departed, having, on the night of the 27th, burned the railroad bridge over Rock Creek, just outside of the town, and the cars that had brought up the militia, and had torn up the track and done other mischief. I became more uneasy about my husband, and I went to see some of the railroad hands to find out what I could relating to him. They told me that he had been captured and paroled, and that he had gone to Harrisburg; so I feel easier, and hope to rest to-night. Three of our scouts came in this morning just after the Rebels left, and report a large force of our soldiers near, making all feel much safer.

JUNE 28. *Sunday.*—About 10 o'clock a large body of our cavalry began to pass through town, and we were all busy feeding them as they passed along. It seemed to me that the long line would never get through. I hope they may catch the Rebels and give them a sound thrashing. Some say we may look for a battle here in a few days, and others say it will be fought near Harrisburg. There is no telling where it will be.

JUNE 29.—Quiet has prevailed all day. Our cavalry came up with the Rebels at Hanover, fourteen miles from here, and had quite a spirited fight, driving them through the town. Their infantry had reached York and had taken possession, as they did here, and demanded goods, stores, and money; threatening, if the demand was not complied with, to burn the town. Dunce-like, the people paid them $28,000, which they pocketed, and passed on to Wrightsville. A company of our militia, guarding the Columbia bridge over the Susquehanna, retreated on the approach of the Rebels, and fired the bridge, which was entirely consumed, preventing the enemy from setting foot on the east bank, and ending their offensive movements for a time.

JUNE 30.—My husband came home last night at 1 o'clock, having walked from Harrisburg, thirty-six miles, since 9 o'clock of yesterday morning. His return has put me in good spirits. I wonder that he escaped the Rebels, who are scouring the country between here and there. Fatigue is all the ill that befell him. This morning the Rebels came to the top of the hill overlooking the town on the Chambersburg pike, and looked over at our place. We had a good view of them from our house, and every moment we expected to hear the booming of cannon, and thought they might shell the town. As it turned out, they were only reconnoitring the town preparatory to an advance if no force opposed them. We were told that a heavy force of our soldiers was within five miles, and the Rebels, learning that a body of cavalry was quite near, retraced their steps, and encamped some distance from town. It begins to look as though we will have a battle soon, and we are in great fear. I see by the papers that General Hooker has been relieved, and the change of commanders I fear may give great advantage to the enemy, and our army may be repulsed.

JULY 1.—I got up early this morning to get my baking done before any fighting would begin. I had just put my bread in the pans when the cannons began to fire, and true enough the battle had begun in earnest, about two miles out on the Chambersburg pike. What to do or where to go, I did not know. People were running here and there, screaming that the town would be shelled. No one knew where to go or what to do. My husband advised remaining where we were,

but all said we ought not to remain in our exposed position,
and that it would be better to go to some part of the town
farther away from the scene of the conflict. As our neighbors
had all gone away, I would not remain, but my husband said
he would stay at home. About 10 o'clock the shells began
to "fly around quite thick," and I took my child and went to
the house of a friend up town. As we passed up the street
we met wounded men coming in from the field. When we
saw them, we, for the first time, began to realize our fearful
situation, and anxiously to ask, Will our army be whipped?
Some said there was no danger of that yet, and pointed to
Confederate prisoners who began to be sent through our
streets to the rear. Such a dirty, filthy set, no one ever saw.
They were dressed in all kinds of clothes, of all kinds and
no kind of cuts. Some were barefooted and a few wounded.
Though enemies, I pitied them. I, with others was sitting
at the doorstep bathing the wounds of some of our brave
soldiers, and became so much excited as the artillery galloped through the town, and the infantry hurried out to
reinforce those fighting, that for a time we forgot our fears
and our danger. All was bustle and confusion. No one can
imagine in what extreme fright we were when our men began to retreat. A citizen galloped up to the door in which
we were sitting and called out, "For God's sake go in the
house! The Rebels are in the other end of town, and all will
be killed!" We quickly ran in, and the cannonading coming
nearer and becoming heavier, we went to the cellar, and in
a few minutes the town was full of the filthy Rebels. They
did not get farther, for our soldiers having possession of the
hills just beyond, shelled them so that they were glad to
give over the pursuit, and the fighting for the day was ended.
We remained in the cellar until the firing ceased, and then
feared to come out, not knowing what the Rebels might do.

How changed the town looked when we came to the light. The street was strewn over with clothes, blankets, knapsacks, cartridge-boxes, dead horses, and the bodies of a few men, but not so many of these last as I expected to see. "Can we go out?" was asked of the Rebels. "Certainly," was the answer; "they would not hurt us." We started home, and found things all right. As I write all is quiet, but O! how I dread to-morrow.

JULY 2.—Of course we had no rest last night. Part of the time we watched the Rebels rob the house opposite. The family had left some time during the day, and the robbers must have gotten all they left in the house. They went from the garret to the cellar, and loading up the plunder in a large four-horse wagon, drove it off. I expected every minute that they would burst in our door, but they did not come near us. It was a beautiful moonlight night, and we could see all they did.

JULY 2.—The cannonading commenced about 10 o'clock, and we went to the cellar and remained a little while until it ceased. When the noise subsided, we came to the light again, and tried to get something to eat. My husband went to the garden and picked a mess of beans, though stray firing was going on all the time, and bullets from sharpshooters or others whizzed about his head in a way I would not have liked. He persevered until he picked all, for he declared the Rebels should not have one. I baked a pan of shortcake and boiled a piece of ham, the last we had in the house, and some neighbors coming in, joined us, and we had the first quiet meal since the contest began. I enjoyed it very much. It seemed so nice after so much confusion to have a little quiet once more. We had not felt like eating before, being worried by danger and excitement. The quiet did not last

long. About 4 o'clock P.M. the storm burst again with terrific
violence. It seemed as though heaven and earth were being
rolled together. For better security we went to the house
of a neighbor and occupied the cellar, by far the most comfortable part of the house. Whilst there a shell struck the
house, but mercifully did not burst, but remained embedded
in the wall, one half protruding. About 6 o'clock the cannonading lessened, and we, thinking the fighting for the day
was over, came out. Then the noise of the musketry was
loud and constant, and made us feel quite as bad as the
cannonading, though it seemed to me less terrible. Very soon
the artillery joined in the din, and soon became as awful as
ever, and we again retreated to our friend's underground
apartment, and remained until the battle ceased, about 10
o'clock at night. I have just finished washing a few pieces
for my child, for we expect to be compelled to leave town
to-morrow, as the Rebels say it will most likely be shelled.
I cannot sleep, and as I sit down to write, to while away
the time, my husband sleeps as soundly as though nothing
was wrong. I wish I could rest so easily, but it is out of the
question for me either to eat or sleep under such terrible
excitement and such painful suspense. We know not what
the morrow will bring forth, and cannot even tell the issue
of to-day. We can gain no information from the Rebels, and
are shut off from all communication with our soldiers. I think
little has been gained by either side so far. "Has our army
been sufficiently reinforced?" is our anxious question. A few
minutes since we had a talk with an officer of the staff of
General Early, and he admits that our army has the best position, but says we cannot hold it much longer. The Rebels
do so much bragging that we do not know how much to
believe. At all events, the manner in which this officer spoke

indicates that our troops have the advantage so far. Can they keep it? The fear they may not be able causes our anxiety and keeps us in suspense.

JULY 3.—To-day the battle opened with fierce cannonading before 4 o'clock A.M. Shortly after the battle began we were told to leave this end of the town, for likely it would be shelled. My husband declared he would not go while one brick remained upon another, and, as usual, we betook ourselves to the cellar, where we remained until 10 o'clock, when the firing ceased. We could not get breakfast on account of our fears and the great danger. During the cessation we managed to get a cold bite. Again, the battle began with unearthly fury. Nearly all the afternoon it seemed as if the heavens and earth were crashing together. The time that we sat in the cellar seemed long, listening to the terrific sound of the strife; more terrible never greeted human ears. We knew that with every explosion, and the scream of each shell, human beings were hurried, through excruciating pain, into another world, and that many more were torn, and mangled, and lying in torment worse than death, and no one able to extend relief. The thought made me very sad, and feel that, if it was God's will, I would rather be taken away than remain to see the misery that would follow. Some thought this awful afternoon would never come to a close. We knew that the Rebels were putting forth all their might, and it was a dreadful thought that they might succeed. Who is victorious, or with whom the advantage rests, no one here can tell. It would ease the horror if we knew our arms were successful. Some think the Rebels were defeated, as there has been no boasting as on yesterday, and they look uneasy and by no means exultant. I hope they are correct, but I fear we are too hopeful. We shall see to-morrow. It will be the 4th of July, and the Rebels have promised us a glorious day. If it only ends the battle and drives them off it will be glorious, and I will rejoice.

JULY 4.—This morning, about 6 o'clock, I heard a great noise in the street, and going to the door I saw a Rebel officer on horseback hallooing to some soldiers on foot, to "Hurry up, the Yankees have possession of the town and all would be captured." I looked up street and saw our men in the public square, and it was a joyful sight, for I knew we were now safe. Soon after, the Rebels sent in a flag of truce, but what was communicated we did not know, and, in consequence, the people were more scared than ever, the report spreading that it was to give notice to remove the women and children before shelling the town. As soon as the flag of truce had gone, our sharpshooters were pushed out to this side of town, and were all around us. We were between two fires, and were kept close prisoners all day, not daring either to go out, or even look out of the windows, on account of the bullets fired at every moving object. The people of other parts of the town could go where they pleased. It has been a dreadfully long day. We know, however, that the Rebels are retreating, and that our army has been victorious. I was anxious to help care for the wounded, but the day is ended and all is quiet, and for the first time in a week I shall go to bed, feeling safe.

JULY 5.—What a beautiful morning! It seems as though Nature was smiling on thousands suffering. One might think, if they saw only the sky, and earth, and trees, that every one must be happy; but just look around and behold the misery made in so short time by man. Early this morning I went out to the Seminary, just outside of town, and which, until the retreat, was in the hands of the enemy. What horrible sights present themselves on every side, the roads being strewn with dead horses and the bodies of some men, though the dead have nearly all been buried, and every step of the way giving evidence of the dreadful contest. Shall we—for I was not alone—enter the building or return home? Can we endure the spectacle of hundreds of men wounded in every conceivable manner, some in the head and limbs, here an arm off and there a leg, and just inside a poor fellow with both legs shot away? It is dreadful to behold, and, to add to the misery, no food has been served for several days. The little we have will not go far with so many. What can we do? is the only question, and the little we brought was distributed. It is heart-sickening to think of these noble fellows sacrificing everything for us, and saving us, and it out of our power to render any assistance of consequence. I turned away and cried. We returned to town to gather up more food if possible, and to get soft material to place under their wounded limbs, to help make them more comfortable. As we returned, our cavalry was moving out to follow the Rebels, and the street was all in an uproar. When I reached home, I found my husband's brother, who had passed through the battle unhurt, and had come to see us. I rejoiced at seeing him, for we feared he had fallen, and at once set to work to prepare a meal to appease his hunger. As I was baking cakes for him, a poor prisoner came to the door and asked me to give him some, for he had had nothing to eat for the past two or three days. Afterward more joined him, and made the same statement and request. I was kept baking cakes until nearly noon, and, in consequence, did not return to the Seminary. The poor fellows in my house were so hungry that they could hardly wait until the cakes were baked.

———

HEAD-QUARTERS, ARMY OF THE POTOMAC,

July 4th, 1863.

General Orders,⎫
   No. 68. ⎬

The Commanding General, in behalf of the country, thanks the Army of the Potomac for the glorious result of the recent operations.

An enemy superior in numbers and flushed with pride of a successful invasion, attempted to overcome and destroy this Army. Utterly baffled and defeated, he has now withdrawn from the contest. The privations and fatigue the Army has endured, and the heroic courage and gallantry it has displayed will be matters of history to be ever remembered.

Our task is not yet accomplished, and the Commanding General looks to the Army for greater efforts to drive from our soil every vestige of the presence of the invader.

It is right and proper that we should, on all suitable occasions, return our grateful thanks to the Almighty Disposer of events, that in the goodness of his Providence He has thought fit to give victory to the cause of the just.

BY COMMAND OF MAJOR GENERAL MEADE:

S. WILLIAMS,
Assistant Adjutant General.

OFFICIAL:

The Fall of Vicksburg

As HURTFUL to Confederate hopes as the failure of the invasion of Pennsylvania—and more immediately apparent in its results—was the Union capture of Vicksburg. Triumph there secured the length of the Mississippi River to Federal control and separated the eastern states of the Confederacy from its trans-Mississippi west.

Vicksburg had repulsed one siege in 1862. In 1863 it could not withstand the long assault of General U. S. Grant. After a valiant and desperate resistance Confederate General John C. Pemberton surrendered the city on July 4.

Here is a Federal soldier's report, a letter written by George W. Driggs on July 5 and published in his history of the Eighth Wisconsin Volunteers, *Opening of the Mississippi.*

YOUNG'S POINT, LA., SUNDAY, July 5th, 1863.

In strange contrast with the startling scenes of carnage, and the deafening roar of artillery around us, is the calm,

sweet serenity of this beautiful Sabbath morning. So quiet
that a feeling of loneliness creeps around the heart of one
accustomed to hearing the constant booming of cannon and
the sharp crack of musketry, and why have the iron throats
of these savage monsters been hushed? Is it because it is the
Sabbath day of rest that this holy calm pervades the hitherto
exciting scenes around us?

No, the tumultuous chaos of two great contending armies
have ceased their struggles, and the Federal arms have
gained another victory over the wily foe. Vicksburg, as you
have long ere this been informed, has surrendered, after
being besieged for forty-seven days. It was a gala day for
our troops, I assure you, and the 4th of July was never before celebrated in Vicksburg with such a right hearty good
feeling as on yesterday. The mortars on the point opposite
the city, with the accompanying chorus from the distant
gunboats had kept our ears in a perfect hum for many long
weeks, until they became like household words, familiar to
the ear, and no longer a terror, as at its introduction. But
the sound of battle strife has ceased for a while, and our
army now breathes the pure air of freedom once again. Victory is perched upon our blood-stained and tattered banners,
and the heart of the great North, which has evinced so much
restlessness and anxiety for the result of our success, may
now leap for joy, and smile at the happy and successful
achievements of the Federal arms. And though we regret that
so much of noble blood has been sacrificed in the attempt
to reduce this stronghold, yet such is the fate of war, and he
whose misfortune it has been to fall while in the discharge
of his duty, will receive the praise and honor due a brave
and noble patriot. Peace and honor to the departed dead—
we honored them for their deeds of bravery while living, we
will now sing a requiem o'er their graves, and entwine

around their head-stones a garland of honor, that their friends may receive the consolation that they are not forgotten by their comrades in arms.

There had been but little firing on either side during the day previous to the surrender, and many were the surmises as to what was the cause of the unusual cessation. It was whispered around in military circles, that Grant intended to celebrate the anniversary of our National Independence in the city—that our approaches were sufficient to warrant another desperate assault upon the enemy's works, and that we were to take the place by storm sometime during the following day. This, I am convinced, was Gen. Grant's intention, and was so believed among his subordinates. It was also surmised, from the appearance of a flag of truce which made its appearance early in the afternoon of Friday the 3d, that Grant and Pemberton were having an interview relative to the surrender of the city, and all waited in breathless suspense the cheering announcement that Vicksburg was ours. While in this suspense, the silence was broken by the appearance of Gen. Pemberton and staff, who approached our lines bearing in his hand a flag of truce, which was received by Gen. Grant with all the courtesy due from one high in rank. They met with a smile, each recognizing the other as old class-mates at West Point—shook hands and dismounted, and while Gen. Grant's staff entertained the gentlemanly officers of Pemberton's staff, the two distinguished generals proceeded arm in arm to the shade of an old oak tree near by—throwing themselves leisurely upon the grassy ground beneath the old shade tree, they reviewed the past in all kindness, and laughed as jocosely as if they had been daily associates and friends, instead of deadly foes. Grant reverted to the national troubles, and regretted that so gross an evil existed between this once prosperous people, and while

Grant sat coolly chewing away upon a stub of a cigar, (one of his peculiar traits,) Pemberton amused himself pulling up tufts of grass, much to the amusement of those that were permitted to gain a peep at long range upon the scene. Pemberton finally broke in upon the point at issue, by stating that he had often been desirous of meeting him since he started his *Correll*, and had called upon him at this time with a view of delivering over the city of Vicksburg—that he had run the thing till the *mule beef* had "gin out," and didn't propose to take charge of the place any longer under the peculiar auspices of the present occasion. Grant agreed to relieve him of his command, and after taking a "chaw of tobacco" in unison, they separated to meet again the following day in the city.

At 11 a. m., yesterday—the 4th of July—Gen. Logan's Division marched into the city, with banners flying and music playing, and at noon the stars and stripes were unfurled from the top of the Court House. It was not long before the city was swarming with Federal soldiery, and the city once more assumed the appearance of life and animation. Admiral Porter, with his fleet, came "rounding to," and soon the shore was closely hemmed in by the steamers which now lined the levee. Bands were playing, troops were marching to and fro through the streets, and the cannon opened the National salute at noon, which was kept up by the gunboats till after 2 o'clock, p. m. Gen. Logan was immediately placed in command of the post, and the prisoners were kept under close guard. The force taken was over 27,000 prisoners, and between 4,000 and 5,000 non-combatants. There were also taken 103 field pieces, 30 siege guns, 5,000 stands of arms, ammunition in vast quantities, locomotives, cars, and 87 stands of colors. Among the distinguished prisoners captured are Lieut. Gen. Pemberton, Major Generals Smith, Forney,

Bowen and Stephenson, fourteen or fifteen brigadier generals, and about one hundred and thirty colonels. Only 15,000 of the garrison are reported able for duty, about 5,000 being sick and wounded in hospitals. Nearly every building in the town is used as a hospital, and great destitution prevailed among them, previous to the surrender, which induced them, no doubt, to surrender the sooner. They were actually reduced to *mule meat!* I am convinced that they could not have maintained their position much longer.

The terms of capitulation allow the officers and men to be paroled here. The former are to retain their side arms, horses and personal property. They are being furnished with subsistence, and rations have been issued to all the prisoners for three days. They seem to take hold of "hard tack" with a hearty good will. The ladies—of whom there are not a few in the city—are quite amused at the rescue; but the officers, when interrogated as to the result, rather disdain the idea of being considered captives. They claim that the surrender was not unconditional, when Gen. Grant, out of courtesy, for their noble defense of the city, allowed them the honors of war to retain their side arms, horses, etc.

Of the surrender. No event since the commencement of the rebellion has caused the nation to rejoice so much as the fall of Vicksburg. It has been universally regarded as the most impregnable point we have been compelled to work against, and many were the doubts of its being reduced, yet, while Gen. Grant was allowed to command the helm, our faith was strong and we only looked for final success, if he was allowed time and means. He has accomplished a great and magnanimous work. Take his movements since our forces left Milliken's Bend on the first of May last; trace his footsteps across the country to the Mississippi river at Grand Gulf, his victories at that point, his march through the enemy's country, capture of Port Gibson, his fight at Champion Hills and later at Raymond, capture of the city of Jackson, Miss., of his victories on the Black river, by driving a superior rebel force from their chosen position, of the fights at Mechanicsburg, Yazoo City and Richmond, and finally, the crowning wreath of his laurels, the capture of Vicksburg on the glorious 4th of July. Gen. Grant has won the confidence of the entire army, as being a general of no ordinary attainments, and should receive the praise of the whole nation.

The Draft

UNTIL 1863 THE UNITED STATES ARMY had been supported by voluntary enlistments. In March the first draft had been enacted by Congress. Many people considered it downright un-American. As a whole it worked smoothly, but there were riots against it in Rutland, Vermont; Portsmouth, New Hampshire; Wooster, Ohio; Boston, and New York. The riots in New York assumed major proportions and resulted in a thousand casualties and heavy property damage.

Here are two items relating to the draft. The first records the words of Henry Clay Work's song "Grafted into the Army"; Americans could laugh even at things they did not like. Following the song is President Lincoln's letter to Governor Seymour answering a communication in which the Governor had suggested a suspension of the draft until its legality could be tested before the Supreme Court.

GRAFTED INTO THE ARMY

Our Jimmy has gone for to live in a tent,
They have grafted him into the army;
He finally pucker'd up courage and went,
When they grafted him into the army.
I told them the child was too young, alas!
At the captain's forequarters, they said he would
    pass—
They'd train him up well in the infantry class—
So they grafted him into the army.

Oh Jimmy farewell! Your brothers fell Way down in
    Alabarmy;
I thought they would spare a lone widder's heir,
But they grafted him into the army.

Drest up in his unicorn—dear little chap;
They have grafted him into the army;
It seems but a day since he sot in my lap,
But they grafted him into the army.
And these are the trousies he used to wear—
Them very same buttons—the patch and the tear—
But Uncle Sam gave him a bran new pair
When they grafted him into the army;

Now in my provisions I see him revealed—
They have grafted him into the army;
A picket beside the contented field,
They have grafted him into the army.
He looks kiner sickish—begins to cry—
A big volunteer standing right in his eye!
Oh what if the ducky should up and die
Now they've grafted him into the army?

———

EXECUTIVE MANSION, WASHINGTON, *Aug.* 7, 1863.
HIS EXCELLENCY, HORATIO SEYMOUR, GOVERNOR OF NEW
    YORK, ALBANY, N. Y.:

Your communication of the 3d instant has been received
and attentively considered. I can not consent to suspend the
draft in New York, as you request, because, among other
reasons, TIME is too important. By the figures you send,
which I presume are correct, the twelve districts represented
fall in two classes of eight and four respectively.

The disparity of the quotas for the draft in these two
classes is certainly very striking, being the difference between an average of 2,200 in one class, and 4,864 in the other.
Assuming that the districts are equal, one to another, in entire population, as required by the plan on which they were
made, this disparity is such as to require attention. Much
of it, however, I suppose will be accounted for by the fact
that so many more persons fit for soldiers are in the city
than are in the country, who have too recently arrived from
other parts of the United States and from Europe to be
either included in the census of 1860, or to have voted in
1862. Still, making due allowance for this, I am yet unwilling to stand upon it as an entirely sufficient explanation of
the great disparity. I shall direct the draft to proceed in all
the districts, drawing, however, at first from each of the four
districts—to wit, the Second, Fourth, Sixth, and Eighth—
only 2,200, being the average quota of the other class. After
this drawing, these four Districts, and also the Seventeenth
and Twenty-ninth, shall be carefully re-enrolled—and, if you
please, agents of yours may witness every step of the process.
Any deficiency which may appear by the new enrollment
will be supplied by a special draft for that object, allowing
due credit for volunteers who may be obtained from these
districts respectively during the interval; and at all points,

so far as consistent with practical convenience, due credits shall be given for volunteers, and your Excellency shall be notified of the time fixed for commencing a draft in each district.

I do not object to abide a decision of the United States Supreme Court, or of the Judges thereof, on the constitutionality of the draft law. In fact, I should be willing to facilitate the obtaining of it. But I can not consent to lose the time while it is being obtained. We are contending with an enemy who, as I understand, drives every able-bodied man he can reach into his ranks, very much as a butcher drives bullocks into a slaughter-pen. No time is wasted, no argument is used. This produces an army which will soon turn upon our now victorious soldiers already in the field, if they shall not be sustained by recruits as they should be. It produces an army with a rapidity not to be matched on our side, if we first waste time to re-experiment wth the volunteer system, already deemed by Congress, and palpably, in fact, so far exhausted as to be inadequate; and then more time to obtain a Court decision as to whether a law is constitutional which requires a part of those not now in the service to go to the aid of those who are already in it; and still more time to determine with absolute certainty that we get those who are to go in the precisely legal proportion to those who are not to go. My purpose is to be in my action just and constitutional, and yet practical, in performing the important duty with which I am charged, of maintaining the unity and the free principles of our common country. Your obedient servant,

A. LINCOLN.

The Gettysburg Address

THE SHORT SPEECH Abraham Lincoln made November 19, 1863, at the dedication of the National Cemetery at Gettysburg is one of the most familiar as well as one of the greatest documents of American history.

⁂

DEDICATORY ADDRESS

OF

PRESIDENT LINCOLN.

FOURSCORE and seven years ago our fathers brought forth upon this continent a new nation, conceived in Liberty, and dedicated to the proposition that all men are created equal.

Now we are engaged in a great civil war, testing whether that nation, or any nation so conceived and so dedicated, can long endure. We are met on a great battle-field of that war. We are met to dedicate a portion of it as the final resting-place of those who here gave their lives that that nation might live. It is altogether fitting and proper that we should do this.

But in a larger sense we cannot dedicate, we cannot consecrate, we cannot hallow this ground. The brave men, living and dead, who struggled here, have consecrated it far above our power to add or detract. The world will little note nor long remember what we say here, but it can never forget what they did here. It is for us, the living, rather to be dedicated here to the unfinished work that they have thus far so nobly carried on. It is rather for us to be here dedicated to the great task remaining before us,—that from these honored dead we take increased devotion to the cause for which they here gave the last full measure of devotion,—that we here highly resolve that the dead shall not have died in vain, that the nation shall, under God, have a new birth of freedom, and that the government of the people, by the people, and for the people, shall not perish from the earth.

The Battle of Chattanooga

THE WESTERN ARMIES, with General U. S. Grant gaining greater reputation each step of the way, made
their way slowly but surely into the heartland of the
Confederacy. They were defeated in September at
Chickamauga, but the Confederates were unable to follow up their victory, and the Federals retired to Chattanooga. Confederate General Bragg held them under
siege there till late November. The siege was broken in
the brilliant battles at Lookout Mountain and Missionary Ridge. Grant's pursuit of the Confederates was
halted at Ringgold Gap, Georgia, and the Union troops
retired once more to Chattanooga, but no longer under
siege. Here is Quartermaster General Montgomery C.
Meigs's report of the Battle of Chattanooga.

HEADQUARTERS U. S. QUARTERMASTER'S DEPARTMENT,

IN THE FIELD,

CHATTANOOGA, TENN., *November 26, 1863.*

HON. E. M. STANTON,
Secretary of War, Washington, D. C.:

SIR: On the 23d, at 11¼, a. m., General Grant ordered a demonstration against Mission [Missionary] Ridge, to develop the force holding it. The troops marched out, formed in order, advanced in line of battle, as if on parade. The rebels watched the formation and movement from their picket lines and rifle pits, and from the summits of Mission Ridge, five hundred feet above us, and thought it was a review and drill, so openly, so deliberately, so regularly was it all done.

As the line advanced, preceded by skirmishers, and at 2, p. m., reached our picket lines, they opened a rattling volley upon the rebel pickets, which replied and ran into their advanced line of rifle pits. After them went our skirmishers, and into them, along the centre of the line of twenty-five thousand troops, which General Thomas had so quickly displayed.

Until we opened fire, prisoners assert that they thought the whole movement was a review and general drill, and then it was too late to send to their camps for reinforcements and they were overwhelmed by force of numbers. It was a surprise in open daylight.

At 3, p. m., the important advanced position of "Orchard Knob" and the lines right and left were in our possession, and arrangements were ordered for holding them during the night.

The next day at daylight General Sherman had five thousand men across the Tennessee, established on its south bank, and commenced the construction of a pontoon bridge about six miles above Chattanooga.

The rebel steamer "Dunbar," repaired at the right moment, rendered effective aid in this crossing, ferrying over some six thousand men.

By nightfall General Sherman had seized the extremity of Mission Ridge nearest the river, and was entrenching himself.

General Howard, with a brigade, opened communication with him from Chattanooga on the south side of the river.

Skirmishing and cannonading continued all day on the left and centre. General Hooker scaled the slopes of Lookout Mountain from the valley of Lookout Creek, drove the rebels around the point, captured some two thousand prisoners, and established himself high up the mountain side, in full view of Chattanooga. This raised the blockade, and our steamers were ordered from Bridgeport to Chattanooga. They had run only to Kelly's Ferry, whence ten miles of hauling over mountain roads and twice crossing the Tennessee on pontoon bridges brought us our supplies.

All night the point of Mission ridge, on the extreme left, and the side of Lookout Mountain, on the extreme right, blazed with the camp fires of loyal troops. The day had been one of driving mists and rains, and much of Hooker's battle was fought above the clouds, which concealed him from our view, but from which his musketry was heard.

At nightfall the sky cleared, and the full moon, the "hunter's moon," shone upon the beautiful scene.

Till 1, a. m., twinkling sparks upon the mountain side showed that picket skirmishing was still going on; then it ceased.

A brigade sent from Chattanooga crossed Chattanooga

creek and opened communication with Hooker soon after nightfall.

General Grant's headquarters during the afternoon of the 23d and the day of the 24th were in Wood's redoubt, except when in the course of the day we rode along the advanced lines, visiting the headquarters of the several commanders in Chattanooga valley.

At daylight on the 25th the stars and stripes were discerned on the peak of Lookout. The rebels had evacuated the mountain. Hooker moved to descend the mountain, and, striking Mission Ridge at the Rossville Gap, to sweep it on both sides and on its summit.

The rebel troops were seen as soon as it was light enough streaming by regiments and brigades along the narrow summit of Mission Ridge, either concentrating on their right to overwhelm Sherman or marching for the railroad and raising the siege. They had evacuated the valley of Chattanooga, would they abandon that of the Chickamauga?

The 30-pounders and 4½-inch rifles of Wood's redoubt opened on Mission Ridge. Orchard Knob sent its compliments to the ridge, which with rifled Parrotts answered, and the cannonade thus commenced continued all day. Shot and shell screamed from Orchard Knob to Mission Ridge, from Mission Ridge to Orchard Knob, and from Wood's redoubt, over the heads of General Grant and General Thomas and their staffs, who were with us in this favorable position, whence the whole could be seen as in an amphitheater.

Headquarters were under fire all day long. Cannonading and musketry were heard from General Sherman. Howard marched the 11th Corps to join him.

Thomas sent out skirmishers, who drove in the rebel pickets, and even shook them in their entrenchments at the foot of Missouri [Missionary] ridge.

Sherman sent an assault against Bragg's right, entrenched on a high knob, next to that on which Sherman himself lay fortified.

The assault was gallantly made, reached the edge of the crest, held its ground for what seemed to me an hour; but was then bloodily repulsed by reserves.

A general advance was ordered, and a strong line of skirmishers, followed by a deployed line of battle, some two miles in length, at the signal of six cannon shots from the headquarters on Orchard Knob, moved rapidly and orderly forward.

The rebel pickets discharged their muskets and ran into their rifle-pits; our skirmishers followed on their heels; the line of battle was not far behind; and we saw the gray rebels swarm out of the long line of rifle-pits in numbers which surprised us, and spread over the base of the hill. A few turned and fired their pieces, but the greater number collected into the various roads which creep obliquely up its steep face, and went on to the top. Some regiments pressed on and began to swarm up the steep sides of the ridge. Here and there a color was advanced beyond the line. The attempt appeared most dangerous; but the advance was supported, and the whole line ordered to storm the heights, upon which not less than forty pieces of artillery, and no one knew how many muskets stood ready to slaughter the assailants.

With cheers answering to cheers, the men swarmed upwards. They gathered to the lines of least difficult ascent and the line was broken. Color after color was planted on the summit, while musketry and cannon vomited their thunder upon them. A well-directed shot from Orchard Knob exploded a rebel caisson on the summit. A gun was seen galloping to the right, its driver lashing his horses. A party of our soldiers intercepted him, and the gun was captured with cheers.

A fierce musketry fight broke out to the left where, between Thomas and Sherman, a mile or two of the ridge, was still occupied by the rebels. Bragg left the house in which he had held his headquarters, and rode to the rear, as our troops crowned the hill on each side of him.

General Grant proceeded to the summit, and then only did we know its height.

Some of the captured artillery was put into position, artillerists were sent for to work the guns, caissons were searched for ammunition. The rebel log breastworks were torn to pieces and carried to the other side of the ridge, and used in forming barricades across it. A strong line of infantry was formed in the rear of Baird's line, hotly engaged in a musketry contest with the rebels to the left, and a secure lodgment was soon effected.

The other assault to the right of our centre gained the summit, and the rebels threw down their arms and fled. Hooker coming in from Rossville swept the right of the ridge and captured many prisoners.

Bragg's remaining troops left early in the night and the battle of Chattanooga, after three days of manœuvring and fighting was won. The strength of the rebellion in the centre was broken; Burnside relieved from danger in East Tennessee; Kentucky, and Tennessee redeemed; Georgia and the southeast threatened in the rear, and another victory added to the chaplet of Unconditional Surrender Grant.

To-night the estimate of captures is several thousand prisoners and thirty pieces of artillery. Loss for so great a victory not severe. Bragg is firing the railroad as he retreats towards Dalton, Sherman is in hot pursuit.

To-day I visited the battle-field, which extends for six

miles along Mission Ridge, and for several miles on Lookout Mountain.

Probably no so well directed, so well ordered a battle has been delivered during the war. But one assault was repulsed, but that assault, by calling to that point the reserves prevented their repulsing any of the others.

A few days since Bragg sent to General Grant a flag of truce to advise him that it would be prudent to remove any non-combatants who might be still in Chattanooga. No reply has been returned, but, the combatants having been removed from this vicinity, it is probable that the non-combatants can remain without imprudence.

May I suggest that your visit to Louisville, with the measures there inaugurated have done the cause in this quarter much good. It would be well to visit us here and also for the President to review an army which has done so much for the country, and which has not yet seen his face.

(Signed.)   M. C. MEIGS,
                              Quartermaster General.

1864

Fresh from Abraham's Bosom

As LINCOLN GREW in stature as President, popular interest in him grew in proportion, particularly in the election year of 1864. The President was roundly criticized by some for his habit of telling jokes. But his readiness with an anecdote endeared him to the masses of Americans who were his greatest supporters. Collections of his jokes and stories were eagerly read. It did not matter that most of the tales they repeated were old jokes revised with an application to Lincoln. The President himself was not averse to putting an old story to new use, and a good laugh is always a good laugh.

In this section is a sketch of "Mr. Lincoln's Daily Life" from *Old Abe's Jokes, Fresh from Abraham's Bosom.* The other items are from *Lincolniana; or, The Humors of Uncle Abe.*

MR. LINCOLN'S DAILY LIFE.

Mr. Lincoln is an early riser, and he thus is able to devote two or three hours each morning to his voluminous private correspondence, besides glancing at a city paper. At nine he breakfasts—then walks over to the war office, to read such war telegrams as they give him, (occasionally some are withheld,) and to have a chat with General Halleck on the military situation, in which he takes a great interest. Returning to the white house, he goes through with his morning's mail, in company with a private secretary, who makes a minute of the reply which he is to make—and others the President retains, that he may answer them himself. Every letter receives attention, and all which are entitled to a reply receive one no matter how they are worded, or how inelegant the chirography may be.

Tuesdays and Fridays are cabinet days, but on other days visitors at the white house are requested to wait in the antechamber, and send in their cards. Sometimes, before the President has finished reading his mail Louis will have a handful of pasteboard, and from the cards laid before him Mr. Lincoln has visitors ushered in, giving precedence to acquaintances. Three or four hours do they pour in, in rapid succession, nine out of ten asking offices, and patiently does the president listen to their application. Care and anxiety have furrowed his rather homely features, yet occasionally he is "reminded of an anecdote" and good humored glances beam from his clear, grey eyes, while his ringing laugh shows that he is not "used up" yet. The simple and natural manner in which he delivers his thoughts makes him appear to those visiting him like an earnest, affectionate friend. He makes little parade of his legal science, and rarely indulges in speculative propositions, but states his ideas in plain Anglo-saxon, illuminated by many lively images and pleasing allusions, which seem to flow as if in obedience to a resistless impulse of his nature. Some newspaper admirer attempts to deny that the President tells stories. Why, it is rarely that any one is in his company for fifteen minutes without hearing a good tale, appropriate to the subject talked about. Many a metaphysical argument does he demolish by simply telling an anecdote, which exactly overturns the verbal structure.

About four o'clock the President declines seeing any more company, and often accompanies his wife in her carriage to take a drive. He is fond of horseback exercise, and when passing the summers' home used generally to go in the saddle. The President dines at six, and it is rare that some personal friends do not grace the round dining table where he throws off the cares of office, and reminds those who have been in Kentucky of the old school gentleman who used to dispense generous hospitality there.— From the dinner table the party retire to the crimson drawing room, where coffee is served, and where the President passes the evening, unless some dignitary has a special interview. Such is the almost unvarying daily life of Abraham Lincoln, whose administration will rank next in importance to that of Washington in our national annals.

UNCLE ABE ON THE WHISKY QUESTION.

A committee, just previous to the fall of Vicksburg, solicitous for the *morale* of our armies, took it upon themselves to visit the President and urge the removal of General Grant.

"What for?" asked Uncle Abe.

"Why," replied the busy-bodies, "he drinks too much whisky."

"Ah!" rejoined Uncle Abe, "can you inform me, gentlemen, where General Grant procures his whisky?"

The committee confessed they could not.

"Because," added Uncle Abe, with a merry twinkle in his

eye, "If I can find out, I'll send a barrel of it to every General in the field!"

The delegation retired in reasonable good order.

A Touching Incident.

The following incident, which occurred at the White House, will appeal to every heart. It reveals unmistakably the deep kindness of Uncle Abe's character:

"At a reception recently at the White House, many persons present noticed three little girls poorly dressed, the children of some mechanic or laboring man, who had followed the visitors into the house to gratify their curiosity. They were passed from room to room, and were passing through the reception room with some trepidation, when Uncle Abe called to them: 'Little girls, are you going to pass me without shaking hands?' Then he bent his tall, awkward form down, and shook each little girl warmly by the hand. Everybody in the apartment was spellbound by the incident, so simple in itself, yet revealing of so much of Uncle Abe's character."

Bushwhackers

THE WAR WOULD BE DECIDED in its Eastern theaters, but it was no less intense in the West. Each battle was supremely important to the men who engaged in it. The Federals slowly restricted Confederate resistance to the confines of Texas, Louisiana, and Arkansas, and territorial inroads were made even into those states. But pro-Southern elements along the border caused flurries of military activity. In August, 1863, William Clarke Quantrill had led a band of Missouri guerrillas into Lawrence, Kansas, and virtually destroyed the town. It was necessary to guard against any possible repetition of such a massacre.

Stationed at Fort Riley, Kansas, were the men of the Second Colorado Cavalry. Even at this isolated post energetic soldiers managed to produce and circulate their own newspaper. Here is a portion of the story of the Second Colorado and its war against the bushwhackers as told in the columns of the *Soldier's Letter.*

263

The Counties of Jackson, Cass, Bates, and part of Vernon —forming the 4th Sub-District, District Central Mo. had been infested by a set of outlaws, consisting in part—of Deserters from the Rebel army, and partly of rebels, who—from cowardice, or some other motive, had failed to join the army—and preferred wreaking their vengeance upon the few persons who were so unfortunate as to be Union citizens. As indicative of their cowardly dispositions, their actions were attended with stealth, seldom daring to risk an open contest, unless vastly superior to the opposing force—in point of numbers; but confining their actions, principally to the bushes—ambushing small parties, and individuals, robbing all who fell into their hands, and showing no quarter to Union Soldiers:—hence, from this mode of warfare, and highway robberies—were termed "Bushwhackers." Sometimes their depredations extended to all parties; but as a general rule, the Union people were the greatest sufferers.

These marauders, or banditti became so numerous, and bold in their nefarious transactions—and such difficulty was experienced in apprehending and punishing the guilty—that it was deemed necessary in order to insure justice to all parties—to cause the immediate abandonment by the inhabitants of these counties; about the 23d of September, 1863, the order was issued by General Ewing, giving them 15 days to leave the Counties, which was speedily obeyed by the inhabitants; troops were stationed in the different parts of the Sub.-District, and the country overrun: houses burned to the ground; grain and farms destroyed—causing the country to resemble a wilderness—with "homes deserted, fields of ground, abandoned by the faithful plow."

On the 14th of January, 1864, Gen. Brown—who was at that time in command of the District of Central Missouri, issued an order—(General Order No. 2 Hd.-Qrs. Dist. Cen-

tral Mo.) allowing all loyally disposed citizens who had been
driven from their homes, to return—on conditions—viz: that
they should ever be ready to assist the Government in its
endeavors to put down the Rebellion, and protect themselves, and their homes, from all enemies; the same General
Order assigned Colonel James H. Ford, Second Colorado
Cavalry, to the command of the 4th Sub.-District District
of Central Missouri, Hd-Qrs. at Kansas City, Mo. Col. Ford
assumed command on the 18th of February, and appointed
Lieut. E. L. Berthoud, Co. E, (now Captain Co. D,) Acting
Assistant Adjutant-General, and Capt. J. C. W. Hall, Co. B,
Assistant Provost Marshal. On assuming command, Colonel
Ford proceeded to distribute his forces throughout the Sub
District, in such a manner as would be best calculated to
conduct the campaign against the squads of Bushwhackers,
and at the same time, be able to concentrate his forces, with
little delay, on the appearance of a superior force of the
enemy. Among the Stations announced, were the following:
Kansas City, Independence—eight miles east—Westport,
three miles south, Hickman's Mills—16 miles south; Pleasant
Hill—thirty-five miles south-east; and Harrisonville—about
45 miles south from Kansas City.

At this time, the Bushwhackers were comparatively quiet,
confining their efforts to an occasional midnight assassination, or robbery; evidently deferring operations on a large
scale, until the leaves came out on the trees—to afford them
protection in their fiendish work; nevertheless, the troops
at the different stations were not idle, but were actively engaged in scouring the country, and becoming acquainted
with its geographical position, the roads and by-ways, as
well the inhabitants—who consisted chiefly of "widows" (!)
whose husbands had gone to the war—and who were strictly
loyal to the Government of the—Southern Confederacy! So

much diligence was exercised by the troops, that, by the 1st of June, there was scarcely a locality, road, or bypath through the country, including the famous "Sni Hills"—with which they were not thoroughly familiar; a very important feature, in hunting Bushwhackers. . . .

On the 29th of April, a detachment of our troops, under command of Lieut. Spencer, pursued on the trail of a party of *Bushwhackers,* between Lone Jack and the Sni Hills; coming up with them, they charged them, but the *Bandits* were well mounted, and succeeded in escaping unharmed, after the first fire, which killed Geo. Wells, Private of K Company, and wounding John Freestone, of Company G, whose horses had led them far in advance of the others.

On the 13th of June, Sergeant-Major Hennion, with an escort of 8 men, and a six mule team in charge, was attacked about 5 o'cl'k in the afternoon, about four miles southwest of Westport, on the Hickman's Mill road, by a band of 25 or 30 *Bushwhackers,* under the infamous desperado, Dick Yeager; the first volley fired, although not over 20 feet distant, had no other effect than the wounding of Hennion slightly in the ankle, and the complete surprise of our little party, who fired several hurried shots, and took to the brush, closely pursued; at the second discharge from the enemy, Hennion's horse was killed, and the cylinder blown from his revolver at the same time; but he succeeded in making his escape into the brush, where he lay until 10 o'clock that night, and reached Kansas City the next morning at 6, a. m., with three bullet-holes in his jacket, and one through his pants. The rest of the party succeeded in getting away unharmed—two of them, who were in the advance, hastened forward to Hickman's Mill for reinforcements, and one of the party lay out during the night and reached Hickman's Mill the next day.

The *Banditti* captured the team, unloaded some goods belonging to Mrs. Johnson of Company L, and directed her to
a house near by, where she could stay until relief would
come; they then set fire to the wagon, killed two of the
mules, and wounded a third one, which they left; the other
three they appropriated to their own use. Some days afterward, a fresh grave was found near the spot, supposed to
be that of a *Bushwhacker* killed in the encounter. The frequency of these attacks, and the increasing temerity of the
assassins, required energetic action, on the part of our troops
—consequently—Colonel Ford, ordered the Regiment into
the field, and established its Head-Quarters near a deserted
village, called Raytown, situated on the Independence and
Hickman's Mill road, and 16 miles distant from Kansas City:
from this point, the troops, under Majors Smith and Pritchard, and other officers of the Regiment, scoured the country,
in every direction—sometimes mounted, and at other times
dismounted—which had the desired effect, of driving these
marauders from that portion of the country, to seek a safer,
and more congenial latitude; during one of these scouts,
Corporal Martin, Co. H. with 10 men, some two miles east
of camp, were quietly passing along, when hearing a noise
as if some persons talking in the distance; quickly conceal-
ing themselves in the brush, our party awaited the approach
of the other party, who, approaching within 50 yards, were
discovered to be Bushwhackers—five in number—and were
immediately fired upon by the scout; a ball from the gun of
private Jones, of H Company, passed through the hips of
one of the enemy named Young—wounding him severely,
but his horse carried him off: pursuing the course taken by
them, and coming up to a house, the alarm was given by
some one who acted as sentinel, and out rushed the same
party, and after a hurried exchange of shots, disappeared

in the brush:—Young, the wounded man, was killed a short time afterwards.

Head-Quarters of the Regiment remained at Raytown about one month, during which time the troops were kept constantly on the move; various expedients were resorted to, to entrap the wary enemy, but they had become aware of the dangerous locality; and quietly decamped, until a more favorable opportunity presented itself.

On the 10th of May, Lt. Gooding, with 20 men of Co's H, and G, started from Pleasant Hill, after night had set in—on a scout of three days duration; on the night of the second day out, while scouting 20 miles north east of Pleasant Hill, they drew up to a house, owned by one Webb; upon entering, although past eleven o'clock, the table was found ready "set," and every necessary preparation made, for a meal; upon inquiry, our party was informed that there were no *Bushwhackers* in the country, but—not being inclined to give credence to the smooth tongues, and unqualified assertions of the "war-widows" who were so numerous in that portion of the country, and who could live there unmolested, while depredations were being committed all around them—our boys kept a sharp look-out, and, after leaving the house, and proceeding cautiously along the road some three miles, they were met by a party of four men, who were just emerging from the brush, and could barely be discerned in the darkness of the night: "Who are you?" challenged their leader: "Who are *you?*" demanded Gooding, while every man grasped his revolver with a firmer grip: without deigning to give answer, the four men wheeled about, put spurs to their horses, and fled through the thick under-brush, amid a shower of bullets from the well directed fire of the advance; the next day, the dead bodies of two of the *Bandits*, were found near the scene of the rencountre.

During the campaign, a portion of the troops had been stationed at Camp Smith, some three miles southwest of Independence, and on the morning of the sixth of July, Captain S. Wagoner, of C. Company, and twenty-five of his men, left Camp, and proceeded in a northeasterly direction, until arriving on the Pleasant Hill and Independence road, and about eight miles distant from the latter mentioned place; here, they saw four men, who immediately took to flight, and while pursuing them, our party was charged upon, by nearly one hundred *Bushwhackers,* who were lying in ambush awaiting their approach; unconscious of the presence of so large a body of the foe, until they rushed forth from the dense thicket, with savage yells, and poured a deadly volley into the midst of the scout, who, nothing daunted, firmly stood their ground, and with their brave Captain leading them on, returned the fire, although outnumbered four to one, by the foe, who came rushing on, until the combatants were mingled together, fighting a hand to hand encounter, midst the fallen dead, and dying, until the gallant Wagoner fell, mortally wounded, and dragging himself a few feet to one side, he gave a farewell shot, that sent an enemy reeling to the ground, with his life-blood spirting from the wound—and shouted "give them death boys," and breathed his last: completely overpowered by numbers, our troops were forced to fall back, and surrender the field to the enemy—with the loss of their valiant Captain, and seven brave men killed, and one wounded: the loss of the enemy were nine men killed, and fifteen wounded; they took the arms and what money was on the persons of our boys, and left their bodies lying as they fell, where a strong force of our troops, who were sent out, found them and brought them to Independence, the next morning, and buried them in a body, in the Cemetery, with a brick wall surrounding the entire number; and the Company, assisted by the Officers of the Regiment, erected a fine Marble Monument, to mark their resting place.— The Monument bears the following inscription, from the pen of Mrs. Williams, of Company A:

"Brave heroes rest beneath this sculptured stone;
In unfair contest slain by murderous hands:
They knew no yielding to a cruel foe—
And thus, this tribute to their memory stands—
Our country's honor, and a Nation's pride;—
'Twas thus they nobly lived, and bravely died."

Captain Wagoner was a brave man, of which his surviving followers can testify, and his loss, and that of the brave men who fell with him, cast a gloom o'er the entire Regiment.

Notwithstanding the increased vigilance of our troops, in scouring the country, in search of these *Brigands*, it was seldom they caught them "napping," for they were cognizant of the danger they were incurring, by remaining in the country, and committing their depredations, and, were cautious of their movements—only making a demonstration, when assured of success, on their part; being intimately acquainted with the entire country, (having resided there for years) and having the advantage of acting on the defensive, when our troops were sent in pursuit of them—they for a long time, succeeded in evading an open collision with them,—feeling uninclined to extend their acquaintance with men who gave them such a rough introduction.

About this time, a desperado by the name of *Thornton*, came into the counties on the North side of the river, and was collecting together all the *Bushwhackers* and other *vagabonds* that would flock to his standard, in order to go

into offensive operations against the Union people, on a
large scale, and finally escape to the Southern army, as it
was getting rather warm for their comfort and safety:
through the spies he had employed to watch the movements
of the enemy—Col. Ford learned of their place of rendezvous,
and about 2 o'clock in the morning of the 13th of July, he
quietly embarked on board the Fanny Ogden, and the
Emilie, with about 300 men, in the midst of a heavy rain-
storm, and proceeded up the river as far as Weston, a town
on the North bank of the Missouri river, about seven miles
above Leavenworth City:—landing at this point, the troops
bivouacked, until 12 o'clock, M, and being reinforced by a
portion of the 16th Kansas Cavalry, under Jennison, the column moved towards Camden Point, a town of 150 inhabitants; arriving within 4 miles of the town, our advance encountered the rebel pickets, who hastily fired a volley, and
retreated, pursued by the advance, who succeeded in killing two of their number; the others made their escape into
the thick brush on the roadside: the Brigade was formed in
fours, and the order "gallop" was given, and the column
moved forward at a rapid rate over the road. Company F,
(Captain West) leading the advance; on arriving at the
town, the rebels were found drawn up in line about 350
strong, ready for battle; West also formed his men in line
at hailing distance, and demanded— "Who are you?" the
question was reiterated by the rebel leader; West replied—
"Captain West, of the Second Colorado!" the reply came
back, proud and defiant— "We do not *recognize* Captain
West, and his party—" and the rebel colors were immediately
displayed. Captain West instantly ordered a charge, and
the rebel ranks were broken and scattered by the fierce
onset of our troops, who bore down on the foe—like an avalanche—sweeping all before them, amid the smoke and din

of battle, and the wild, deafening cheers of our men, that
rang out clear and loud upon the air, and was echoed, and
re-echoed through the surrounding forest: the rebel forces,
after exchanging a few volleys, fled in every direction in the
wildest confusion—in many instances, leaving their horses
and equipments, and quite a number throwing down their
arms, and taking to the brush, pursued closely by our troops,
who, having become exasperated by their former fiendish
transactions—shot them down like so many dogs—without
mercy: the main portion fled on the road leading east of
town, and were hotly pursued, for nearly five miles, but
being mounted on fresh horses, they finally escaped—and our
troops returned, and camped on the same ground occupied
previously, by their forces. Our loss was one man killed,
(private Flannegan) and 1 wounded, (Serg't Crane,) both
of Co. F: that of the rebels was 21 killed; if any were
wounded, they made their escape. In this action, the rebel
colors, which was presented to them, by the ladies of Platte
City, and bore the motto—"Protect Missouri"—was captured
by Company F.

The *Alabama* and the *Kearsarge*

NEXT IN FAME to the fight between the *Monitor* and the *Merrimac* among naval battles of the Civil War is the engagement between the Confederate *Alabama* and the Federal *Kearsarge* fought off Cherbourg on June 19, 1864.

In a career a few weeks short of two years the *Alabama*, commanded by Raphael Semmes, had burned, sunk, or captured more than sixty Federal ships. Her very name was anathema to the Union Navy, and the fear his ship incited seems to have been counted on by Semmes, who is quoted in this account by Frederick Milnes Edge as having observed with surprise the efficient conduct of the Federal sailors and to have remarked, "Confound them; they've been fighting twenty minutes, and they're as cool as posts."

Edge was distinctly Northern in his sympathies. His is, nevertheless, a careful and considered report of the fight and is a good antidote for the histrionic sensationalism which marks many of the contemporary accounts of the sea battle.

The loss of the *Alabama* did not end the Confederate Navy, but it left only the cruisers *Florida* and *Shenandoah* as major dangers to Federal shipping. The *Florida* surrendered at Bahia, Brazil, in October, 1864. The *Shenandoah* survived the war and finally gave herself up to British authorities at Liverpool in November, 1865.

By the summer of 1864 the Federal Navy had been built up to controlling strength. Slowly its blockade was throttling commercial activity in Southern ports. Its gunboats were exceedingly efficient in operations in inland waters. It could be used for the transport of troops and for joint operations with the army. From virtually nothing in 1861 it had been made into an effective war force.

Within a few days of the fight, the writer of these pages crossed from London to Cherbourg for the purpose of obtaining by personal examination full and precise information in reference to the engagement. It would seem as though misrepresentation, if not positive falsehood, were inseparable from everything connected with the *Alabama,* for on reaching the French naval station he was positively assured by the people on shore that nobody was permitted to board the *Kearsarge.* Preferring, however, to substantiate the truth of these allegations, from the officers of the vessel themselves, he hired a boat and sailed out to the sloop, receiving on his arrival an immediate and polite reception from Captain Winslow and his gallant subordinates. During the six days he remained at Cherbourg, he found the *Kearsarge* open to the inspection, above and below, of any and everybody who chose to visit her; and he frequently heard surprise expressed by English and French visitors alike that representations on shore were so inconsonant with the truth of the case.

I found the *Kearsarge* lying under the guns of the French ship-of-the-line *Napoleon*, two cables' length from that vessel, and about a mile and a half from the harbour; she had not moved from that anchorage since entering the port of Cherbourg, and no repairs whatever had been effected in her hull since the fight. I had thus full opportunity to examine the extent of her damage, and she certainly did not look at all like a vessel which had just been engaged in one of the hottest conflicts of modern times.

The *Kearsarge*, in size, is by no means the terrible craft represented by those who, for some reason or other, seek to detract from the honour of her victory; she appeared to me a mere yacht in comparison with the shipping around her, and disappointed many of the visitors who came to see her. The relative proportions of the two antagonists were as follows:—

	ALABAMA.	KEARSARGE.
Length over all..........	220 ft.	232 ft.
" of keel	210 "	198½ "
Beam	32 "	33 "
Depth	17 "	16½ "
Horse power, 2 engines of 300 each		400 h.p.
Tonnage	1,040	1,031*

The *Alabama* was a barque-rigged screw propeller, and the heaviness of her rig, and, above all, the greater size and height of her masts would give her the appearance of a much larger vessel than her antagonist. The masts of the

* The *Kearsarge* has a four-bladed screw, diameter 12 ft 9-in. with a pitch of 20-ft.

latter are disproportionately low and small; she has never carried more than top-sail yards, and depends for her speed upon her machinery alone. It is to be questioned whether the *Alabama,* with all her reputation for velocity, could, in her best trim, outsteam her rival. The log book of the *Kearsarge,* which I was courteously permitted to examine, frequently shows a speed of upwards of fourteen knots the hour, and her engineers state that her machinery was never in better working order than at the present time. I have not seen engines more compact in form, nor, apparently, in finer condition; looking in every part as though they were fresh from the workshop, instead of being, as they are, half through the third year of the cruise. . . .

Numerous facts serve to prove that Captain Semmes had made every preparation to engage the *Kearsarge,* and that wide-spread publicity had been given to his intention. As soon as the arrival of the Federal vessel was known at Paris, an American gentleman of high position came down to Cherbourg, with instructions for Captain Winslow; but so desirous were the French authorities to preserve a really honest neutrality, that permission was only granted to him to sail to her after his promise to return to shore immediately on the delivery of his message. Once back in Cherbourg, and about to return to Paris, he was advised to remain over night, *as the Alabama intended to fight the Kearsarge next day* (Sunday). On Sunday morning, an excursion train arrived from the Capital, and the visitors were received at the terminus of the railway by the boatmen of the port, who offered them boats for the purpose of seeing *a genuine naval battle which was to take place during the day.* Turning such a memorable occurrence to practical uses, Monsieur Rondin, a celebrated photographic artist on the *Place d'Armes* at Cherbourg, prepared the necessary chemicals, plates, and *camera,* and placed himself on the summit of the old church tower which the whilom denizens of Cherbourg had very properly built in happy juxtaposition with his establishment. I was only able to see the negative, but that was quite sufficient to show that the artist had obtained a very fine view indeed of the exciting contest. Five days, however, had elapsed since Captain Semmes sent his challenge to Captain Winslow through the Confederate agent, Monsieur Bonfils; surely time sufficient for him to make all the preparations which he considered necessary. Meanwhile the *Kearsarge* was cruising to and fro at sea, outside the breakwater.

The *Kearsarge* reached Cherbourg on the 14th, and her Captain only heard of Captain Semmes' intention to fight him on the following day. Five days, however, elapsed before the *Alabama* put in an appearance, and her exit from the harbour was heralded by the English yacht *Deerhound.* The officer on watch aboard the *Kearsarge* made out a three-masted vessel steaming from the harbour, the movements of which were somewhat mysterious; after remaining a short time only, this steamer, which subsequently proved to be the *Deerhound,* went back into port; only returning to sea a few minutes in advance of the *Alabama,* and the French ironclad *La Couronne.* Mr. Lancaster, her owner, sends a copy of his log to the *Times,* the first two entries being as follows:

"Sunday, June 19, 9 A.M.—Got up steam and proceeded out of Cherbourg harbour.

"10.30.—Observed the 'Alabama' steaming out of the harbour towards the Federal steamer 'Kearsarge.'" *

* The following is the copy of the log of the *Kearsarge* on the day in question:
"June 19, 1864.   "From 8 to Merid.
        "Moderate breeze from the Wd. weather b. c. At 10 o'clock, inspected crew at quarters. At 10.20, discovered the Alabama steaming out

Mr. Lancaster does not inform us why an English gentleman should choose a Sunday morning, of all days in the week, to cruise about at an early hour with ladies on board, nor does he supply the public with information as to the movements of the *Deerhound* during the hour and a half which elapsed between his exit from the harbour and the appearance of the *Alabama.* The preceding paragraph, however, supplies the omission.

At length the *Alabama* made her appearance in company with the *Couronne,* the latter vessel conveying her outside the limit of French waters. Here let me pay a tribute to the careful neutrality of the French authorities. No sooner was the limit of jurisdiction reached, than the *Couronne* put down her helm, and without any delay, steamed back into port, not even lingering outside the breakwater to witness the fight. Curiosity, if not worse, anchored the English vessel in handy vicinity to the combatants. Her presence proved to

---

from the port of Cherbourg, accompanied by a French iron-clad steamer, and a fore and-aft rigged steamer showing the white English ensign and a yacht flag. Beat to General Quarters, and clear the ship for action. Steamed ahead standing off shore. At 10.50, being distant from the land about two leagues, altered our course and approached the Alabama. At 10.57, the Alabama commenced the action with her starboard broadside at 1,000 yards range. At 11, we returned her fire, and came fairly into action, which we continued until Merid., when observing signs of distress in the enemy, together with a cessation of her fire, our fire was withheld. At 12.10, a boat with an officer from the Alabama came alongside and surrendered his vessel, with the information that she was rapidly sinking, and a request for assistance. Sent the Launch and 2d Cutter, the other boats being disabled by the fire of the enemy. The English yacht before mentioned, coming within hail, was requested by the Captain (W.) to render assistance in saving the lives of the officers and crew of the surrendered vessel. At 2.24, the Alabama went down in forty fathoms of water, leaving most of the crew struggling in the water. Seventy persons were rescued by the boats, two pilot boats and the yacht also assisted. One pilot boat came alongside us, but the other returned to the port. The yacht steamed rapidly away to the Nd. without reporting the number of our prisoners she had picked up.

(Signed) JAMES S. WHEELER, Actg. Master."

be of much utility, for she picked up no less than fourteen of the *Alabama*'s officers, and among them the redoubtable Semmes himself.

So soon as the *Alabama* was made out, the *Kearsarge* immediately headed seaward and steamed off the coast, the object being to get a sufficient distance from the land so as to obviate any possible infringement of French jurisdiction; and, secondly, that in case of the battle going against the *Alabama*, the latter could not retreat into port. When this was accomplished, the *Kearsarge* was turned shortly round and steered immediately for the *Alabama*, Captain Winslow desiring to get within close range, as his guns were shotted with five-seconds shell. The interval between the two vessels being reduced to a mile, or thereabouts, the *Alabama* sheered and discharged a broadside, nearly a raking fire, at the *Kearsarge*. More speed was given to the latter to shorten the distance, and a slight sheer to prevent raking. The *Alabama* fired a second broadside and part of a third while her antagonist was closing; and at the expiration of ten or twelve minutes from the *Alabama*'s opening shot, the *Kearsarge* discharged her first broadside. The action henceforward continued in a circle, the distance between the two vessels being about seven hundred yards; this, at all events, is the opinion of the Federal commander and his officers, for their guns were sighted at that range, and their shell burst in and over the privateer. The speed of the two vessels during the engagement did not exceed eight knots the hour.

At the expiration of one hour and two minutes from the first gun, the *Alabama* hauled down her colours and fired a lee gun (according to the statements of her officers), in token of surrender. Captain Winslow could not, however, believe that the enemy had struck, as his own vessel had received so little damage, and he could not regard his antagonist as much more injured than himself; and it was only when a boat came off from the *Alabama* that her true condition was known. The 11-inch shell from the *Kearsarge*, thrown with fifteen pounds of powder at seven hundred yards range, had gone clean through the starboard side of the privateer, bursting in the port side and tearing great gaps in her timber and planking. This was plainly obvious when the *Alabama* settled by the stern and raised the forepart of her hull high out of water.

The *Kearsarge* was struck twenty-seven times during the conflict and fired in all one hundred and seventy-three (173) shots. These were as follows:

Two 11-inch guns	55 shots.
Rifle in forecastle	48　"
Broadside 32-pdrs.	60　"
12-pdr. boat howitzer	10　"
Total,	173 shots.

The last-named gun performed no part whatever in sinking the *Alabama,* and was only used in the action to create laughter among the sailors. Two old quartermasters, the two Dromios of the *Kearsarge,* were put in charge of this gun, with instructions to fire when they received the order. But the two old salts, little relishing the idea of having nothing to do while their messmates were so actively engaged, commenced peppering away with their pea-shooter of a piece, alternating their discharges with vituperation of each other. This low-comedy by-play amused the ship's company, and the officers good-humoredly allowed the farce to continue until the single box of ammunition was exhausted. . . .

The first accounts received of the action led us to suppose that Captain Semmes' intention was to lay his vessel alongside the enemy, and to carry her by boarding. Whether this information came from the Captain himself or was made out of "whole cloth" by some of his admirers, the idea of boarding a vessel under steam—unless her engines, or screw, or rudder be disabled—is manifestly ridiculous. The days of boarding are gone by, except under the contingencies above stated; and any such attempt on the part of the *Alabama* would have been attended with disastrous results to herself and crew. To have boarded the *Kearsarge*, Semmes must have possessed greater speed to enable him to run alongside her; and the moment the pursuer came near her victim, the latter would shut off steam, drop astern in a second of time, sheer off, discharge her whole broadside of grape and canister, and rake her antagonist from stern to stem. Our pro-southern sympathizers really ought not to make their *protegé* appear ridiculous by ascribing to him such an egregious intention.

Andersonville

MOST DREADED of Confederate prisons was Camp Sumter at Anderson Station, Georgia. The prison had been designed with humane motives, to take care of the overload of prisoners at Belle Isle caused by the suspension by the Federals of the cartel for exchange. The site was selected with care to provide a healthy, watered area. But the prison was severely overcrowded almost as soon as it opened, and proper preparations for housing had not been made. The drain by the armies on supplies of food in the Confederacy was responsible for a ration far below any humane or healthy standard. By the summer of 1864 more than thirty thousand prisoners were crowded into twenty-six acres. Exposure, a complete lack of even rudimentary sanitation, lack of decent food and medical care, and overcrowding combined to make the prison pen a veritable pesthouse and to cause more than twelve thousand deaths.

Andersonville was a national outrage in the North. In the summer of 1864 a few of the prisoners were exchanged. Their stories of imprisonment were widely publicized and effectively used as propaganda for the strenuous prosecution of the war. Their testimony was most widely circulated in a pamphlet, *Narrative of the Privations and Sufferings of United States Officers and Privates While Prisoners of War in the Hands of Rebel Authorities,* a portion of which is included here.

Deposition of PRIVATE TRACY:—

I am a private in the 82d New York Regiment of Volunteers, Company G. Was captured with about eight hundred Federal troops, in front of Petersburg, on the 22d of June, 1864. We were kept at Petersburg two days, at Richmond, Belle Isle, three days, then conveyed by rail to Lynchburg. Marched seventy-five miles to Danville, thence by rail to Andersonville, Georgia. At Petersburg we were treated fairly, being under the guard of old soldiers of an Alabama regiment; at Richmond we came under the authority of the notorious and inhuman Major Turner, and the equally notorious Home Guard. Our ration was a pint of beans, four ounces of bread, and three ounces of meat, a day. Another batch of prisoners joining us, we left Richmond sixteen hundred strong.

All blankets, haversacks, canteens, money, valuables of every kind, extra clothing, and in some cases the last shirt and drawers, had been previously taken from us.

At Lynchburg we were placed under the Home Guard, officered by Major and Captain Moffett. The march to Danville was a weary and painful one of five days, under a torrid sun, many of us falling helpless by the way, and soon filling the empty wagons of our train. On the first day we received a little meat, but the *sum* of our rations for the five days was thirteen crackers. During the six days by rail to Anderson-ville, meat was given us twice, and the daily ration was four crackers.

On entering the Stockade Prison, we found it crowded with twenty-eight thousand of our fellow-soldiers. By *crowded*, I mean that it was difficult to move in any direction without jostling and being jostled. This prison is an open space, sloping on both sides, originally seventeen acres, now twenty-five acres, in the shape of a parallelogram, without trees or shelter of any kind. The soil is sand over a bottom of clay. The fence is made of upright trunks of trees, about twenty feet high, near the top of which are small platforms, where the guards are stationed. Twenty feet inside and parallel to the fence is a light railing, forming the "dead line," beyond which the projection of a foot or finger is sure to bring the deadly bullet of the sentinel.

Through the ground, at nearly right-angles with the longer sides, runs or rather creeps a stream through an artificial channel, varying from five to six feet in width, the water about ankle deep, and near the middle of the enclosure, spreading out into a swamp of about six acres, filled with refuse wood, stumps and debris of the camp. Before entering this enclosure, the stream, or more properly sewer, passes through the camp of the guards, receiving from this source, and others farther up, a large amount of the vilest material, even the contents of the sink. The water is of a dark color, and an ordinary glass would collect a thick sediment. This was our only drinking and cooking water. It was our custom to filter it as best we could, through our remnants of haversacks, shirts and blouses. Wells had been dug, but the water either proved so productive of diarrhœa, or so limited in quantity that they were of no general use. The cook-house was situated on the stream just outside the stockade, and its refuse of decaying offal was thrown into the water, a greasy coating covering much of the surface. To these was added the daily large amount of base matter from the camp itself. There was a system of policing, but the means was so limited, and so large a number of the men was rendered irresolute and depressed by imprisonment, that the work was very imperfectly done. One side of the swamp was naturally used as a sink, the men usually going out some distance into the water. Under the summer sun this place early became corruption too vile for description, the men breeding disgusting life, so that the surface of the water moved as with a gentle breeze.

The new-comers, on reaching this, would exclaim: "Is this hell?" yet they soon would become callous, and enter unmoved the horrible rottenness. The rebel authorities never removed any filth. There was seldom any visitation by the officers in charge. Two surgeons were at one time sent by President DAVIS to inspect the camp, but a walk through a small section gave them all the information they desired, and we never saw them again.

The guards usually numbered about sixty-four—eight at each end, and twenty-four on a side. On the outside, within three hundred yards, were fortifications, on high ground, overlooking and perfectly commanding us, mounting twenty-four twelve-pound Napoleon Parrotts. We were never permitted to go outside, except at times, in small squads, to gather our firewood. During the building of the cook-house, a few, who were carpenters, were ordered out to assist.

Our only shelter from the sun and rain and night dews was what we could make by stretching over us our coats or scraps of blankets, which a few had, but generally there was no attempt by day or night to protect ourselves.

The rations consisted of eight ounces of corn bread (the

cob being ground with the kernel), and generally sour, two ounces of condemned pork, offensive in appearance and smell. Occasionally, about twice a week, two tablespoons of rice, and in place of the pork the same amount (two table-spoonfuls) of molasses were given us about twice a month.* This ration was brought into camp about four o'clock, P. M., and thrown from the wagons to the ground, the men being arranged in divisions of two hundred and seventy, subdi-vided into squads of nineties and thirties. It was the custom to consume the whole ration at once, rather than save any for the next day. The distribution being often unequal some would lose the rations altogether. We were allowed no dish or cooking utensil of any kind. On opening the camp in the winter, the first two thousand prisoners were allowed skillets, one to fifty men, but these were soon taken away. To the best of my knowledge, information and belief, our ration was in quality a starving one, it being either too foul to be touched or too raw to be digested.

The cook-house went into operation about May 10th, prior to which we cooked our own rations. It did not prove at all adequate to the work, (thirty thousand is a large town,) so that a large proportion were still obliged to prepare their own food. In addition to the utter inability of many to do this, through debility and sickness, we never had a supply of wood. I have often seen men with a little bag of meal in

---

* Our regular army ration is:
¾ lb. Pork or 1¼ lbs. Fresh Beef,
18 ozs. Hard Bread, or 20 ozs. Soft Bread or Flour,
1-10 lb. Coffee,
1-6 lb. Sugar,
1-10 lb. Rice, or
1-10 lb. Beans or Hominy.
   Vegetables—Fresh or
    Desiccated,
   Molasses,   Irregularly.
   Vinegar.

hand, gathered from several rations, starving to death for want of wood, and in desperation would mix the raw material with water and try to eat it.

The clothing of the men was miserable in the extreme. Very few had shoes of any kind, not two thousand had coats and pants, and those were late comers. More than one-half were indecently exposed, and many were naked.

The usual punishment was to place the men in the stocks, outside, near the Captain's quarters. If a man was missing at roll-call, the squad of ninety to which he belonged was deprived of the ration. The "dead-line" bullet, already referred to, spared no offender. One poor fellow, just from Sherman's army—his name was Roberts—was trying to wash his face near the "dead-line" railing, when he slipped on the clayey bottom, and fell with his head just outside the fatal border. We shouted to him, but it was too late—"another guard would have a furlough," the men said. It was a common belief among our men, arising from statements made by the guard, that General WINDER, in command, issued an order that any one of the guard who should shoot a Yankee outside of the "dead-line" should have a month's furlough, but there probably was no truth in this. About two a day were thus shot, some being cases of suicide, brought on by mental depression or physical misery, the poor fellows throwing themselves, or madly rushing outside the "line."

The mental condition of a large portion of the men was melancholy, beginning in despondency and tending to a kind of stolid and idiotic indifference. Many spent much time in arousing and encouraging their fellows, but hundreds were lying about motionless, or stalking vacantly to and fro, quite beyond any help which could be given them within their prison walls. These cases were frequent among those who had been imprisoned but a short time. There were those who were captured at the first Bull Run, July 1861, and had known Belle Isle from the first, yet had preserved their physical and mental health to a wonderful degree. Many were wise and resolute enough to keep themselves occupied—some in cutting bone and wood ornaments, making their knives out of iron hoops—others in manufacturing ink from the rust from these same hoops, and with rude pens sketching or imitating bank notes, or any sample that would involve long and patient execution.

Letters from home very seldom reached us, and few had any means of writing. In the early summer, a large batch of letters—five thousand we were told—arrived, having been accumulating somewhere for many months. These were brought into camp by an officer, under orders to collect ten cents on each—of course most were returned, and we heard no more of them. One of my companions saw among them three from his parents, but he was unable to pay the charge. According to the rules of transmission of letters over the lines, these letters must have already paid ten cents each to the rebel government.

As far as we saw General Winder and Captain Wirtz [Wirz], the former was kind and considerate in his manners, the latter harsh, though not without kindly feelings.

It is a melancholy and mortifying fact, that some of our trials came from our own men. At Belle Isle and Andersonville there were among us a gang of desperate men, ready to prey on their fellows. Not only thefts and robberies, but even murders were committed. Affairs became so serious at Camp Sumter that an appeal was made to General Winder, who authorized an arrest and trial by a criminal court. Eighty-six were arrested, and six were hung, beside others who were severely punished. These proceedings effected a marked change for the better.

Some few weeks before being released, I was ordered to act as clerk in the hospital. This consists simply of a few scattered trees and fly tents, and is in charge of Dr. White, an excellent and considerate man, with very limited means, but doing all in his power for his patients. He has twenty-five assistants, besides those detailed to examine for admittance to the hospital. This examination was made in a small stockade attached to the main one, to the inside door of which the sick came or were brought by their comrades, the number to be removed being limited. Lately, in consideration of the rapidly increasing sickness, it was extended to one hundred and fifty daily. That this was too small an allowance is shown by the fact that the deaths within our stockade were from thirty to forty a day. I have seen one hundred and fifty bodies waiting passage to the "dead house," to be buried with those who died in hospital. The average of deaths through the earlier months was thirty a day: at the time I left, the average was over one hundred and thirty, and one day the record showed one hundred and forty-six.

The proportion of deaths from *starvation*, not including those consequent on the diseases originating in the character and limited quantity of food, such as diarrhœa, dysentery and scurvy, I cannot state; but to the best of my knowledge, information and belief, there were scores every month. We could, at any time, point out many for whom such a fate was inevitable, as they lay or feebly walked, mere skeletons, whose emaciation exceeded the examples given in Leslie's Illustrated for June 18, 1864. For example: in some cases the inner edges of the two bones of the arms, between the elbow and the wrist, with the intermediate blood vessels, were plainly visible when held toward the light. The ration, in quantity, was perhaps barely sufficient to sustain life, and the cases of starvation were generally those whose stomachs could not retain what had become entirely indigestible.

For a man to find, on waking, that his comrade by his side was dead, was an occurrence too common to be noted. I have seen death in almost all the forms of the hospital and battle-field, but the daily scenes in Camp Sumter exceeded in the extremity of misery all my previous experience.

The work of burial is performed by our own men, under guard and orders, twenty-five bodies being placed in a single pit, without head-boards, and the sad duty performed with indecent haste. Sometimes our men were rewarded for this work with a few sticks of fire-wood, and I have known them to quarrel over a dead body for the *job.*

Dr. White is able to give the patients a diet but little better than the prison rations—a little flour porridge, arrow-root, whiskey and wild or hog tomatoes. In the way of medicine, I saw nothing but camphor, whiskey, and a decoction of some kind of bark—white oak, I think. He often expressed his regret that he had not more medicines. The limitation of military orders, under which the surgeons in charge was placed, is shown by the following occurrence: A supposed private, wounded in the thigh, was under treatment in the hospital, when it was discovered that he was a major of a colored regiment. The assistant-surgeon, under whose immediate charge he was, proceeded at once not only to remove him, but to kick him out, and he was returned to the stockade, to shift for himself as well as he could. Dr. White could not or did not attempt to restore him.

After entering on my duties at the hospital, I was occasionally favored with double rations and some wild tomatoes. A few of our men succeeded, in spite of the closest examination of our clothes, in secreting some green-backs, and with those were able to buy useful articles at exorbitant prices:—a tea-cup of flour at one dollar; eggs, three to six dollars a dozen; salt, four dollars a pound; molasses, thirty dollars a gallon; nigger beans, a small, inferior article, (diet of the slaves and pigs, but highly relished by us,) fifty cents a pint. These figures, multiplied by ten, will give very nearly the price in Confederate currency. Though the country abounded in pine and oak, sticks were sold to us at various prices, according to size.

Our men, especially the mechanics, were tempted with the offer of liberty and large wages to take the oath of allegiance to the Confederacy, but it was very rare that their patriotism, even under such a fiery trial, ever gave way. I carry this message from one of my companions to his mother: "My treatment here is killing me, mother, but I die cheerfully for my country."

Some attempts were made to escape, but wholly in vain, for, if the prison walls and guards were passed and the protecting woods reached, the bloodhounds were sure to find us out.

Tunneling was at once attempted on a large scale, but on the afternoon preceding the night fixed on for escape, an officer rode in and announced to us that the plot was discovered, and from our huge pen we could see on the hill above us the regiments just arriving to strengthen the guard. We had been betrayed. It was our belief that spies were kept in the camp, which could very easily be done.

The number in camp when I left was nearly thirty-five thousand, and daily increasing. The number in hospital was about five thousand. I was exchanged at Port Royal Ferry, August 16th.

PRESCOTT TRACY,
Eighty-second Regiment, N. Y. V.

Sherman

IN VIRGINIA in the summer of 1864 the war had ground slow. Grant had set out on a new campaign in May. Despite heavy losses at the Wilderness, Spotsylvania Court House, Second Cold Harbor, and the Crater before Petersburg, he had kept Richmond under continuous threat and had forestalled any effective counteroffensive against the Federals. The greater manpower and greater war potential of the North was beginning to pay off, though slowly, and the Confederacy found itself faced with a war of attrition it could hardly hope to win.

Grant was the most effective of Lincoln's many choices as commander of the army in Virginia. The President stuck by his general. But a campaign which lost soldiers by the thousand could hardly be a popular one, and Lincoln and his administration were heavily criticized for their conduct of the war.

Lincoln was renominated for the Presidency, on a "National Union" ticket, by a convention which met in Baltimore early in June. The Democrats tried to capitalize on the personal popularity of General McClellan and, meeting at Chicago in late August, named him as their candidate and adopted a "peace platform" (virtually repudiated by their candidate) which called for an immediate end to the war and restoration of the Union by peaceful means.

The military situation at the end of the summer made Democratic victory in the November election a real possibility. Grant had been fighting on the Virginia line all summer, with the real extent of his success still not apparent. Sherman had followed Johnston deep into Georgia, and, though his campaign had been definitely successful, he still had not achieved a decisive victory. Lincoln badly needed a decisive victory by one of his generals, both to assure his re-election and to have a mandate through the vote of the people for thorough and complete prosecution of the war.

William Tecumseh Sherman gave him that victory. On September 1 he telegraphed the President: "Atlanta is ours and fairly won."

Sherman did not plan to garrison the city indefinitely. There would be no profit in bottling himself up there. To prepare for his further campaign he ordered all civilians to evacuate Atlanta. His order was regarded by General John B. Hood and the civilian authorities in Atlanta as one of extreme cruelty. But Sherman knew that war itself was cruelty and that if, for military purposes, the city must be destroyed before he could continue his campaign, it would be far less cruel to remove its inhabitants before the destruction. Here is his exchange of letters with the authorities in Atlanta.

THE AUTHORITIES TO GEN. SHERMAN.

ATLANTA, GA., Sept. 11, 1864.

Major-General W. T. Sherman—*Sir:* The undersigned, Mayor and two members of Council for the city of Atlanta, for the time being the only legal organ of the people of said city to express their wants and wishes, ask leave most earnestly but respectfully to petition you to reconsider the order requiring them to leave Atlanta. At first view, it struck us that the measure would involve extraordinary hardship and loss, but since we have seen the practical execution of it, so far as it has progressed, and the individual condition of many of the people, and heard the statements as to the inconvenience, loss and suffering attending it, we are satisfied that the amount of it will involve in the aggregate consequences appalling and heart-rending.

Many poor women are in an advanced state of pregnancy; others having young children, whose husbands, for the greater part, are either in the army, prisoners, or dead. Some say: "I have such a one sick at my house; who will wait on them when I am gone?" Others say: "what are we to do; we have no houses to go to, and no means to buy, build, or rent any; no parents, relatives or friends to go to." Another says: "I will try and take this or that article of property; but such and such things I must leave behind, though I need them much." We reply to them: "Gen. Sherman will carry your property to Rough and Ready, and then Gen. Hood will take it thence on;" and they will reply to that: "But I want to leave the railroad at such a place, and cannot get conveyance from thence on."

We only refer to a few facts to illustrate, in part, how this measure will operate in practice. As you advanced, the people north of us fell back, and before your arrival here a

large portion of the people here had retired south; so that
the country south of this is already crowded, and without
sufficient houses to accommodate the people, and we are
informed that many are now staying in churches and other
outbuildings. This being so, how is it possible for the people
still here (mostly women and children) to find shelter, and
how can they live through the winter in the woods; no shelter or subsistence; in the midst of strangers who know them
not, and without the power to assist them much if they were
willing to do so?

This is but a feeble picture of the consequences of this
measure. You know the woe, the horror, and the suffering
cannot be described by words. Imagination can only conceive to it, and we ask you to take these things into consideration. We know your mind and time are continually
occupied with the duties of your command, which almost
deters us from asking your attention to the matter, but
thought it might be that you had not considered the subject
in all of its awful consequences, and that, on reflection, you,
we hope, would not make this people an exception to all
mankind, for we know of no such instance ever having occurred—surely not in the United States. And what has this
helpless people done that they should be driven from their
homes, to wander as strangers, outcasts and exiles, and to
subsist on charity?

We do not know as yet the number of people still here.
Of those who are here a respectable number, if allowed to
remain at home, could subsist for several months without assistance; and a respectable number for a much
longer time, and who might not need assistance at any
time.

In conclusion, we most earnestly and solemnly petition
you to reconsider this order, or modify it, and suffer this un-

fortunate people to remain at home and enjoy what little means they have.

Respectfully submitted,

JAMES M. CALHOUN, Mayor

E. E. RAWSON, S. C. WELLS, Councilmen.

GEN. SHERMAN'S REPLY

HDQRS. MILITARY DIVISION OF THE MISSISSIPPI, IN THE FIELD,
ATLANTA, GA., Sept. 12, 1864.

JAMES M. CALHOUN, *Mayor*, E. E. RAWSON and S. C. WELLS, *representing City Council of Atlanta.*

Gentlemen: I have your letter of the 11th, in the nature of a petition to revoke my orders removing all the inhabitants from Atlanta. I have read it carefully, and give full credit to your statements of the distress that will be occasioned by it, and yet shall not revoke my order, simply because my orders are not designed to meet the humanities of the case, but to prepare for the future struggles, in which millions, yea hundreds of millions of good people outside of Atlanta have a deep interest. We must have *Peace*, not only at Atlanta, but in all America. To secure this, we must stop the war that now desolates our once happy and favored country. To stop war we must defeat the Rebel armies that are arrayed against the laws and Constitution which all must respect and obey. To defeat these armies we must prepare the way to reach them in their recesses, provided with the arms and instruments which enable us to accomplish our purpose.

Now, I know the vindictive nature of our enemy, and that we may have many years of military operations from this quarter, and therefore deem it wise and prudent to prepare in time. The use of Atlanta for warlike purposes is inconsistent with its character as a home for families. There will

be no manufactures, commerce or agriculture here for the
maintenance of families, and sooner or later want will com-
pel the inhabitants to go. Why not *go now*, when all the
arrangements are completed for the transfer, instead of
waiting till the plunging shot of contending armies will renew the scene of the past month? Of course I do not appre-
hend any such thing at this moment, but you do not suppose
that this army will be here till the war is over. I cannot discuss this subject with you fairly, because I cannot impart
to you what I propose to do, but I assert that my military
plans make it necessary for the inhabitants to go away, and
I can only renew my offer of services to make their exodus
in any direction as easy and comfortable as possible. You
cannot qualify war in harsher terms than I will.

War is cruelty, and you cannot refine it; and those who
brought war on the country deserve all the curses and male-
dictions a people can pour out. I know I had no hand in
making this war, and I know I will make more sacrifices
to-day than any of you to secure peace. But you cannot have
peace and a division of our country. If the United States
submits to a division now, it will not stop, but will go on
until we reap the fate of Mexico, which is eternal war. The
United States does and must assert its authority wherever
it has power; if it relaxes one bit to pressure it is gone, and
I know that such is not the national feeling. This feeling
assumes various shapes, but always comes back to that of
Union. Once admit the Union, once more acknowledge the
authority of the National Government, and instead of devot-
ing your houses and streets and roads to the dread uses of
war, I, and this army, become at once your protectors and
supporters, shielding you from danger, let it come from what
quarters it may. I know that a few individuals cannot resist
a torrent of error and passion such as has swept the South

into rebellion; but you can point out, so that we may know those who desire a Government and those who insist on war and its desolation.

You might as well appeal against the thunderstorm as against these terrible hardships of war. They are inevitable, and the only way the people of Atlanta can hope once more to live in peace and quiet at home is to stop this war which can alone be done by admitting that it began in error and is perpetuated in pride. We don't want your negroes or your horses, or your houses or your land, or anything you have; but we do want and will have a just obedience to the laws of the United States. That we will have, and if it involves the destruction of your improvements, we cannot help it. You have heretofore read public sentiment in your newspapers, that live by falsehood and excitement, and the quicker you seek for truth in other quarters the better for you.

I repeat, then, that, by the original compact of the government, the United States had certain rights in Georgia which have never been relinquished, and never will be; that the South began war by seizing forts, arsenals, mints, customhouses, etc., etc., long before Mr. Lincoln was installed, and before the South had one jot or tittle of provocation. I myself have seen in Missouri, Kentucky, Tennessee, and Mississippi, hundreds and thousands of women and children fleeing from your armies and desperadoes, hungry and with bleeding feet. In Memphis, Vicksburg, and Mississippi we fed thousands upon thousands of the families of rebel soldiers left on our hands, and whom we could not see starve. Now that war comes home to you, you feel very different—you deprecate its horrors, but did not feel them when you sent car-loads of soldiers and ammunition and molded shell and shot to carry war into Kentucky and Tennessee, and

desolate the homes of hundreds and thousands of good people, who only asked to live in peace at their old homes, and
under the government of their inheritance. But these com-
parisons are idle. I want peace, and believe it can only be
reached through Union and war, and I will ever conduct
war purely with a view to perfect and early success.

But, my dear sirs, when that peace does come, you may
call on me for anything. Then will I share with you the last
cracker, and watch with you to shield your homes and families against danger from every quarter. Now, you must go,
and take with you the old and feeble; feed and nurse them,
and build for them in more quiet places proper habitations
to shield them against the weather, until the mad passions
of men cool down, and allow the Union and peace once more
to settle on your old homes at Atlanta.

Yours, in haste,

W. T. SHERMAN, Maj.-Gen.

Sheridan at Winchester

B Y THE FALL of 1864 the generals who the North, in 1861, had expected to be the heroes of the war were gone from the scene. In their stead there had risen a new breed of generals, a new breed of heroes. Schooled in the war itself, Grant, Sherman, Phil Sheridan, George Thomas asked no quarter and gave none. They knew war was rough and cruel and were willing to accept it on its own terms.

The next selection describes Sheridan's victory over Confederate General Jubal A. Early in September, 1864. This was the second Battle of Winchester, "Stonewall" Jackson having bested General Banks there in 1862, and the town had changed hands a number of times during the course of the war. After his win over Early, Sheridan proceeded systematically to destroy the supplies and the potential for supplies in the Valley of Virginia. He defeated Early a second time a month later at Cedar Creek in the battle made famous by T. Buchanan Read's poem "Sheridan's Ride."

This description of the September battle is by John William DeForest, a veteran of the campaigns of the

300

Army of the Gulf, who was here in his first fighting in Virginia. DeForest later became known as the author of the first truly realistic Civil War novel, *Miss Ravenel's Conversion from Secession to Loyalty.*

SHERIDAN'S BATTLE OF WINCHESTER.

On the morning of the 19th of September, 1864, I was marching at the head of my company along the narrow and wooded gorge through which the Berryville and Winchester pike winds between the Opequan Creek and the town of Winchester. My regiment belonged to the Second Brigade of the First Division of the Nineteenth Army Corps, and formed a fraction of the Army of Major-General Philip Sheridan, which, at two o'clock that morning, had quitted its intrenched position near Berryville.

For a month Sheridan had been watching his opportunity. He had advanced to Front Royal, and retreated to Halltown; he had manœuvred in face of a superior enemy with curious and happy dexterity; he had guarded himself, where it was necessary to make a stand, with miles of field-fortifications; he had parried Early's threatened second raid upon Washington and Pennsylvania; and now, when his antagonist was weakened by the departure of Kershaw's division, he promptly resumed the offensive.

The army at this moment was engaged in the perilous movement of filing through a narrow gorge and deploying in face of a strongly-posted and veteran enemy. The road was crowded with artillery, ammunition-wagons, and ambulances, all hurrying forward. On each side of it a line of infantry in column of march stumbled over the rocky, guttered ground, and struggled through the underbrush. The multitudes of men who belong to an army, yet who do not fight—the cooks, the musicians, the hospital attendants, the quarter-masters' and commissaries' people, the sick, and the skulkers—sat on every rock and under every bush, watching us pass. Here, too, were jammed the troopers of the cavalry advance, who, for the present, had finished their fighting, having cleared the passage of the Opequan Creek, and opened the way thus far for the infantry and artillery. Presently we met litters loaded with pale sufferers, and passed a hospital-tent, inside of which I saw surgeons surrounding a table, and amputated limbs and pools of blood underneath it. The stern and sad business of the day had evidently begun in front, although the sound of it was not yet audible to us, excepting an occasional boom of cannon, deadened to a dull *pum pum* by the woods and the distance.

The battle of Winchester was fought on this plan: A narrow ravine, winding among hills so steep and thickly wooded as to be impassable for any troops but light infantry, debouches into an irregular, undulating valley, faced on the south by an amphitheatre of stony heights, laid, with regard to each other, like detached fortifications. The object of Sheridan was to pass through this ravine, deploy in the valley, amuse the enemy's right, fight his centre vigorously, turn and force his left. The object of Early was to allow us to deploy up to a certain extent; then to beat in our attacking columns and throw them back in confusion on our line of advance; lastly, to ruin us by pushing his strong left through our right, and reaching the mouth of the gorge so as to cut off our retreat. To effect this final purpose his army was not drawn up at right angles to the pike, but diagonally to it, so as to bring his left nearer to our vital debouching point. And this fatal stroke he attempted early in the day, with a strong column, pushed with remarkable vigor, and for a time with terrible promise of success.

At about ten o'clock the head of the Sixth Corps emerged from the ravine, took ground rapidly to the left, and advanced in two lines, the first of which presently carried a rifle-pit and wood that formed the outwork of the enemy's right. This right being refused, or held aloof, our extreme left had throughout the day, so far as I could learn, no very serious fighting. The opening struggle of supreme importance came in the centre, where it was necessary, firstly, to gain ground enough to bring up our second line: and, secondly, to hold the approaches to the ravine at no matter what cost of slaughter. I beg the reader to remark that if this was not done our striking right could not be deployed, and our retreat could not be secured; that if this was not done there could be no victory, and there must be—if the enemy pushed us with energy—calamitous defeat. Upon the Nineteenth Corps and upon Ricketts' Division of the Sixth Corps devolved this bloody task. They were to sustain the principal burden of the battle during the long hours which would be necessary to let the Eighth Corps sweep around on its more enviable and brilliant mission of turning the hostile position. How the Nineteenth Corps performed its portion of the task is shown by its list of killed and wounded. Swept by musketry and artillery from the front, enfiladed by artillery from the right, pressed violently by the one grand column of attack which Early massed to decide the battle, it bled, but it stood, and, after hours of suffering, advanced.

Closely following the Sixth Corps—lapping its rear, indeed—Grover's Division emerged from the defile at a little before eleven o'clock, and forming in two lines, each consisting of two brigades, moved promptly forward in superb order.

Steep hills and a thick wood, impracticable for artillery until engineered, rendered it necessary for the infantry to open the contest without the support of cannon. In face of a vigorous shelling the column swept over the hills, struggled through the wood, and emerged upon a broad stretch of rolling fields, on the other side of which lay the rebel force, supported by another wood and by a ledge of rocks, which answered the purpose of a fortification, with the semicircular heights of Winchester in the rear, as a final rallying base. As the lines of advance from the gorge were divergent, opening outward like the blades of a fan, General Emory found it necessary, in order to keep up a connection with the Sixth Corps, to hurry Molineux's brigade from the rear to the front. This was done at a double-quick, in face of the hostile musketry, without checking the general advance. And now the division quickened its pace into a charge of unusual and unintended impetuosity, the officers being dragged on by the eagerness of the men, the skirmishers firing as they ran, and the brigades following at a right-shoulder-shift, with deafening yells. Birge's men carried the detached wood with a rush: they were ordered to halt there and lie down, but it was impossible to stop them; they hurried on, pell-mell, and drove the enemy three hundred yards beyond. The rebel General Rhodes [Rodes] was killed while placing a battery in position. Three colonels taken by Sharpe's Brigade were sent back to Emory as prisoners. Early's first line in the centre was every where thrown back in confusion.

But an advance as vehement as this is liable to sudden reverse when the attacked party has a strong second line well in hand, as was the case on the present occasion. It is possible even that Grover's opening success changed the plans of Early, and forced him quicker than he had intended into decisive action. At all events he suddenly developed at

this early stage of the battle the greatest mass of troops that
he showed at any period of the day. From the position where
it had been lying sheltered a force estimated at two divisions
of infantry rose up, poured in a stunning volley, followed by
a steady file-fire, and moved forward against the ranks of
Grover and Ricketts, already disordered by their rapid push.
Artillery on a height near Winchester, firing over the heads
of the rebel troops, and other artillery on a height far to our
right, enfilading our line, supported the movement with
shell, grape, and canister. For a while this powerful and well-
timed advance was fearfully successful, and threatened Sheridan with repulse, if not with serious disaster. Ricketts' Division was forced, after a bloody though brief struggle, up
the Berryville and Winchester pike toward the mouth of
that gorge which was so vital to our army. Grover's line
fought for a time at close quarters; for instance his extreme
left regiment, the One Hundred and Fifty-Sixth New York
(Lieutenant-Colonel Neafie), faced a rebel regiment at
thirty yards distance; and around the colors of the latter not
more than forty men remained, the rest having fled or fallen.
But now the One Hundred and Fifty-Sixth, and presently
the entire brigade, was exposed to a fatal fire from the left
flank as well as from the front. Neafie's loss of one hundred
and fifteen men nearly all occurred at this time and within
a few minutes. Colonel Sharpe, commanding the brigade,
and all the regimental commanders except one, were disabled. To attempt to hold the position longer was to be
slaughtered uselessly or to be taken prisoners. The order to
retire was given, and passed rapidly down the division line
from left to right, being obeyed by each brigade in succession. The bloody but victorious advance was changed into
a bloody and ominous retreat.

And here let me beg the reader to conceive the inevitable

circumstances of hopeless, unresisting slaughter which attend the withdrawal of troops from the immediate presence
of a powerful enemy. There is no inspiriting return of blow
for blow; there is no possibility of quelling the hostile fire
by an answering fire; the soldier marches gloomily in his file,
imagining that his foe is ever gaining on him; the ranks are
rapidly thinned, and the organization of the companies shattered; and thus, from both physical and moral causes, the
bravest battalions go to pieces. Rarely does it happen, if
ever, that a force is extricated from this fearful trial without
breaking. Grover's and Ricketts' commands reached the base
from which they had advanced in a state of confusion which
threatened wide-spread disaster. Sixth Corps men and Nineteenth Corps men were crowding together up the line of
the Berryville pike, while to the right and left of it the fields
were dotted with fugitives, great numbers of them wounded,
bursting out of the retiring ranks and rushing toward the
cover of the forest. Some regiments disappeared for a time
as organizations. Early's veterans advanced steadily, with
yells of triumph and a constant roll of murderous musketry,
threatening to sweep away our centre and render our struggle a defeat almost before it had become a battle. It was the
bloodiest, the darkest, the most picturesque, the most dra-
matic, the only desperate moment of the day. General Emory
and General Grover, with every brigade commander and
every staff officer present, rode hither and thither through
the fire, endeavoring by threats, commands, and entreaties
to halt and re-form the panic-stricken stragglers.

"Halt here, men," Emory cried to group after group.
"Here is good cover. Halt and form a line here."

"I am looking for my own regiment," was the usual reply.

"Never mind your own regiments. Never mind if you belong to fifty regiments. Make a regiment here."

Pointing out other groups to this and that officer of his staff, he would say, "My God! look at these men; ride over to them, and bring them up here."

Captain Yorke of the staff seized a regimental flag and bore it forward, shouting, "Men, don't desert your colors," when a spent ball struck him in the throat, paralyzing him for a time and causing him to drop his burden. Of the other staff officers Captain Wilkinson had his horse killed under him. Captain Coley had a bullet pass through his coat collar, and Major Walker received a spent shot in his shoulder.

One instance of coolness and discipline, which contrasted curiously with the general panic, was noticed by Captain Bradbury of the First Maine Battery, now Major and Chief of Artillery on General Emory's staff. Through the midst of the confusion came a captain of infantry, Rigby of the Twenty-fourth Iowa, leading a sergeant and twelve men, all marching as composedly as if returning from drill.

"Captain, you are not going to retreat any further, I hope?" said Bradbury.

"Certainly not," was the reply. "Halt; front. Three cheers, men; hip, hip, hurrah!"

The little band cheered lustily. It was the first note of defiance that broke the desperate monotony of the panic; it gave heart to every one who heard it, and made an end of retreat in that part of the field. In a few minutes the platoon swelled to a battalion composed of men from half a dozen regiments.

"Bradbury," said General Grover, "you must push a section into the gap. We *must* show a front there."

Under a heavy fire of musketry and artillery two pieces galloped into the open, under the charge of Bradbury himself, and, unsupported by infantry, commenced a cannonade which assisted greatly in checking the rebel advance and encouraging our men to rally. A Confederate line which attempted to carry these pieces was repulsed in a somewhat singular manner. General Emory had personally aided in rallying the One Hundred and Thirty-first New York, and had posted it in a narrow grove projecting from the wood which now formed Grover's base of resistance. The charging rebels were allowed to pass this point, and then a volley was poured into their backs. As they staggered under the unexpected shock a fire was opened upon their front by another rallied line, and breaking ranks, they fled pell-mell across the fields to cover.

Thus piece by piece our shattered first line was picked up and reunited. The rebel attack was checked, and a large portion of the lost ground recovered. On the left Neafie, now commanding the Third Brigade, made a second charge nearly up to his original position, while on the right Molineux pushed a line to within two hundred yards of the isolated wood which Birge had carried and lost. And now came into action the famous First Division of the Nineteenth Corps—a division that had never been put to shame on any field of battle, the division that under Weitzel had triumphed at Camp Bisland and Port Hudson, that under Emory had prevented defeat at Sabine Cross Roads and Pleasant Hill. From this moment my story of the battle will become to some extent a record of personal observation.

We of the First Division were already out of the defile, and drawn up in two columns behind Grover, when the failure of his attack became evident. The difficulty was, not that we were not in hand, but that, as we had only two brigades present (the Third having been left at Halltown), we were hardly strong enough to face the enemy's left, which far outreached our right, and at the same time make head against the vehement attack which threatened our centre.

It had been intended that we should remain in reserve until the time came for us to join the Eighth Corps, in the grand turning movement of the day. Now we must fill up gaps, run from one imperiled point to another, and, in short, be used as the urgency of circumstances required.

Lying in a hollow across which the rebel shell screamed harmlessly, I saw our First Brigade disappear over the crest of the hill in our front. Then we of the Second Brigade moved in column to the right, and halted on a lofty slope, where we could discover some parts of the field of battle, and where the earth was occasionally furrowed by the shot of hostile artillery. Far away to the left I saw a part of the Sixth Corps mount an aclivity and charge into a wood on its summit from which the smoke of musketry issued. I distinguished their distant cheer, and rejoiced in their gallantry and triumph. We knew nothing all this while of the disaster which had occurred in our front, and did not doubt that we should have our customary success. Presently we advanced into the wood, on the extreme verge of which Grover's men were rallying and resuming the conflict. We did not see them, but we plainly heard the incessant rattle of their musketry, and, not knowing the rolling nature of the ground, wondered that the bullets did not hum more frequently through our ranks. Soon we turned to the right again, and emerged into an opening from which we obtained our first clear view of the fighting. Nearly a quarter of a mile in advance of us we saw our First Brigade in line behind a rail-fence, the men kneeling or lying down and keeping up a violent file-firing. Two hundred yards beyond them was the wood which Early had retaken from Birge, a smoke of rebel musketry now rising from it, although not a rebel was visible. As we looked our men rose up, formed, faced about and came slowly toward us, the officers running hither and thither to check a momentary confusion in the ranks. The report flew along our line that they were ordered back to the fence where we stood, and that we were to relieve them; but while we watched the unaccomplished movement two of our four regiments, the Twelfth Connecticut and Eighth Vermont, were faced to the left and hurried back through the wood which we had just traversed. The last thing that I saw as I re-entered the covert was the One Hundred and Sixteenth New York facing about with a cheer and charging back to the fence. I afterward learned that the whole brigade followed it; that the line was a second time ordered back, and then again resumed its position. Here it was that the One Hundred and Fourteenth New York offered up its glorious sacrifice of one hundred and eighty-eight men and officers, being three-fifths of the number which it took into battle. After the engagement the position of the brigade was distinguishable by a long, straight line of dead and dying, here and there piled one upon another, the prostrate and bloody ranks telling with matchless eloquence how the American soldier can fight.

While the One Hundred and Sixtieth New York and Forty-seventh Pennsylvania remained to support the First Brigade and share its fatal honors my regiment and the Eighth Vermont moved back to the centre. We were apparently wanted in many places at once. Pressing and contradictory orders repeatedly changed our direction and position. It was, "Forward!" and "About face!" "By the right flank!" and "By the left flank!" "Double quick!" and "Halt!" until our heads were half turned by the confusion. At last we came to the outskirt of the wood, and looked out upon Grover's field of battle. No ranks of enemies were visible athwart those undulating fields, but there were long light lines of smoke from musketry and great piles of smoke from batteries, while the rush and crash of shell tore through the forest. Bradbury was putting two of his pieces in position, and we lay down in their rear to support them. General Emory and General Dwight, mounted and surrounded by staff officers, were a little to the front surveying the position. "My God!" remarked the former as he saw men and horses falling around him, "this is a perfect slaughterhouse. It must be held; it is the key of the position. But tell Captain Bradbury to keep his people covered as much as possible."

Here fell one of the best and bravest gentlemen in the service, the only field-officer present with our regiment, Lieutenant-Colonel Peck. He had just given the command, "Officers rectify the alignment," as we were about to move forward, when a shell burst among us, one piece of it shattering his knee and mortally mangling the arteries. A moment afterward the Eighth and Twelfth were ordered to move into the open, wheel to the right, and relieve a portion of Molineux's brigade, which lay about two hundred yards from the isolated wood. At a double quick we went nearly a quarter of a mile over gently-rolling fields, pulling up occasionally from pure lack of breath, and then hurrying on again, until we flung ourselves on the ground among the Fourteenth New Hampshire and One Hundred and Thirty-first New York. As the enemy were firing low we suffered very little in our advance; but we had not been in position five minutes before we felt how coolly and surely Lee's veterans could aim; for, stretched at full length as we all were, and completely concealed by tall grass, the bullets searched out our covert with fatal certainty. A groan here, a shriek of agony there, a dying convulsion, a plunge of some wounded wretch to the rear, showed from instant to instant how rapidly our men were being disabled. We lay on a gentle, very gentle slope, and aimed upward, so that our fire was probably even more fatal than that of our adversaries, an ascending range being more sure of its mark than a descending one. After a quarter of an hour here (what a Frenchman would call a *mauvais quart d'heure*), our commander, Captain Clarke, ordered a volley. With the usual cautionary commands from the officers of "Steady men!" "Wait for the word!" "Aim low!" the regiment rose up, closed its ranks, and poured in a splendid crash of musketry, dropping immediately that it was delivered. For a few minutes our antagonists were silenced. Perhaps we had slaughtered them; perhaps the venomous flight of hissing Miniés had frightened them into taking cover; perhaps they simply saved their powder because they supposed that we were about to charge. But presently the steady file-firing was resumed. On each side the men fired low, fired slowly, fired calmly, knowing full well the hostile position, although able to discover no hostile sign except the light opposing line of musketry smoke. For two or more hours this tranquil, changeless, mortal contest continued. For two or more hours the bullets whizzed through the grass which scarcely concealed us, striking into our prostrate ranks so frequently that every one occasionally searched the branches of the trees in our front to discover the forms of hostile sharp-shooters. It seemed impossible that they could strike so many of us, and yet not see us. Of the seventy men and officers whom our regiment lost during the day, at least sixty must have been hit on this line. But the enemy fired much more rapidly and continuously than we did. The word was repeatedly passed along our ranks to spare the cartridges, for we were a long way from our supports, or from any chance of replenishing ammunition, and it was necessary to save shots enough to repulse the rebels in case they should charge us with the bayonet.

"Fire down to ten cartridges a piece, and then stop," was the order of our commander.

A curious change came over our men during this long trial. At first they were grave and anxious, but this passed away as they became accustomed to the position; at the last they laughed, jested, and recklessly exposed themselves. Corporal Gray, of Company C, dashed to the front, and with his shelter-tent beat out a flame which was kindling in the autumn grass, returning unhurt out of a frightful peril. "Here's one for Corporal Gray!" shouted several men, leaping up and pulling trigger. Then followed, "Here's one for Sheridan!" and "Here's one for Lincoln!" and "Here's one for M'Clellan, who'll pay us off in gold!" and "Here's one for Jeff Davis!" until the grim joke was played out for lack of cartridges.

All this time our dead and wounded lay among us, with the exception of a few of the latter who crawled a little to the rear, and found shelter in a ditch. Among us, too, were the dead and wounded of the regiments which we had relieved; and the ground in front of us was strewn with other sufferers who had fallen there when Birge met his reverse. The position of these last was horrible; the musketry of both sides passed over them in a constant stream; the balls of friend and foe added to their agony, or closed it in death. One of our men, Private Brown, of Company C, was mortally wounded while giving a drink of water to an officer of an Iowa regiment who lay within ten paces of us, pierced by three bullets. We could not carry away these children of suffering, not even our own, until the battle should be over. It was forbidden by orders; it was contrary to the regulations of the United States Army; it would have been simply an act of well-meant folly and cruelty. We could not spare the men who would surely be killed or wounded in the attempt; or who, reaching the shelter of the rear with their dangerous burdens, would not find their way back again.

I have been thus minute in describing this experience of our regiment in close line-fighting, because it was a picture of what passed in every part of the field during the central period of the battle. Along the entire front each side clung to its own positions, too exhausted or too cautious to advance, and too obstinate to recede. The duty of the Sixth and Nineteenth Corps now was to hold the enemy desperately occupied until the Eighth Corps could execute the turning movement with which Sheridan meant to decide the combat.

At three o'clock the hour of defeat for Early struck. To our right, *where* precisely I could not see because of the rolling nature of the ground, but in the direction of the spot where our First Brigade was forming those prostrate and bloody ranks which I have previously mentioned, we heard a mighty battle-yell, which never ceased for ten minutes, telling us that Crook and his men were advancing. To meet this yell there arose from the farthest sweep of the isolated wood, where it rounded away toward the rebel rear, the most terrific, continuous wail of musketry that I ever heard. It was not a volley, nor a succession of volleys, but an uninterrupted explosion without a single break or tremor. As I listened to it I despaired of the success of the attack, for it did not seem to me possible that any troops could endure such a fire. The captain of our right company, who was so placed that he could see the advance, afterward described it to me as magnificent in its steadiness; the division which accomplished it moving across the open fields in a single line without visible supports, the ranks kept well dressed, in spite of the stream of dead and wounded which dropped to the

rear, the pace being the ordinary quick-step, and the men
firing at will, but coolly and rarely.

At this moment our whole army assumed the offensive.
Looking back I saw General Emory's reserves emerging from
the wood in our rear. And now occurred one of those happy
dashes, almost spontaneous in their character, which so frequently aid in deciding a battle. At the first yell of Crook's
charge our men reopened fire violently, exhausting their ammunition in five minutes; and then Colonel Thomas, of the
Eighth Vermont, regardless of unloaded muskets and empty
cartridge-boxes, led on his command at a double quick with
the bayonet. General officers and staff officers, misunder-
standing the orders of General Emory, which were to advance, came up at a gallop, telling us that we were to be
relieved by the One Hundred and Sixtieth New York, warning us to wait for our supports, and shouting, "Halt! Lie
down!" But it was impossible to check the crowd of yelling,
running madmen; a few would hesitate, and stare around at
their advancing comrades, then they would dash on with
renewed speed to make up the lost distance. While the
regiment thus wavered between discipline and impulse, a
mounted officer belonging, as I afterward heard, to Sheridan's staff—a florid, dashing young fellow, in a gayly-em-
broidered blue shirt, with trowsers tucked into his long boots
—galloped in front of us from the direction of the Eighth
Corps, and pointed to the wood with his drawn sabre. It was
the most chivalrous, the most picturesque equestrianism of
battle that I ever saw. It was as fine as a painting of Horace
Vernet or of Wouvermans. As a contrasting picture, let me
introduce an infantry officer whom I noticed at the same
moment, running breathless, twenty feet in advance of the
line, his blanket-roll over his shoulders, and his sword
sheathed, but waving his men forward with a large brier-

wood pipe, for he was smoking when the charge was ordered. From the instant that that American St. George in the embroidered shirt appeared all hope of stopping us vanished. The men sprang out with a yell like wild beasts, and the wood was carried on a full run, while the rebels rushed out of it at the top of their speed, many of them throwing away their guns and accoutrements. As we came in from one side Crook's troops entered from another, the two commands converging, and for a moment mingling together in the tumultuous triumph.

Thus passed the crisis of the battle. Early had used up at least two divisions of infantry in retaking and endeavoring to hold this wood, which was so essential to him; firstly, as covering his centre, and secondly, as being his most favorable base whence to launch an attack against our course of retreat, the Berryville and Winchester Pike. The slaughter in and around the grove proved the importance which each party attached to the possession of it. Looking down the gentle slopes over which our troops had advanced, retreated, and again advanced, we saw piles and lines of dead and wounded which could hardly be estimated at less than fifteen hundred men. In the wood lay the slaughtered skirmishers of Birge's brigade, mingled with the dead and severely wounded of the rebels, who also dotted the fields beyond. I noticed that most of our slain here had been stripped of their clothing, probably to cover the backs of Early's ragged soldiers. Colonel Thomas observed one of our officers propped against a tree with a wounded rebel on each side of him.

"Courage, my friend," said he. "We will take care of you soon; but first we want to finish the enemy."

The sufferer waved his hand feebly, and answered in a low voice, "Colonel, you are doing it gloriously."

Thomas started, for he now recognized in this mortally wounded man his old companion in arms, the brave Lieutenant-Colonel Babcock, of the Seventy-fifth New York, formerly of our brigade.

"Don't trouble yourself about me now," said Babcock. "But when you have done your fighting, will you spare me a couple of men to carry me away?"

Thomas promised, and followed his regiment. Colonel Babcock's watch and money had been taken by a rebel officer, probably with the intention of preserving them for him; but he had also been plundered in cruel earnest by the soldiers, who roughly dragged off his boots although one of his thighs was shattered by a musket-ball.

The Eighth Corps now moved against the heights, where Early made his final stand. The Eighth Vermont and One Hundred and Sixtieth New York, in conjunction with Upton's men of the Sixth Corps, followed the troops who had been forced out of the wood, and, flanking them with a heavy enfilading fire, drove them successively from a rail-fence and a stone-wall, where they attempted to rally. Lieutenant-Colonel Van Petten, of the One Hundred and Sixtieth, already had a bullet through the thigh, but refused to give up the command of his regiment until the fighting was over. As he led off at the head of it General Emory said to him, "Colonel, you are going into a hot fire; you had better dismount."

"Can't walk, Sir," replied Van Petten, pointing to his bandaged thigh, and rode onward.

Our regiment halted in the grove, and waited for ammunition. Twice it wheeled into column of companies to give passage to Birge's and Molineux's brigades of Grover's Division, which were now pushed up as supports to the general advance. I could not see that these commands bore any trace of the repulse of the morning; the ranks moved steadily, and the air of the men was composed and resolute. It must be observed, however, that up to this time I did not know that our line had suffered any disaster. They had just passed when a mounted officer, followed by a single orderly, galloped up to us. As he reined in his horse a rebel shell, one of the many which were now tearing through the wood, burst within a few feet of him, actually seeming to crown his head with its deadly halo of smoke and humming fragments.

"That's all right, boys," he said, with careless laugh. "No matter; we can lick them."

The men laughed; then a whisper ran along the ranks that it was Sheridan; then they burst into a spontaneous cheer.

"What regiment is this?" he asked, and dashed off toward the firing.

Presently we advanced, in support of a battery of artillery, over high ground lately occupied by Early's centre. Our close fighting was over, and for the rest of the day we were spectators. At the distance of half a mile from us, too far away to distinguish the heroism of individuals, but near enough to observe all the grand movements and results, the last scene of the victorious drama was acted out. Crook's column carried the heights and the fort which crowned them. We could see the long, dark lines moving up the stony slopes; we could see and hear the smoke and clatter of musketry on the deadly summit; then we could hear our comrades' cheer of victory. Early's battle was rapidly reduced to a simple struggle to save himself from utter rout. His mounted force had been beaten as usual by Averell, Torbert, and Custer. His infantry, dreadfully weakened by killed, wounded, prisoners, and stragglers, was retreating in confusion, presenting no reliable line of resistance. And now, just in the nick of time, our cavalry formed its connection with the extreme right of our infantry, so that Sheridan was able to use it

promptly to complete his victory. I saw a brigade of these
gallant troopers gallop in a long, straight line along the crest
of the hill, rush upon Early's rear, and break up and sweep
away his disorganized regiments as easily, to all appearance,
as a billow tosses its light burden of sea-weed. Seven hundred prisoners and two guns were the results of this well-
timed and brilliant onslaught. It was, I believe, the most
effective cavalry charge that has been delivered during the
war; and it was certainly one of the most spirit-stirring and
magnificent spectacles conceivable.

The victory was now won, and our infantry quietly bivouacked two miles beyond the field of battle, while the cavalry pushed on picking up materiel and prisoners.

The fruit of the battle, gathered on the spot or during the
pursuit of the next day, were five cannon, fifteen flags, six or
seven thousand small arms, and three thousand prisoners,
besides two thousand wounded who were left on the field, or
in the town of Winchester, or on the road between there and
Strasburg. The entire loss of the enemy in killed, wounded,
and prisoners, and in stragglers who did not again rejoin him,
could not have been less than seven thousand men. But the
results of this bloody and successful combat did not stop
here. It thoroughly demoralized Early's remaining troops,
thus rendering possible, indeed rendering easy, the extraordinary victory of Strasburg, which was but the sequel, the
moral consequence, of that of Winchester.

Of the loss of our own army I can not speak with certainty
for lack of official information. But the heaviest slaughter
must have fallen, I think, upon the Nineteenth Corps, which
had nineteen hundred and forty killed and wounded, besides
losing some prisoners, most of whom, however, were recap-
tured.

It was the first battle of our corps in Virginia; and I must say that Lee's veterans somewhat disappointed us. They made desperate fighting, but not more desperate than we had been accustomed to see. They were neither better nor worse soldiers than the Texans, Louisianians, Arkansans, and Alabamians, whom we had met, and had beaten too, in the Department of the Gulf.

Victory for Christmas

SHERMAN MOVED SOUTHEAST from Atlanta in mid-November. Hood had marched north in a vain attempt to carry the war to Federal territory. Sherman had no serious opposition to impede his course to Savannah. In Tennessee Hood ran headlong into the well-trained Union veterans under General George H. Thomas. Sherman took Savannah almost without incident. Thomas repulsed Hood in decisive battles at Nashville and Franklin, Tennessee.

Sherman was in Savannah, in contact with Federal navy units, and poised to attack Charleston or to aim a march north toward Virginia. His old foe, the Confederate Army of Tennessee, had been wrecked by Thomas and could no longer give him trouble. With only General Joe Wheeler to harass him on a march or General William J. Hardee to oppose him with an outnumbered and worn-out army at Charleston there was every reason for this to be a happy Christmas in the loyal states.

The "Official Bulletin" released by the War Department and published in the *Army and Navy Official Gazette* reflected the heightened pace with which the war entered its final stages. A high spot in them is General Sherman's Christmas message to President Lincoln.

SAVANNAH, GA., *December* 22, 1864,
Via FORTRESS MONROE, *Dec.* 25.

To His Excellency President LINCOLN:

I beg to present you, as a Christmas gift, the city of Savannah, with one hundred and fifty heavy guns and plenty of ammunition; and also about twenty-five thousand (25,000) bales of cotton.　　　W. T. SHERMAN,
Major General.

1865

Peace Conference

BY FEBRUARY, 1865, the Confederates were anxious, even desperate, for peace. Confederate Vice-President Alexander H. Stephens, John A. Campbell, and Robert M. T. Hunter met with President Lincoln and Secretary of State Seward in an informal conference at Hampton Roads on February 3 to discuss possible peace terms.

President Lincoln would not accede to any conditions on less than the terms he had already enunciated: "no cessation or suspension of hostilities, except on the basis of the disbandment of the insurgent forces, and the restoration of the national authority throughout all the States in the Union" and no departure "from the positions he had heretofore assumed in the proclamation of emancipation and other documents."

The conference produced no immediate results, but the end grew nearer.

Here is Secretary Seward's letter to Charles Francis Adams in London, written to keep the ambassador apprised of developments at home.

DEPARTMENT OF STATE,
Washington, February, 7, 1865.

SIR: It is a truism, that in times of peace there are always instigators of war. So soon as a war begins there are citizens who impatiently demand negotiations for peace. The advocates of war, after an agitation, longer or shorter, generally gain their fearful end, though the war declared is not unfrequently unnecessary and unwise. So peace agitators in time of war ultimately bring about an abandonment of the conflict, sometimes without securing the advantages which were originally expected from the conflict.

The agitators for war in time of peace, and for peace in time of war, are not necessarily, or perhaps ordinarily, unpatriotic in their purposes or motives. Results alone determine whether they are wise or unwise. The treaty of peace concluded at Guadalupe Hidalgo was secured by an irregular negotiator, under the ban of the government. Some of the efforts which have been made to bring about negotiations with a view to end our civil war are known to the whole world, because they have employed foreign as well as domestic agents. Others, with whom you have had to deal confidentially, are known to yourself, although they have not publicly transpired. Other efforts have occurred here which are known only to the persons actually moving in them and to this government. I am now to give, for your information, an account of an affair, of the same general character, which recently received much attention here, and which, doubtless, will excite inquiry abroad.

A few days ago Francis P. Blair, esq., of Maryland, obtained from the President a simple leave to pass through our military lines, without definite views known to the government. Mr. Blair visited Richmond, and on his return he showed to the President a letter which Jefferson Davis had written to Mr. Blair, in which Davis wrote that Mr. Blair was at liberty to say to President Lincoln that Davis was now, as he always had been, willing to send commissioners, if assured they would be received, or to receive any that should be sent; that he was not disposed to find obstacles in forms. He would send commissioners to confer with the President, with a view to a restoration of peace between the two countries, if he could be assured they would be received. The President thereupon, on the 18th of January, addressed a note to Mr. Blair, in which the President, after acknowledging that he had read the note of Mr. Davis, said that he was, is, and always should be willing to receive any agents that Mr. Davis or any other influential person now actually resisting the authority of the government might send to confer informally with the President, with a view to the restoration of peace to the people of our one common country. Mr. Blair visited Richmond with this letter, and then again came back to Washington. On the 29th instant we were advised from the camp of Lieutenant General Grant that Alexander H. Stephens, R. M. T. Hunter, and John A. Campbell were applying for leave to pass through the lines to Washington, as peace commissioners, to confer with the President. They were permitted by the Lieutenant General to come to his headquarters, to await there the decision of the President. Major Eckert was sent down to meet the party from Richmond at General Grant's headquarters. The major was directed to deliver to them a copy of the President's letter to Mr. Blair, with a note to be addressed to them, and signed by the major, in which they were directly informed that if they should be allowed to pass our lines they would be understood as coming for an informal conference, upon the basis of the aforenamed letter of the 18th of January to Mr. Blair. If they should express their assent to this condition in writing, then Major Eckert was directed to give them safe conduct to Fortress Monroe, where a person coming from the President would meet them. It being thought probable, from a report of their conversation with Lieutenant General Grant, that the Richmond party would, in the manner prescribed, accept the condition mentioned, the Secretary of State was charged by the President with the duty of representing this government in the expected informal conference. The Secretary arrived at Fortress Monroe in the night of the first day of February. Major Eckert met him on the morning of the second of February with the information that the persons who had come from Richmond had not accepted, in writing, the condition upon which he was allowed to give them conduct to Fortress Monroe. The major had given the same information by telegraph to the President, at Washington. On receiving this information, the President prepared a telegram directing the Secretary to return to Washington. The Secretary was preparing, at the same moment, to so return, without waiting for instructions from the President; but at this juncture Lieutenant General Grant telegraphed to the Secretary of War, as well as to the Secretary of State, that the party from Richmond had reconsidered and accepted the conditions tendered them through Major Eckert, and General Grant urgently advised the President to confer in person with the Richmond party. Under these circumstances, the Secretary, by the President's direction, remained at Fortress Monroe, and the President joined him there on the night of the 2d of February. The Richmond party was brought down the James river in a United States steam transport during the day, and the transport was anchored in Hampton Roads.

On the morning of the 3d the President, attended by the Secretary, received Messrs. Stephens, Hunter, and Campbell on board the United States steam transport River Queen, in Hampton Roads. The conference was altogether informal. There was no attendance of secretaries, clerks, or other witnesses. Nothing was written or read. The conversation, although earnest and free, was calm, and courteous, and kind on both sides. The Richmond party approached the discussion rather indirectly, and at no time did they either make categorical demands, or tender formal stipulations, or absolute refusals. Nevertheless, during the conference, which lasted four hours, the several points at issue between the government and the insurgents were distinctly raised, and discussed fully, intelligently, and in an amicable spirit. What the insurgent party seemed chiefly to favor was a postponement of the question of separation, upon which the war is waged, and a mutual direction of efforts of the government, as well as those of the insurgents, to some extrinsic policy or scheme for a season, during which passions might be expected to subside, and the armies be reduced, and trade and intercourse between the people of both sections resumed. It was suggested by them that through such postponement we might now have immediate peace, with some not very certain prospect of an ultimate satisfactory adjustment of political relations between this government and the States, section, or people now engaged in conflict with it.

This suggestion, though deliberately considered, was nevertheless regarded by the President as one of armistice or truce, and he announced that we can agree to no cessation or suspension of hostilities, except on the basis of the disbandment of the insurgent forces, and the restoration of the national authority throughout all the States in the Union. Collaterally, and in subordination to the proposition which was thus announced, the anti-slavery policy of the United States was reviewed in all its bearings, and the President announced that he must not be expected to depart from the positions he had heretofore assumed in his proclamation of emancipation and other documents, as these positions were reiterated in his last annual message. It was further declared by the President that the complete restoration of the national authority everywhere was an indispensable condition of any assent on our part to whatever form of peace might be proposed. The President assured the other party that, while he must adhere to these positions, he would be prepared, so far as power is lodged with the Executive, to exercise liberality. His power, however, is limited by the Constitution; and when peace should be made, Congress must necessarily act in regard to appropriations of money and to the admission of representatives from the insurrectionary States. The Richmond party were then informed that Congress had, on the 31st ultimo, adopted by a constitutional majority a joint resolution submitting to the several States the proposition to abolish slavery throughout the Union, and that there is every reason to expect that it will be soon accepted by three-fourths of the States, so as to become a part of the national organic law.

The conference came to an end by mutual acquiescence, without producing an agreement of views upon the several matters discussed, or any of them. Nevertheless, it is perhaps of some importance that we have been able to submit our opinions and views directly to prominent insurgents, and to hear them in answer in a courteous and not unfriendly manner.

I am, sir, your obedient servant,

WILLIAM H. SEWARD

The Second Inaugural

ABRAHAM LINCOLN'S ADDRESS at his second inauguration
as President ranks with his address at Gettysburg as
an eloquent document. The President himself wrote of
it, in a letter to Thurlow Weed, March 15: "Every one
likes a compliment. Thank you for yours on my little
notification speech, and on the recent Inaugural Address.
I expect the latter to wear as well as—perhaps better
than—anything I have produced; but I believe it is not
immediately popular. Men are not flattered by being
shown that there has been a difference of purpose between the Almighty and them. To deny it, however, in
this case, is to deny that there is a God governing the
world. It is a truth which I thought needed to be told,
and, as whatever of humiliation there is in it, falls most
directly on myself, I thought others might afford for me
to tell it."

INAUGURAL ADDRESS.
MARCH 4, 1865.

FELLOW-COUNTRYMEN: At this second appearing to take the oath of the presidential office, there is less occasion for an extended address than there was at the first. Then, a statement, somewhat in detail, of a course to be pursued, seemed fitting and proper. Now, at the expiration of four years, during which public declarations have been constantly called forth on every point and phase of the great contest which still absorbs the attention and engrosses the energies of the nation, little that is new could be presented. The progress of our arms, upon which all else chiefly depends, is as well known to the public as to myself; and it is, I trust, reasonably satisfactory and encouraging to all. With high hope for the future, no prediction in regard to it is ventured.

On the occasion corresponding to this four years ago, all thoughts were anxiously directed to an impending civil war. All dreaded it—all sought to avert it. While the inaugural address was being delivered from this place, devoted altogether to *saving* the Union without war, insurgent agents were in the city seeking to *destroy* it without war—seeking to dissolve the Union, and divide effects, by negotiation. Both parties deprecated war; but one of them would *make* war rather than let the nation survive; and the other would *accept* war rather than let it perish. And the war came.

One-eighth of the whole population were colored slaves, not distributed generally over the Union, but localized in the southern part of it. These slaves constituted a peculiar and powerful interest. All knew that this interest was, somehow, the cause of the war. To strengthen, perpetuate and extend this interest was the object for which the insurgents would rend the Union, even by war; while the government claimed no right to do more than to restrict the territorial enlargement of it. Neither party expected for the war the magnitude or the duration which it has already attained. Neither anticipated that the *cause* of the conflict might cease with, or even before, the conflict itself should cease. Each looked for an easier triumph, and a result less fundamental and astounding. Both read the same Bible, and pray to the same God; and each invokes His aid against the other. It may seem strange that any men should dare to ask a just God's assistance in wringing their bread from the sweat of other men's faces; but let us judge not, that we be not judged. The prayers of both could not be answered—that of neither has been answered fully. The Almighty has His own purposes. "Woe unto the world because of offences! for it must needs be that offences come; but woe to that man by whom the offence cometh." If we shall suppose that American slavery is one of those offences which, in the providence of God, must needs come, but which, having continued through His appointed time, He now wills to remove, and that He gives to both north and south this terrible war, as the woe due to those by whom the offence came, shall we discern therein any departure from those divine attributes which the believers in a living God always ascribe to Him? Fondly do we hope—fervently do we pray—that this mighty scourge of war may speedily pass away. Yet, if God wills that it continue until all the wealth piled by the bondsman's two hundred and fifty years of unrequited toil shall be sunk, and until every drop of blood drawn with the lash shall be paid by another drawn with the sword, as was said three thousand years ago, so still it must be said, "The judgments of the Lord are true and righteous altogether."

With malice toward none; with charity for all; with firmness in the right, as God gives us to see the right, let us strive on to finish the work we are in; to bind up the nation's wounds; to care for him who shall have borne the battle, and for his widow, and his orphan—to do all which may achieve and cherish a just and a lasting peace among ourselves, and with all nations.

All Going Finely

A S SPRING WEATHER made possible the renewal of active
campaigning, the war in Virginia moved swiftly to
a close. Grant's generalship met that severest and truest
of all tests of military ability—victory.

The Confederate lines at Petersburg broke, and Lee's
army retreated to the southwest, hoping to join with
Johnston and the remnants of his Army of Tennessee
somewhere in North Carolina for at least one more desperate offensive. But destiny, hunger, and Grant's army
met together at Appomattox Court House, and the war
in Virginia was over.

These bulletins from the *Army and Navy Official Gazette* illustrate the staccato pace with which event succeeded event in the final days of March and the first
days of April.

No. 162

WAR DEPARTMENT,

WASHINGTON, *April* 1, 1865, 10 a. m.

Major General J. A. DIX, *New York:*

The following telegram, in relation to military operations now going on at the front, was received this morning.

Nothing later has reached this Department.

EDWIN M. STANTON,

Secretary of War.

CITY POINT, VA., *March* 31, 8.30 p. m.

Hon. EDWIN M. STANTON, *Secretary of War:*

At 12.30 p. m., to-day, General Grant telegraphed me as follows:

"There has been much hard fighting this morning. The enemy drove our left from near Dabney's house back well toward the Boydtown plank road.

"We are now about to take the offensive at that point, and I hope will more than recover the lost ground."

Later he telegraphed again, as follows: "Our troops, after being driven back on to the Boydtown plank road, turned and drove the enemy in turn, and took the White Oak road, which we now have. This gives us the ground occupied by the enemy this morning.

"I will send you a rebel flag captured by our troops in driving the enemy back. There have been four flags captured to-day."

Judging by the two points from which General Grant telegraphs, I infer that he moved his headquarters about one mile since he sent the first of the two dispatches.

A. LINCOLN.

No. 163.

WAR DEPARTMENT,
WASHINGTON CITY, *April* 1, 1865, 11 p. m.
Major General DIX, *New York:*

The following dispatch from the President, received to-night, shows that the desperate struggle between our forces and the enemy continues undecided, although the advantage appears to be on our side.

EDWIN M. STANTON,
Secretary of War.

CITY POINT, VA., *April* 1, 1865, 5.30 p. m.
Hon. EDWIN M. STANTON, *Secretary of War:*

Dispatch just received showing that Sheridan, aided by Warren, had at 2 p. m. pushed the enemy back so as to retake the five forks and bring his own headquarters up to J. Boisseau's. The five forks were barricaded by the enemy, and carried by Diven's division of cavalry. This part of the enemy seem to now be trying to work along the White Oak road to join the main force in front of Grant, while Sheridan and Warren are pressing them as closely as possible.

A. LINCOLN.

No. 164.

WAR DEPARTMENT, *April* 2, 6 a. m.
Major General J. A. DIX, *New York:*

A dispatch just received from General Grant's Adjutant General at City Point announces the triumphant success of our arms after three days of hard fighting, during which the forces on both sides exhibited unsurpassed valor.

EDWIN M. STANTON,
Secretary of War.

CITY POINT, VA., *April 2, 1865, 5.30 a. m.*

A dispatch from General Grant states that General Sheridan, commanding cavalry and infantry, has carried everything before him. He captured three brigades of infantry, a wagon train, and several batteries of artillery. The prisoners captured will amount to several thousand.

Respectfully,

T. S. BOWERS, A. A. G.

No. 165.

WAR DEPARTMENT,

WASHINGTON, *April 2, 1865, 11 a. m.*

Major General DIX, *New York:*

The following telegram from the President, dated at City Point, at half past 8 o'clock this morning, gives the latest intelligence from the front, where a furious battle was raging, with continued success to the Union arms.

EDWIN M. STANTON,

Secretary of War.

CITY POINT, V., *April 2, 8.30 a. m.*

Hon. EDWIN M. STANTON, *Secretary of War:*

Last night General Grant telegraphed that General Sheridan, with his cavalry and the Fifth corps, had captured three brigades of infantry, a train of wagons, and several batteries, prisoners amounting to several thousands. This morning General Grant, having ordered an attack along the whole line, telegraphs as follows:

"Both Wright and Parke got through the enemy's lines.

"The battle now rages furiously. General Sheridan with his cavalry, the Fifth corps, and Miles's division of the Second corps, which was sent to him since 1 o'clock this morning, is now sweeping down from the west. All now looks highly favorable. General Ord is engaged, but I have not yet heard the result in his front."

A. LINCOLN.

No. 166.

WAR DEPARTMENT,
April 2, 1865, 12.30 p. m.

Major General DIX, *New York:*

The President, in the subjoined telegram, gives the latest news from the front.

EDWIN M. STANTON,
Secretary of War.

CITY POINT, VA., *April 2, 1865, 11 a. m.*

Hon. EDWIN M. STANTON, *Secretary of War:*

Dispatches frequently coming in. All going finely. Parke, Wright, and Ord, extending from the Appomattox to Hatcher's run, have all broken through the enemy's intrenched lines, taking some forts, guns, and prisoners.

Sheridan, with his own cavalry, Fifth corps, and part of the Second, is coming in from the west on the enemy's flank, and Wright is already tearing up the Southside railroad.

A. LINCOLN.

No. 167.

WASHINGTON, D. C., *April 2, 11 p. m.*

Major General John A. DIX, *New York:*

The following telegrams report the condition of affairs at half past 4 o'clock this afternoon.

EDWIN M. STANTON,
Secretary of War.

City Point, Va., *April* 2, 1865, 2 p. m.

Hon. Edwin M. Stanton, *Secretary of War:*

At 10.45 a. m. General Grant telegraphs as follows:

"Everything has been carried from the left of the Ninth corps. The Sixth corps alone captured more than 3,000 prisoners. The Second and Twenty-Fourth corps both captured forts, guns, and prisoners from the enemy, but I cannot tell the numbers. We are now closing around the works of the line immediately enveloping Petersburg. All looks remarkably well. I have not yet heard from Sheridan."

His headquarters have been moved up to T. Banks's house, near the Boydtown road, about three miles southwest of Petersburg.

A. LINCOLN.

City Point, Va., *April* 2, 1865, 8.30 p. m.

Hon. Edwin M. Stanton, *Secretary of War:*

At 4.30 p. m. to-day General Grant telegraphs as follows:

"We are now up and have a continuous line of troops, and in a few hours will be intrenched from the Appomattox, below Petersburg, to the river above.

"The whole captures since the army started out will not amount to less than 12,000 men and probably 50 pieces of artillery. I do not know the number of men and guns accurately, however. A portion of Foster's division, Twenty-Fourth corps, made a most gallant charge this afternoon and captured a very important fort from the enemy with its entire garrison."

All seems well with us, and everything quiet just now.

A. LINCOLN.

No. 168.

WAR DEPARTMENT,
WASHINGTON CITY, *April* 3, 1863, 10 a. m.
Major General DIX, *New York:*

The following telegram from the President, announcing the evacuation of Petersburg and probably of Richmond, has just been received by this Department.

EDWIN M. STANTON,
Secretary of War.

This morning General Grant reports Petersburg evacuated, and he is confident Richmond also is. He is pushing forward to cut off, if possible, the retreating army.

A. LINCOLN.

No. 169.

WAR DEPARTMENT,
WASHINGTON CITY, *April* 3, 1865, 10.45 a. m.
Major General DIX, *New York:*

It appears from a dispatch of General Weitzel, just received by this Department, that our forces under his command are in Richmond, having taken it at 8.15 this morning.

EDWIN M. STANTON,
Secretary of War.

Raising the Flag at Sumter

EVEN BEFORE THE SURRENDER at Appomattox plans were under way to celebrate on the fourth anniversary of the fall of Fort Sumter the long-term reversal of the immediate outcome of that battle.

The same flag that Major Robert Anderson had ceremoniously lowered on April 14, 1861, would be as ceremoniously raised by that same officer, now a general but broken in health ever since his ordeal of four years before. Formalities would be kept to a minimum in deference to General Anderson's health, but there would be an accomplished speaker to commemorate the occasion, the Rev. Henry Ward Beecher, most famous and most sought-after of the orators of the day. President Lincoln was invited to attend, but the press of duties in Washington would not permit his presence. Instead he would choose the evening of that same day to try to relax from the cares of the Presidency by attending a performance at Ford's Theater.

GENERAL ORDERS,⎫
    No. 50.   ⎭

WAR DEPARTMENT,
ADJUTANT GENERAL'S OFFICE,
Washington, March 27, 1865.

ORDERED—

First. That at the hour of noon, on the 14th day of April, 1865, Brevet Major General ANDERSON will raise and plant upon the ruins of Fort Sumter, in Charleston harbor, the same United States flag which floated over the battlements of that Fort during the rebel assault, and which was lowered and saluted by him and the small force of his command when the works were evacuated on the 14th day of April, 1861.

Second. That the flag, when raised, be saluted by one hundred guns from Fort Sumter, and by a National salute from every fort and rebel battery that fired upon Fort Sumter.

Third. That suitable ceremonies be had upon the occasion, under the direction of Major General WILLIAM T. SHERMAN, whose military operations compelled the rebels to evacuate Charleston, or, in his absence, under the charge of Major General Q. A. GILLMORE, commanding the Department. Among the ceremonies will be the delivery of a public address by the Reverend HENRY WARD BEECHER.

Fourth. That the naval forces at Charleston, and their Commander on that station, be invited to participate in the ceremonies of the occasion.

BY ORDER OF THE PRESIDENT OF THE UNITED STATES:

EDWIN M. STANTON,
Secretary of War.

OFFICIAL:

Assistant Adjutant General.

Rev. Henry Ward Beecher's

FORT SUMTER ORATION.

April 14th, 1865.

On this solemn and joyful day we again lift to the breeze our father's flag, now again the banner of the United States, with the fervent prayer that God would crown it with honor, protect it from treason, and send it down to our children with all the blessings of civilization, liberty, and religion. Terrible in battle, may it be beneficent in peace. Happily no bird or beast of prey has been inscribed upon it. The stars that redeem the night from darkness, and the beams of red light that beautify the morning, have been united upon its folds. As long as the sun endures, or the stars, may it wave over a nation neither enslaved nor enslaving.

Once, and but once, has treason dishonored it. In that insane hour, when the guiltiest and bloodiest rebellion of time hurled its fires upon this fort, you, sir (turning to General Anderson), and a small heroic band stood within these now crumbled walls, and did gallant and just battle for the honor and defence of the nation's banner. In that cope of fire this glorious flag still peacefully waved to the breeze above your head, unconscious of harm as the stars and skies above it. Once it was shot down; a gallant hand, in whose care this day it has been placed, plucked it from the ground, and reared it again, "cast down but not destroyed." After a vain resistance, with trembling hand and sad heart, you withdrew it from its height, closed its wings, and bore it far away, sternly to sleep amid the tumults of rebellion and the thunder of battle.

The first act of war had begun. The long night of four years had set in. While the giddy traitors whirled in a maze

of exhilaration, dim horrors were already advancing, that
were ere long to fill the land with blood. To-day you are
returned again; we devoutly join with you in thanksgiving
to Almighty God, that He has spared your honored life, and
vouchsafed to you the glory of this day. The heavens over
you are the same; the same shores are here. Morning comes
and evening as they did. All else how changed! What grim
batteries crowd the burdened shores! What scenes have
filled this air and disturbed these waters! These shattered
heaps of shapeless stones are all that is left of Fort Sumter.
Desolation broods in yonder sad city. Solemn retribution
hath avenged our dishonored banner.

You have come back with honor who departed hence four
years ago, leaving the air sultry with fanaticism. The surging
crowds that rolled up their frenzied shouts as the flag came
down are dead, or scattered, or silent, and their habitations
are desolate. Ruin sits in the cradle of treason, rebellion has
perished, but there flies the same flag that was insulted!
With starry eyes it looks all over this bay for that banner
that supplanted it, and sees it not. You, that then for the day
were humbled, are here again to triumph once and forever.
In the storm of that assault this glorious ensign was often
struck, but, memorable fact, not one of its *stars* was torn out
by shot or shell. It was a prophecy. It said, "Not one State
shall be struck from this nation by treason." The fulfilment
is at hand. Lifted to the air, to-day, it proclaims, that after
four years of war, "Not a State is blotted out." Hail to the
flag of our fathers and our flag! Glory to the banner that has
gone through four years, black with tempests of war, to
pilot the nation back to peace without dismemberment! And
glory be to God who, above all hosts and banners, hath ordained victory and shall ordain peace!

Wherefore have we come hither, pilgrims from distant

places? Are we come to exult that Northern hands are stronger than Southern? No! but to rejoice that the hands of those who defend a just and beneficent Government are mightier than the hands that assaulted it. Do we exult over fallen cities? We exult that a nation has not fallen! We sorrow with the sorrowful, we sympathize with the desolate, we look upon the shattered fort and yonder dilapidated city with sad eyes, grieved that men should have committed such treason; but glad that God hath set such a mark upon treason, that all ages shall dread and abhor it. We exult, not for a passion gratified, but for a sentiment victorious; not for temper, but conscience; not, as we devoutly believe, that *our* will is done, but that God's will hath been done. We should be unworthy of that liberty intrusted to our care if, on such a day as this, we sullied our hearts by feelings of aimless vengeance, and equally unworthy if we did not devoutly thank Him who hath said, "Vengeance is mine, I will repay, saith the Lord," that He hath set a mark upon arrogant rebellion ineffaceable while time lasts.

Since this flag went down, on that dark day, who shall tell the mighty woes that have made this land a spectacle to angels and men! The soil has drunk blood and is glutted; millions mourn for millions slain, or, envying the dead, pray for oblivion; towns and villages have been razed; fruitful fields have turned back to wilderness. It came to pass, as the prophet said: *The sun was turned to darkness and the moon to blood.* The course of law was ended. The sword sat chief magistrate in half the nation; industry was paralyzed, morals corrupted; the public weal invaded by rapine and anarchy; whole States were ravaged by avenging armies. The world was amazed. The earth reeled. When the flag sunk here, it was as if political night had come, and all beasts of prey had come forth to devour. That long night is ended, and for this returning day we have come from afar to rejoice and give thanks. No more war! No more accursed secession! No more slavery that spawned them both! Let no man misread the meaning of this unfolding flag. It says, Government hath returned hither; it proclaims, in the name of vindicated Government, peace and protection to loyalty; humiliation and pains to traitors. This is the flag of sovereignty. The nation, not the State, is sovereign! Restored to authority, this flag commands, not supplicates. There may be pardon, but no concession. There may be amnesty and oblivion, but no honeyed compromises. The nation to-day has peace for the peaceful, and war for the turbulent. The only condition of submission is to submit. There is the Constitution, there are the laws, there is the Government. They rise up like mountains of strength that shall not be moved. They are the conditions of peace. One nation under one Government, without slavery, has been ordained and shall stand. There can be peace on no other basis. On this basis reconstruction is easy, and needs neither architect nor engineer. Without this basis no engineer or architect shall ever reconstruct these rebellious States.

We do not want your cities or your fields; we do not envy you your prolific soil, nor heavens full of perpetual summer. Let agriculture revel here; let manufactures make every stream twice musical; build fleets in every port; inspire the arts of peace with genius second only to that of Athens, and we shall be glad in your gladness and rich in your wealth. All that we ask is unswerving loyalty and universal liberty; and that, in the name of this *high sovereignty of the United States of America,* we demand, and that, with the blessing of Almighty God, *we will have!*

We raise our fathers' banner, that it may bring back better blessings than those of old, that it may cast out the devil of discord; that it may restore lawful government and a prosperity purer and more enduring than that which it protected before; that it may win parted friends from their alienation; that it may inspire hope and inaugurate universal liberty; that it may say to the sword, *Return to thy sheath,* and to the plough and sickle, *Go forth;* that it may heal all jealousies, unite all policies, inspire a new national life, compact our strength, purify our principles, ennoble our national ambitions, and make this people great and strong; not for aggression and quarrelsomeness, but for *the peace of the world;* giving to us the glorious prerogative of leading all nations to juster laws, to more humane policies; to sincerer friendship, to rational instituted civil liberty, and to universal Christian brotherhood. Reverently, piously, in hopeful patriotism, we spread this banner on the sky, as of old the bow was planted on the cloud, and with solemn fervor, beseech God to look upon it, and make it the memorial of an everlasting covenant and decree, that never again on this fair land shall a deluge of blood prevail.

Why need any eye turn from this spectacle? Are there not associations which, overleaping the recent past, carry us back to times when, over North and South, this flag was honored alike by all! In all our colonial days we were one; in the long Revolutionary struggle, and in the scores of prosperous years succeeding we were united. When the passage of the Stamp Act, in 1765, aroused the colonies, it was Gadsden, of South Carolina, that cried with prescient enthusiasm: *"We stand on the broad common ground of those natural rights that we all feel and know as men.* There ought to be no New England man, no New Yorker known on this continent, but all of us," said he, "Americans." That *was* the voice of South Carolina, that *shall be* again the voice of South Carolina!

Faint is the echo; but it is coming; we now hear it sighing sadly through the pines, but it shall yet break in thunder upon the shore—no North, no West, no South, but the United States of America! There is scarcely a man born in the South who has lifted his hand against this banner, but had a father who would have died for it. Is memory dead? Is there no historic pride? Has a fatal fury struck blindness or hate into eyes that used to look kindly toward each other, that read the same Bible, that hung over the historic pages of our national glory, that studied the same Constitution?

Let this uplifting bring back all of the past that was good, but leave in darkness all that was bad. The flag was never before so wholly unspotted, so clear of all wrong, so purely and simply the sign of justice and liberty. Did I say that we brought back the same banner that you bore away, noble and heroic sir? It is not the same—it is more and better than it was.

The land is free from slavery since that banner fell. When God would prepare Moses for emancipation, he overthrew his first steps, and drove him for forty years to brood in the wilderness. When our flag came down, four years it lay brooding in darkness; it cried to the Lord, Wherefore am I deposed? Then arose before it a vision of its sin. It had strengthened the strong and forgotten the weak. It proclaimed Liberty, but trod upon slaves. In that seclusion it dedicated itself to liberty. Behold, to-day it fulfils its vows. When it went down, four millions of people had no flag; to-day it rises, and four million people cry out, Behold *our* flag! Hark, they murmur; it is the Gospel that they recite in sacred words: "It is a Gospel to the poor, it heals our broken hearts; it preaches deliverance to captives; it gives sight to the blind; it sets at liberty them that are bruised." Rise up, then, glorious Gospel banner, and roll out these messages of God! Tell the air that not a spot now sullies thy whiteness. Thy red is not the blush of shame, but the flush of joy. Tell the dews that wash thee that thou art pure as they. Say to the night that thy stars lead toward the morning, and to the morning, that a brighter day arises with healing in its wings. And then, oh glowing flag, bid the sun pour light on all thy folds with double brightness, while thou art bearing round and round the world, the solemn joy—a race set free! a nation redeemed!

The mighty hand of Government made strong in war by the favor of the God of battles, spreads wide to-day the Banner of Liberty, that went down in darkness, that arose in light; and there it streams like the sun above it, neither parcelled out nor monopolized, but flooding the air with light for all mankind. Ye scattered and broken, ye wounded and dying, bitten by the fiery serpents of oppression, everywhere, in all the world, look upon this sign lifted up, and live! Ye homeless and houseless slaves, look, and ye are free. At length *you*, too, have put part and lot in this glorious ensign, that broods with impartial love over small and great, over the poor and the strong, the bond and the free.

In this solemn hour let us pray for the quick coming of reconciliation and happiness under this common flag. But we must build again from the foundations in all these now free Southern States. No cheap exhortations to forgetfulness of the past, to restore all things as they were, will do. God does not stretch out His hand as He has for four dreadful years, that men may easily forget the might of His terrible acts. Restore things as they were? What, the alienations and jealousies, the discords and contentions, and the causes of them? No! In that solemn sacrifice on which a nation has offered up for its sins so many precious victims loved and lamented, let our sins and mistakes be consumed utterly and forever. No! Never again shall things be restored as before the war!

It is written in God's decree of events fulfilled, "Old things have passed away." That new earth in which dwelleth righteousness draws near. Things as they were? Who has an omnipotent hand to restore a million dead, slain in battle, or wasted by sickness, or dying of grief, broken-hearted? Who has omniscience to search for the scattered ones? Who shall restore the lost to broken families? Who shall bring back the squandered treasure, the years of industry wasted, and convince you that four years of guilty rebellion and cruel war are no more than dirt upon the hand which a moment's washing removes, and leaves the hand clean as before? Such a war reaches down to the very vitals of society. Emerging from such a prolonged rebellion, he is blind who tells you that the State, by a mere amnesty and benevolence of government, can be put again, by a mere decree, in its old place. It would not be honest—it would not be kind or fraternal for me to pretend that Southern revolution against the Union has not reacted and wrought revolution in the Southern States themselves, and inaugurated a new dispensation. Society here is like a broken loom, and the piece which rebellion put in and was weaving has been cut, and every thread broken. You must put in new warp, and new woof, and weaving anew, as the fabric slowly unwinds, we shall see in it no gorgon figures, no hideous grotesques of the old barbarism, but the figures of liberty,—vines, and golden grains, framing in the heads of justice, love, and liberty. The august convention of 1787 framed the Constitution with this memorable preamble: "We the people of the United States, in order to form a more perfect union and establish justice, insure domestic tranquillity, provide for the common defence, promote the general welfare, and secure the blessings of liberty to ourselves and our posterity, do ordain this Constitution for the United States of America."

Again, in an awful convention of war, the people of the United States, for the very ends just recited, have debated, settled, and ordained certain fundamental truths which must henceforth be accepted and obeyed; nor is any State or any individual wise who shall disregard them. They are to civil affairs what the natural laws are to health—indispensable conditions of peace and happiness. What are the ordinances given by the people speaking out of fire and darkness of war, with authority inspired by that same God who gave the law from Sinai amid thunders of trumpet voices?

1. That these United States shall be one and indivisible.

2. That States have not absolute sovereignty, and have no right to dismember the Republic.

3. That universal liberty is indispensable to Republican Government, and that slavery shall be utterly and forever abolished.

Such are the results of war; these are the best fruits of the war. They are worth all they have cost. They are foundations of peace. They will secure benefits to all nations as well as to ours. Our highest wisdom and duty is to accept the facts as the decrees of God. We are exhorted to forget all that has happened. Yes, the wrath, the conflict, the cruelty, but not those overruling decrees of God which this war has pronounced as solemnly as on Mount Sinai. God says: "Remember—*remember*,"—hear it to-day. Under this sun, under that bright child of the sun, our banner, with the eyes of this nation and of the world upon us, we repeat the syllables of God's providence, and recite the solemn decrees—

No MORE DISUNION!

No MORE SECESSION!

No MORE SLAVERY! . . .

We have shown by all that we have suffered in war how great is our estimate of the importance of the Southern States to this Union, and we will honor that estimate now in peace by still greater exertions for their rebuilding. Will reflecting men not perceive, then, the wisdom of accepting established facts, and with alacrity of enterprise begin to retrieve the past? Slavery cannot come back. It is the interest, therefore, of every man to hasten its end. Do you want more war? Are you not yet weary of contest? Will you gather up the un-exploded fragments of this prodigious magazine of all mischief, and heap them up for continued explosions? Does not the South need peace? And since free labor is inevitable, will you have it in its worst forms or its best? Shall it be ignorant, impertinent, indolent, or shall it be educated, self-respecting, moral, and self-supporting? Will you have men as drudges, or will you have them as citizens? Since they have vindicated the Government and cemented its foundation stones with their blood, may they not offer the tribute of their support to maintain its laws and its policy? It is better for religion, it is better for political integrity, it is better for industry, it is better for *money*, if you will have that ground-motive, that you should educate the black man, and by education make him a citizen. They who refuse education to the black man would turn the South into a vast poorhouse, and labor into a pendulum incessantly vibrating between poverty and indolence.

From this pulpit of broken stone, we speak forth our earnest greeting to all our land. We offer to the President of these United States our solemn congratulations that God has sustained his life and health under the unparalleled burdens and sufferings of four bloody years, and permitted him to behold this auspicious consummation of that national unity for which he has waited with so much patience and fortitude, and for which he has labored with such disinterested wisdom. To the members of the Government associated with him in the administration of perilous affairs in critical times; to the Senators and Representatives of the United States, who have eagerly fashioned the instruments by which the popular will might express and enforce itself, we tender our grateful thanks.

To the officers and men of the army and navy, who have so faithfully, skilfully, and gloriously upheld their country's authority by suffering, labor, and sublime courage, we offer a heart-tribute beyond the compass of words. Upon those true and faithful citizens, men and women, who have borne up with unflinching hope in the darkest hour, and covered the land with their labors of love and charity, we invoke the the divinest blessing of Him whom they have so truly imitated.

But chiefly to Thee, God of our fathers! we render thanksgiving and praise for that wondrous providence that has brought forth from such a harvest of war the seed of so much liberty and peace. We invoke peace upon the North; peace be to the West; peace be upon the South. In the name of God, we lift up our banner, and dedicate it to Peace, Union, and Liberty, now and forevermore. Amen!

Index

Abstract of the Cruise of the U.S. Steam Frigate Wabash . . . 1861–'62 & '63, quoted: 65–72
Acker, William H., 118
Adams, Charles, 205
Adams, Charles Francis, 325
"Address of the Legislative Assembly of Mexico," 75; quoted, 77–82
Address to the People of Maryland by the General Assembly, 27; quoted, 28–29
Alabama (ship), 273–81
Alcott, Louisa May, 185; quoted, 185–99
Aldie, Va., 177
Alexander, Colonel, 59
Alexandria, La., 213
Allen's Farm, Battle of, 144
Anderson, Lieutenant, 93
Anderson, Robert, 5–11, 13, 15–18, 20–23, 342–44
Anderson Station, Ga., 282
Andersonville prison, 282–91
Anthony, Scott J., 86
Appomattox Court House, Va., 335, 342
Appomattox River, 339, 340
Aquia Creek, 177
Arkansas, 263
Arlington Heights, Va., 35
Army and Navy Official Gazette, 321, 335; quoted, 322, 336–41
arrests, arbitrary, 3
Ashby's cavalry, 172
Ashby's Gap, Va., 177
Atchafalaya River, 212
Atlanta, 127, 293–99, 321
Atlanta, Mayor of. *See* Calhoun, James M.
Augur, Christopher C., 213
Augusta (ship), 70
Averell, William W., 318

Babcock, Willoughby, 317
Bahia, Brazil, 274
Baird, Absalom, 255
Baird, Henry Carey, 212

Baker, John, 91, 92
Baltic (ship), 21, 22
Baltimore, 227, 292
Baltimore and Ohio Railroad, 123
Banks, Nathaniel P., 123, 160, 211, 212, 300; quoted, 212–15
Banks, T., 340
"Barbara Frietchie" (poem), 156–58
Barnes, J. S., 68
Bates, John F., 41, 43, 44, 46
Bates County, Mo., 264
Baton Rouge, La., 213
Bay Point, S.C., 66, 68, 69
Bayou Sara, 212, 213
Beach, Ben, 46
Beauregard, P. G. T., 5, 6, 15–18, 20, 22, 112, 114
Beecher, Henry Ward, 342, 343; quoted, 344–54
Belle Isle prison, 282, 283, 288
Berryville, Va., 305
Berryville and Winchester Pike, 316
Berryville Pike, 306
Berthoud, E. L., 265
Bienville (ship), 67, 70, 71
Bingham, Corporal, 16
Birge, Henry W., 304, 308, 309, 313
Birge's brigade, 316, 317
Bivouac and Battlefield, 24
Black River, 243
Blackistone, D. C., 29
Blair, Francis P., 326, 327
Blatchford, E. W., 155
Blenker's division, 122
blockade, 109, 110, 274
Blue Ridge Mountains, 176, 177
Boisseau, J., 337
Boker, George H., 97; quoted, 97–99
bone jewelry, 134, 135, 165
Boone, H. H., 86
Booneville, Mo., 41–43, 45
Boston, 110, 244
Bowen, John S., 242

355

Bowers, T. S., 338
Box Elder, Colo. Ter., 56
Boynton (soldier), 207
Bradburn, Albert W., 307, 310
Bradley, S. J., 29
Bragg, Braxton, 250, 254–56
Bridgeport, Ala., 252
Bristol, Colonel, 89
Brooke, John B., 29
Brown, Private, 313
Brown, Egbert B., 264
Buckeystown, Md., 160
Buell, Don Carlos, 112, 114, 115, 117
Buffalo House, Denver, 51
Bull Run, First Battle of. *See* Manassas, First Battle of
Bull Run, Second Battle of. *See* Manassas, Second Battle of
Burchsted, Benjamin F., 205
Burnside, Ambrose E., 109, 173, 178, 180, 184, 203, 255; quoted, 179
bushwhackers, 263–72
Butler, Benjamin F., 109, 137, 211; quoted, 138–43

Cache-a-la-Poudre River, 56, 57
Calhoun, James M., quoted, 294–96
Camden Point, Mo., 271
Cameron, Simon, 22
Camp Banks, 35
Camp Bisland, Battle of, 308
Camp Cameron, 43
Camp Ellsworth, 41
Camp Fires of the Twenty-Third, 180
Camp Floyd, 55
Camp Jackson, 32
Camp Oglethorpe (prison), 125–36
Camp "Paul," 180
Camp Rufus King, 180
Camp Sigel, 42
Camp Smith, 269
Camp Sumter. *See* Andersonville prison
Camp Weld, 53, 54
Campbell, John A., 325, 327, 328
Cass County, Mo., 264
Castle, Lieutenant, 159
Catskill (ship), 110
Cedar Creek, Battle of, 300
censorship, 142
Centreville, Va., 38
Chambers, Lieutenant, 92
Chambersburg, Pa., 226
Chambersburg Pike, 225, 230
Champion's Hill, Miss., 243
Chancellorsville, Battle of, 208–10, 223
Charleston, S.C., 110, 321
Chattanooga, 127, 252, 256; Battle of, 250–56
Chattanooga Creek, 252
Cherbourg, France, 273, 274, 276–78
Chesapeake Bay, 124
Chester, Pa., 110

Chester Gap, Va., 178
Chicago, 292
Chickahominy Raid, 144
Chickahominy River, 144
Chickamauga, Battle of, 250
Chivington, J. M., 53, 82, 84, 85, 90, 94, 95
City Point, Va., 336–40
Claflin, Ira W., 87, 90
Claflin's battery, 91, 93
Clarke, Sidney E., 312
Cobb, Alfred S., 93
Cobb, Howell, 170
Cold Harbor, Second Battle of, 292
Cole (soldier), 47
Coley, Captain, 307
Columbia, Tenn., 111
Confederate money, 141, 142, 162, 167–69, 291
Confederate prisoners, 231
Confederate States, Army of Tennessee, 321, 335
Congress (ship), 102, 103
Constitution (ship), 107
Cook, Sam H., 50, 51, 83–85
Copperheads, 216, 217
Corning, Erastus, 3
Coslosky's ranch, New Mex. Ter., 89
Couronne, La (ship), 277, 278
Cox (hospital steward), 159
Crane, Sergeant, 272
Crane, N. M., 183
Crater, The, 292
Crawford, S. W., 8, 19
Crittenden, Thomas T., 115, 120
Crocker, Sergeant, 161
Crook, George, 314–16, 318
Crow Creek, 55, 57
Culpeper Court House, Va., 176
Cumberland (ship), 102, 103
Cumming's Point, S.C., 9, 15
Cummins, Captain, 46
Curlew (ship), 70
Curtenius (soldier), 121
Curtin, A. G., 224
Curtis, Colonel, 41
Curtiss, Captain, 119
Custer, George A., 318

Dahlgren, John A., 106
Dalton, Ga., 255
Danville, Va., 283
Dashiell, James F., 29
Davidson, Joseph C., 92
Davis, Jefferson, 285, 326, 327
Davis, Jefferson C., 8, 15, 16
Deerhound (ship), 277, 278
DeForest, John William, 300, 301; quoted, 301–20
Demeritt, C. H., 205
Democrats, 292
Denver, 51–53

disaffection in East Tennessee and West-
  ern Virginia, 216
disaffection in the North, 219, 220
Diven's division, 337
Dix, John A., 336–39, 341
"Dixie" (song), 25, 161
Dixon (soldier), 86
Doubleday, Abner, 8, 183
Downing, Jacob, 86, 91, 92
draft, 244–47
draft riots, 244
Driggs, George W., 238; quoted, 238–43
Dunbar (ship), 252
DuPont, S. F., 65, 71
Dutro, Martin, 87, 89
Duvall, Washington, 29
Dwight, William, 311

Early, Jubal A., 233, 300–304, 309, 314,
  316, 318, 319
East Tennessee, 216, 255
Eckert, Thomas T., 327, 328
Edge, Frederick Milnes, 273; quoted, 274–
  81
emancipation, 149–55
Emilie (ship), 271
Emmett, Daniel Decatur, 24, 180
Emmitsburg, Md., 225
Emory, William H., 213, 304, 306–8,
  310, 315, 317
England, 110
Ericsson, John, 104, 106, 109, 110
"European Legion" of New Orleans, 139
Evangelical Reformed Church, Frederick,
  Md., 165
Ewing, Thomas, 264
Examiner Printing Office, Frederick, Md.,
  164

Fair Oaks, Battle of, 144, 145
Fairfax, Va., 35, 39
Falmouth, Va., 209
Falvey, John, 90
Fanny Ogden (ship), 271
Farragut, David Glasgow, 137
Fielding, George, 20
First Maine Battery, 307
Fitzgerald (hospital steward), 172
Five Forks, Battle of, 337
Flanders, F. M., 205
Flannegan, Private, 272
Fletcher, Miss A., 5; quoted, 5–23
Florida (ship), 274
Ford, James H., 90, 265, 267, 271
Ford's Theater, Washington, 342
Forney, John H., 241
Fort Albany, 35
Fort Beauregard, 66, 70
Fort Bliss, 53
Fort Corcoran, 35
Fort Darling, 105, 107
Fort Donelson, 219; Battle of, 109

Fort Fillmore, 53, 80
Fort Henry, Battle of, 109
Fort Jackson, 137
Fort Laramie, 56, 58–64
Fort Moultrie, 9, 10, 13
Fort Pulaski, Battle of, 109
Fort Riley, 263
Fort St. Philip, 137
Fort Sumter, 342–54; Battle of, 4–23
Fort Union, 89
Fort Walker, 66, 68, 70
Fortress Monroe, 102, 106, 328
Foster, John G., 15, 16
Foster's division, 340
Franklin, Battle of, 321
Frederick, Md., 156–74
Frederick Herald, 166
Fredericksburg, Va., 177; Battle of, 180–
  84, 219
Freestone, John, 266
Frietchie, Barbara, 157, 158
Front Royal, Va., 301

Gaines' Mi" \ Battle of, 144, 219
Galena (ship), 107
Galisteo, New Mex. Ter., 90
Gallegos, J. M., 75; quoted, 77–82
Galway, Edward, 20, 21
Gardner, J. B., 205
Georgia, 293
Gettysburg address, 248, 331; quoted,
  248–49
Gettysburg campaign, 223–37
Gettysburg National Cemetery, 248
Gibson, W. H., 120
Gillmore, Quincy A., 343
Gilpin, William, 51, 53–56
Glendale, Battle of, 144
Gloire, La (ship), 110
Glorietta Pass, Battle of, 76
Goldsboro, N.C., 203
Goldsborough, C. F., 29
Goldsborough, H. H., 29
Gooding, Lieutenant, 268
Governor (ship), 66
"Grafted into the Army" (song), 244, 245
Grand Gulf, Miss., 242
Grand River, 44
Grant, U. S., 112–15, 117, 238, 240–43,
  250, 251, 253, 255, 256, 261, 292,
  293, 300, 313, 327, 328, 335–38, 340,
  341
Greeley, Horace, 219
Green Point, N.Y., 110
Gregory, Idaho Ter., 53
Gregory's Gap, Va., 177
Grover, Cuvier, 213, 305–10
Grover's division, 303, 317
Gunnison, Norman, 217; quoted, 217–22

Hagerstown, Md., 172
"Hail to the Chief" (song), 20

Hall, J. C. W., 265
Hall, Norman J., 8, 14, 15
Halleck, Henry W., 145, 175, 212
Halltown, Va., 301, 308
Hamburg, Tenn., 112
Hampton Legion, 172
Hampton Roads, 328, 329; Battle of, 101–10
Hampton Roads peace conference. *See* peace conference, Hampton Roads
Hannibal, Mo., 41, 42
Hannibal and St. Joseph Railroad, 41
Hanover, Pa., 229
Hanover Court House, Va., 145
Hardin, George H., 92, 93
Harney, William S., 27; quoted, 29–33
Harper's Ferry, Va., 176, 177
Harrisburg, Pa., 227, 229, 230
Harrison's Landing, Va., 145; Battle of, 109
Harrisonville, Mo., 265
Hart, Peter, 15
Hartstene, Henry J., 18
Hatcher's Run, 339
Haughey, John V., 118
Hawley, Charles C., 55
Haymarket, Va., 177
Heard (editor), 166
Heckart, J. J., 29
Hennion, Martin, 266
Hero of Medfield, The, 34
Hiawatha (ship), 114
Hickman's Mills, Mo., 265, 266
Hight, G. W., 205
Hill, D. H., 165, 171
Hilton Head, S.C., 66–68
History of the First Regiment of Colorado Volunteers, 48, 49, 75, 76
History of the First Regiment of Iowa Volunteers, 40
Hollister, Ovando J., 48, 75; quoted, 48–64, 76, 82–95
Holmes, Oliver Wendell, quoted, 4–5
Hood, John B., 293, 294, 321
Hooker, Joseph, 180, 208, 252, 253, 255; quoted, 209–10
Howard, H., 205
Howard, O. O., 252, 253
Howard, W., 205
Howe, Daniel, 20, 21
Howland, George W., 83
Hunter, Robert M. T., 325, 327, 328

Immortalité (ship), 71
imperialism, 220–21
Independence, Mo., 265, 269
Indians, 77
Iowa, 40, 41
"Iowa Gray Hounds," *See* U.S. Army: Regiments: Iowa: Ist Infantry
Isaac Smith (ship), 70

Jackson, Claiborne F., 41, 43–45, 53
Jackson, Thomas, 68
Jackson, Thomas Jonathan ("Stonewall"), 144, 157, 158, 160, 161, 165, 168, 208, 211, 300
Jackson, Miss., 243
Jackson County, Mo., 264
Jackson's Valley campaign, 144
James River, 104, 107, 110, 145, 328
Jenkins, Micah, 228
Jennison, Charles R., 271
Jersey City, N.J., 110
Johnson, Mrs., 267
Johnson, Bradley T., 160, 166
Johnson, Jude W., 55, 89
Johnston, Albert Sidney, 112, 114
Johnston, Joseph Eggleston, 144, 293, 335
Jones, Private, 267
Jones, D. R., 18
"Jordan Is a Hard Road to Travel" (song), 180

Kansas City, Mo., 265, 266
Kansas Militia, 51
Kearsarge (ship), 273–81
Keel (soldier), 89
Kelly's Ferry, 252
Kemp Hall, Frederick, Md., 159, 161
Kentucky, 255, 298
Keokuk, Iowa, 40–42
Keokuk (ship), 109
Kerber, Charles, 92
Kershaw's division, 301
Keteltas, Captain, 119
Kiggins, Sergeant, 119
Killink, Sergeant, 119
Kimmel, Anthony, 29
Kiner, F. F., 125; quoted, 125–36
King, John H., 116, 118, 121
Kingsbury, Allen A., 34; quoted, 35–39
Knights of the Golden Circle, 217, 219

Lancaster (shipowner), 277, 278
Lane, James H., 50, 51
Laporte, Colo. Ter., 57
Laramie Creek, 58, 63
Lawrence, Kans., 263
Leavenworth, Kans., 51
Leavenworth City, Mo., 271
Lee, Francis L., 207
Lee, Robert E., 144, 165, 223, 335
Lehigh (ship), 110
Leighton, J. E., 205
lice, 136
Lincoln, Abraham, 3, 122, 144, 149, 150, 154, 175, 179, 224, 244, 248, 256–62, 292, 293, 298, 322, 325–28, 330, 331, 336, 337, 339–42, 353; quoted, 3–4, 96–97, 122–24, 175–78, 217, 246–47, 248–49, 331, 332–34
Lincolniana; or, The Humors of Old Abe, 259; quoted, 261–62

Little Thompson, Colo. Ter., 56
Liverpool, England, 274
Logan, John A., 241
Logan, Samuel M., 86, 87, 89
London, England, 274
Lone Jack, Mo., 266
Longstreet, James, 165
Lookout Creek, 252
Lookout Mountain, 252, 253, 256; Battle of, 250
Lord, R. S. C., 89
Louisiana, 263
Louisville, Ky., 256
Lovell, Mansfield, 137
Lowe, George W., 86
Lynchburg, Va., 283
Lyon, Nathaniel, 41, 43–45, 47
Lyster, Sergeant, 119

Macon City, Mo., 42
Mahin (editor), 42
Malvern Hill, Battle of, 144
Manassas, Va., 124, 218; First Battle of, 34, 53, 65, 288; Second Battle of, 156
Manassas Gap, Va., 178
Manassas Junction, Va., 123
Marshall, W. F., 51, 55, 56, 59, 62, 86, 88
martial law in New Orleans, 143
Martin, Corporal, 267
Marye's Hill, 180
Maryland, 28, 29, 156–74; General Assembly of, 28, 29; Governor of, 28
Maxson, William P., 180; quoted, 180–84
McClellan, George B., 96, 97, 122, 144, 145, 156, 160, 174, 175, 178, 292; quoted, 99–100, 145–46, 146–47, 178–79
McCook, Alexander McD., 115
McCook's division, 117
McCulloch, Ben, 44
McDowell, Irvin, 123
McKaig, Thomas J., 29
Meade, George G., 224; quoted, 224, 237
Meade, R. K., 8
Mechanicsburg, Battle of, 243
Mechanicsville, Battle of, 144
Medfield, Mass., 34
Meigs, Montgomery C., 250; quoted, 251–56
"Memorial of the Christian Men of Chicago," quoted, 150–55
Memphis, 298
Mercury (ship), 68, 70
Merrimac (ship), 101–8, 273
Merritt, Lieutenant Colonel, 47
Miles, Oscar, 29
Miles, William Porcher, 18
Miles's division, 338
Milliken's Bend, La., 242
Milroy, R. H., 228

Miss Ravenel's Conversion from Secession to Loyalty, 301
Missionary Ridge, Ga., 251–53, 256; Battle of, 250
Mississippi, 298
Mississippi River, 109, 110, 211, 238
Missouri, 27, 29–33, 41, 264–72, 298
Missouri artillery, 116
Missouri guerillas, 263
Missouri River, 41, 271
Mitchel, Ormsby MacKnight, 127
Mitchell, Edward L., 119
Mobile, Ala., 128
Moffat's farm, Md., 160
Moffett, Captain, 283
Moffett, Major, 283
Molineux, Edward L., 308
Molineux's brigade, 304, 311, 317
Monitor (ship), 101–9, 273
Monocacy River, 159
Monrovia, Md., 159
Montauk (ship), 110
Montgomery, Ala., 127
Morris Island, S.C., 13
mule meat at Vicksburg, 242
"My Maryland" (song), 161

Nahant (ship), 110
Nantucket (ship), 110
Napoleon (ship), 275
Narrative of the Privations and Sufferings of United States Officers and Privates While Prisoners of War in the Hands of Rebel Authorities, 283; quoted, 283–91
Nashville, Battle of, 321; fall of, 111
Naugatuck (ship), 107
Neafie, Alfred, 305, 308
Negro troops, 169, 211–15
Negroes, education of, 353
Nelson, George, 50, 55, 56, 85
Nelson, William, 115, 120
New Bern, N.C., 203, 204
New Mexico Territory, 54, 59, 75–95
New Orleans, 211; capture and occupation of, 109, 137–43; Fire Department, 143
New York, 109, 244
Newell, C. D., 205
Nicholson, John Page, 76, 111
Norfolk, 102–4
North Carolina, 335
Noyes, George F., quoted, 24
Nuttle, Tilghman, 29

O'Connor, Henry, 40, 41; quoted, 40–41, 42–47
Ogalallah Sioux Indians, 63, 64
Ohio volunteers, 173
Old Abe's Jokes, Fresh from Abraham's Bosom, 259; quoted, 259–61

Olmsted, Frederick Law, 158
Opequan Creek, 302
Orchard Knob, 251, 253, 254
Ord, Edward O. C., 339
Osage River, 44, 47
Osceola (ship), 66
Otis, L. B., 155
Ottawa (ship), 68, 70
Our Stars, 217
Ozark Mountains, 42

Paine, Charles J., 213
Parke, John G., 338, 339
Passaic (ship), 110
Patapsco (ship), 110
Patterson, M. A., 89
Pawnee (ship), 70
Pawnee Indians, 63
peace conference, Hampton Roads, 325–30
Peck, Frank H., 311
Peerless (ship), 66
Pemberton, John C., 238, 240, 241
Pembina (ship), 70
Penguin (ship), 70
Peninsular campaign, 34, 144
Pennsylvania, 167, 176, 223, 225, 238, 301
Petersburg, Va., 283, 335, 340, 341
Peterson, Samuel G. W., 118
Philadelphia, 212
Pickens, Francis W., 18, 20
Pigeon's Ranche, 82, 87, 89, 90; Battle of, 90–95
Pike's Peakers. *See* U.S. Army: Regiments: Colorado: 1st Infantry
Pino, Facundo, 75; quoted, 77–82
Pittsburg Landing, Battle of, 109, 112, 114–16
Platte City, Mo., 272
Platte River, 53, 58
Pleasant Hill, La., Battle of, 308
Pleasant Hill, Mo., 265, 268, 269
Pocahontas (ship), 70
Pope, John, 145, 156; quoted, 147–48
Port Gibson, Miss., 243
Port Hudson, Miss., 211–13; Battle of, 308
Port Royal, Battle of, 65–72, 109
Port Royal Ferry, S.C., 291
Porter, A. B., 44, 47
Porter, David D., 241
Portsmouth, N.H., 244
Potomac River, 35, 123, 158, 160, 176, 177
Pratt, Azro B., 89
Price, Sterling, 41
prisoners and prisons, 125–36, 282–91
Pritchard, Jesse L., 267
Pryor, Roger, 18
punishments, 47

Quantrill, William Clarke, 263

Rappahannock River, 123, 184, 209
Rawson, E. E., 296
Raymond, Miss., 243
Raytown, Mo., 267, 268
R. B. Forbes (ship), 70
Read, T. Buchanan, 300
Record of News, History and Literature, The (Richmond), 157
Rectortown, Va., 178
Red River campaign, 211
Reed, W. G., 205
Renick, Mo., 42
Reynolds, John F., 183
Rice, Dan, 87
Richardson, Israel B., 35
Richmond, Miss., 243
Richmond, Va., 110, 123, 176–78, 219, 283, 292, 326–28, 341
Richmond *Examiner*, 157; quoted, 157–58
"Richmond Is a Hard Road to Travel" (song), 180
Ricketts, James B., 305, 306
Ricketts' division, 303, 305
Rigby, William T., 307
Ringgold Gap, Ga., 250
Ritter, Simon, 90
Ritter's battery, 91, 92
River Queen (ship), 329
Roanoke Island, N.C., 203
Robbins, Samuel M., 93
Roberts (prisoner), 287
Rock Creek, 229
Rodes, Robert E., 304
Rodgers, C. R. P., 68
Rodgers, John, 68
Rogers, Colonel, 182, 183
Rondin (photographer), 276
Root, George F., 24
Ross, W. G., 164
Rossville, Ga., 255
Rough and Ready, Ga., 294
Rousseau, Lovell H., 117, 120
Rutland, Vt., 244

Sabine Cross Roads, Battle of, 308
St. Louis, Mo., 30, 41
St. Vrain's Creek, 55
Sandy Creek, 213
Sangamon (ship), 110
Santa Fe, New Mex. Ter., 53, 90, 94, 95
Satterlee, George, 46
Savage's Station, Battle of, 144
Savannah, Ga., 321, 322
Savannah, Tenn., 111–13, 115
Savery, W. E., 205
Sawyer, Charles Carroll, 24
Sayer, F. A., 205
secession, 4, 27

secession sympathies in the Old North-
    west, 216
secret societies, 219
*Secretary Seward's Review of Recent
    Military Events*, 211–12
Seminole (ship), 70
Semmes, Raphael, 273, 276, 277, 280,
    281
Seneca (ship), 70
Seven Days' Battles, 144
Seward, William H., 211, 325, 328;
    quoted, 212, 326–30
Seymour, Horatio, 244
Seymour, Truman, 8
Sharpe, Jacob, 304
Shenandoah (ship), 274
Shenandoah River, 176
Sheridan, Philip, 300–302, 305, 318, 337–
    40
"Sheridan's Battle of Winchester," 301–
    20
"Sheridan's Ride" (poem), 300
Sherman, Thomas W., 65
Sherman, William Tecumseh, 109, 213,
    251, 253–55, 293, 294, 300, 321, 343;
    quoted, 212, 296–99, 322
Shiloh, Battle of, 111–22
Shiloh prisoners, 127
Sigel, Franz, 44, 45
Simonds, Joe, 205
slaves and slavery, 79, 149–55, 330, 332,
    333, 353
Slough, J. P., 53, 90
Smith, J. Nelson, 267
Smith, John E., 29
Smith, Martin L., 241
Sni Hills, 266
Snicker's Gap, Va., 177
Snyder, G. W., 8
Soldier's Letter, 263; quoted, 264–72
Sommesport, La., 212
Soule, Silas S., 93
South Clear Creek, 49
Southside Railroad, 339
Southworth, Mrs. E. D. E. N., 156
Spencer, Lieutenant, 266
Spotsylvania Court House, Battle of, 292
Springfield, Mo., 42, 45
Stanton, Edwin McMasters, 123, 328, 336–
    41; quoted, 343
Stanwood, H. D., 205
Steiner, Lewis H., 156; quoted, 158–
    74
Stephenson, C. L., 242
Strasburg, Va., 123, 319
Strong, George C., 143
Stuart, J. E. B., 144, 172
Stuart's cavalry, 172, 173
Sturgis, Samuel D., 44
Sullivan's Island, S.C., 9
Sumner, Edwin V., 123
Susquehanna (ship), 70

Susquehanna River, 230
Swaine, P. T., 116, 119–21

Tappan, S. F., 53, 54, 93
"Tardy George" (poem), 97; quoted,
    97–99
Tennessee, 255, 298, 321
Tennessee, East. *See* East Tennessee
Tennessee River, 115, 116
Texans, 52, 75, 77–79, 82, 84–95
Texas, 77, 83, 263
Thomas, George H., 251, 253, 255, 300,
    321
Thomas, Stephen, 315–17
Thompson, George, 89
Thornton (desperado), 270
Thornton's Gap, Va., 178
Times (London), 277
Torbert, Alfred T. A., 318
Townsend, Teagle, 29
Tracy, Prescott, deposition of, quoted,
    283–91
Trent (ship), 106
Turner, Thomas P., 283
Tyler, Daniel, 35

Unadilla (ship), 70
Union (ship), 66
U.S. Army:
    Army of the Gulf, 212, 300
    Army of the Potomac, 97, 99, 100, 109,
        145, 146, 178, 208, 209, 224, 237
    Army of Virginia, 145, 147
    Department of the West, 29, 30
    Military Division of the Mississippi, 296
    II Corps, 338–40
    V Corps, 338–40
    VI Corps, 303, 306, 309, 314, 317
    VIII Corps, 303, 309, 314, 315, 317
    IX Corps, 340
    XIX Corps, 301, 303, 306, 308, 314,
        319
    XXIV Corps, 340
    Regiments:
        Colorado: 1st Infantry, 48–64, 75,
            82–95
            2nd Cavalry, 90, 263–72
            5th Cavalry, 90
        Connecticut: 12th Infantry, 310, 311
        Iowa: 1st Infantry, 40–47
            24th Infantry, 307
        Kansas: 1st Infantry, 47
            16th Cavalry, 172
        Louisiana: 2nd Infantry, 211–15
            1st Engineers, 214
        Massachusetts: 1st Infantry, 35
            44th Infantry, 203–7
            1st Cavalry, 172
        Michigan: 2nd Infantry, 35
            3rd Infantry, 35
        New Hampshire: 14th Infantry, 311

U.S. Army, Regiments (*continued*)
    New York: 12th Infantry, 35
        21st Infantry, 182
        23rd Infantry, 180–84
        69th Infantry, 38
        75th Infantry, 316
        82nd Infantry, 283
        114th Infantry, 310
        116th Infantry, 310
        131st Infantry, 308, 311
        156th Infantry, 305
        160th Infantry, 310, 315, 317
    Pennsylvania: 47th Infantry, 310
    Wisconsin: 8th Infantry, 238
    U.S. Infantry, 15th, 118, 119, 121
        16th, 118, 119
        19th, 118, 119
U.S. flag: at Fort Sumter, 14, 16–21,
    343–50; at Frederick, Md., 164, 167,
    172, 173; in New Orleans, 139, 140
U.S. President. *See* Lincoln, Abraham
U.S. Sanitary Commission, 156, 158
U.S. Supreme Court, 244, 247
U.S. War Department, 321
Upham, Corporal, 207
Upham, Emerson O., 43
Urbana, Md., 165

Vallandigham, Clement L., 3, 217
Valley of Virginia, 300
Van Petten, John B., 317
Vandalia (ship), 70
Vanderbilt (ship), 107
Vernal Spring, New Mex. Ter., 90
Vernon County, Mo., 264
Vestal's Gap, Va., 177
Vicksburg, 110, 211, 298; Battle of, 109,
    238–43
"Victory's Band" (song), quoted, 25–26
Vienna, Va., 36
Virginia, 36, 208, 292, 321, 335
Virginia (ship). *See Merrimac* (ship)

Wabash (ship), 66–70
Wagoner, S., 269, 270
Walker, Aldace F., 307
Walker, Charles J., 91
Warren, Gouverneur K., 337
Warrenton, Va., 179
Warrior (ship), 110
Washington, 35, 39, 123, 177, 178, 223,
    301, 327, 328
*Washington and Jackson on Negro Sol-
    diers,* 212
Washington family, 173
Watkins, J. S., 29
Webb, Mr., 268
Weehawken (ship), 110

Weir (surgeon), 159
Weitzel, Godfrey, 213, 308, 341
Wells, George, 266
Wells, S. C., 296
West, Captain, 271
West Point, Va., 145
Weston, Mo., 271
Westport, Mo., 265
Wheeler, James S., 278
Wheeler, Joseph, 321
Whitaker, F., 29
White, Lieutenant, 206
White, E. V., 166
White (doctor), 289, 290
Whitehall, N.C., 203
Whittier, John Greenleaf, 156, 157
Wigfall, Louis T., 15–17
Wilder, William F., 92
Wilderness, Battle of the, 292
Wilkinson, Robert F., 307
Williams, Mrs., 270
Williams, John, 119
Williams, S., 30, 210, 237
Williams, West, 207
Williamsburg, Battle of, 144, 145, 218
Willich, August, 121
Wilmington, Del., 110
Wilson, Luther, 50, 51
Winchester, Va., 123, 176, 177; Second
    Battle of, 300–320
Winder, John H., 287, 288
Winslow, John A., 274, 276–79
Wirz, Henry, 288
Within Fort Sumter, 5
Wood's redoubt, 253
Wool, John E., 124
Wooster, Ohio, 244
Work, Henry Clay, 24, 244; quoted, 245
Worthington, W. W., 111; quoted, 111–
    21
Wright, Horatio G., 69, 338, 339
Wrightsville, Pa., 229
Wykoff, Lieutenant, 119
Wynkoop, Edward W., 86

"Yankee Doodle" (song), 20, 35
"Yankee Muse in History, The," 157
Yazoo City, Miss., 243
Yeager, Dick, 266
Yellot, Captain, 161
Yellott, Coleman, 29
York, Pa., 229
Yorke, Captain, 307
Yorktown, Battle of, 144, 218
Young, Mr., 268
Young's Point, La., 238

Zacharias, Daniel, 165